ROUTLEDGE LIBRARY EDITIONS: WOMEN AND CRIME

Volume 5

ANNALS OF CRIME

ANNALS OF CRIME
Some Extraordinary Women

W. H. WILLIAMSON

LONDON AND NEW YORK

First published in 1930 by George Routledge & Sons, Ltd.

This edition first published in 2016
by Routledge
2 Park Square, Milton Park, Abingdon, Oxon OX14 4RN

and by Routledge
711 Third Avenue, New York, NY 10017

Routledge is an imprint of the Taylor & Francis Group, an informa business

© 1930 W. H. Williamson

All rights reserved. No part of this book may be reprinted or reproduced or utilised in any form or by any electronic, mechanical, or other means, now known or hereafter invented, including photocopying and recording, or in any information storage or retrieval system, without permission in writing from the publishers.

Trademark notice: Product or corporate names may be trademarks or registered trademarks, and are used only for identification and explanation without intent to infringe.

British Library Cataloguing in Publication Data
A catalogue record for this book is available from the British Library

ISBN: 978-1-138-18723-8 (Set)
ISBN: 978-1-315-64317-5 (Set) (ebk)
ISBN: 978-1-138-12595-7 (Volume 5) (hbk)
ISBN: 978-1-138-12600-8 (Volume 5) (pbk)

Publisher's Note
The publisher has gone to great lengths to ensure the quality of this reprint but points out that some imperfections in the original copies may be apparent.

Disclaimer
The publisher has made every effort to trace copyright holders and would welcome correspondence from those they have been unable to trace.

ANNALS OF CRIME

SOME EXTRAORDINARY WOMEN

By
W. H. WILLIAMSON

LONDON
GEORGE ROUTLEDGE & SONS, Ltd.
BROADWAY HOUSE: 68-74 CARTER LANE, E.C.
1930

PRINTED IN GREAT BRITAIN BY
M. F. ROBINSON & CO. LTD., AT THE LIBRARY PRESS, LOWESTOFT.

CONTENTS

		PAGE
I	JEANNE DE LA COUR	1
II	MRS MAYBRICK	20
III	MADAME LAFARGE	62
IV	CHRISTIANA EDMUNDS	85
V	MARIE DE MORELL	110
VI	HELENE JAGADO	141
VII	MADELEINE SMITH	163
VIII	MARIE MICHEL	198
IX	CONSTANCE KENT	222
X	CELESTINE DOUDET	238
XI	MADAME JONIAUX	264

PREFACE

THERE are many ways in which we can approach the study of crime. Some get their full satisfaction in the thrill of the narrative. There are legally minded people, who are primarily interested in the forensic points, in the weighing of evidence, in the way the prosecution and the defence are conducted, and in the summing up of the judge. But everybody, we think, will be interested in the light these cases throw on human nature.

The stories that are set out in this volume are of a kind no student of humanity can afford to overlook. We see the behaviour of abnormal people. But we are made to wonder at times how much of the criminal is in us all. "There go I, but for circumstance . . ."

Would these creatures, whose stories are set out here, have been criminals if some circumstance (small or big) had not turned their feet in the evil way? What made Constance Kent do what she did? Some strange brooding, that in a more enlightened age would have been noticed and dissipated. We are thrown straightway against those odd complexes and inhibitions, that disturb our serenity and turn us to savage paths. If we knew more of the springs of human conduct we should be able to take young people by the hand and train them so that they should *not* go in certain unhappy ways. The brooding woman, the girl in early teens, is here seen to be positively dangerous in certain circumstances. Some people fling off their spleen by back-biting, by sneers, by cattishness; but some go forward to crime.

The young are a problem, and few there be who tackle it. One can readily believe that an observing, understanding parent might have disposed of Constance Kent's imaginary grievance by the exercise of sympathy and sense. Marie de Morell needed someone to discern the fantastic things that were darting in the hidden pools of her mind. Her mother thought if she limited her to the reading of the Bible and provided her with an English governess all would be well! It is tragic. Parents have no knowledge of their children's secret thoughts; and those are the thoughts that matter; those are the things that mould them. Many parents are superb at discipline, many at leniency, but few at understanding. Parents should observe and discern and sympathize. The tactful would find the way of grappling effectively with the strange longings of budding youth.

Another point that emerges from the reading of the cases that comprise this book is the empirical nature of the doctor's calling.

"The ancient physicians," wrote Dr Hart of Northampton three centuries ago, " did divide Physicke principally into two parts, to wit, that which we commonly call Therapeuticke . . . and that part which we call Diagnosticke, whose most common scope is to discern the whole and sound from the like, and the sick and infirme from the whole, being unlike the one to the other. And this part of Physicke doth farre excell the other, to wit the Therapeuticke, the which without the Diagnosticke is of small use and profit . . ."

If Dr Watson learned nothing else from Sherlock Holmes than how to develop and cultivate his observation, he then did well. The diagnosis of the doctor in many instances spells tragedy.

Many of the cases herewith treat of poisons and we are amazed at the leaping fact that people can be poisoned without any suspicion being aroused in the doctor. Read the story of Hélène Jagado. She poisoned about thirty people, using arsenic all the time. The symptoms of arsenic poisoning are very well known; they are set out in all the text-books. Yet doctors see patients die of arsenical poisoning and presumably sign a certificate setting out gastro-enteritis or peritonitis or . . . as the cause of death.

One sees the doctor's difficulty, but he should overcome it. That's what difficulties are for. When the medical man suspects, he shakes his head and the patient dies. He shrinks from action, because, if he should be mistaken, his practice is ruined. We venture to say that a great number of doctors in this (and every) country could mention cases of suspected poisoning where nothing was done.

Here is an excerpt from the evidence in the Maybrick case. Dr Carter was the witness.

" But you did not suspect the presence of any poison ? "

" No."

" As a doctor you would not do so ? "

" No—decidedly not. It is the last thing—the very last thing—we would think of . . ."

But people are poisoned, and a doctor should not put the idea on one side till it is too late, as most of them do. In the case of arsenic poisoning it would be quite easy for a doctor to say in his best professional manner that he would take some of the vomit for analysis . . . Why not ? If the doctors who had attended Hélène Jagado's victims had done that she wouldn't have poisoned thirty people. As we are of opinion that a person who has once committed a murder and been unsuspected is liable to essay another, it is essential in the interests of society that the murderer should be suspected and, if possible, caught at the first attempt. When Armstrong was charged with poisoning his wife criminologists were almost ready to believe him guilty because it will be remembered, he attempted to poison someone else for a motive that was inadequate for a first murder.

In the Brighton poisoning case the doctor who was called in to see Mr Miller never suspected poison, with the consequence that the chocolate creams were not examined and the boy died.

Madame Joniaux used morphia, and she had safely disposed of (at least) two victims before she was discovered. And then it was rather the suspicion of shrewd Insurance people than the diagnosis of the doctors that forced the issue.

The doctor in the Road murder never guessed that the weapon used to kill the little boy was a razor.

And note how the doctors differed over the strength of the hands of Marie Michel. Whenever there is a case where medical evidence is essential there will always be some doctors to swear a thing is white, and others that it is black. But that is perhaps true of most experts.

THE AUTHOR.

I

JEANNE DE LA COUR: OR THE WIDOW GRAS

THESE ideas of our childhood, what do they become? What do these ardent suppressed desires to be as others, who seem to have the favours of Fortune, make of us?

Wisdom is knowledge well handled. But if knowledge tarries . . .

Take Jeanne Amenaide Brécourt.

It is not the name one would ordinarily suggest for the child of a *concierge* who sells carrots and cabbages. Jeanne Amenaide Brécourt, one of four children, must have had something about her out of the ordinary, for neighbours not only took notice of her but helped her. She had to help herself too. From the age of five till she was eleven she had *de la chance*, whatever it was worth.

A rich neighbour, the Baroness de Pallandt, adopted her, and this daughter of the *concierge* then turned up her nose at her old companions.

"The daughter of a lady," she is reported to have said, "doesn't play with a wine-merchant's."

This "daughter of a lady" sticks. It marks the child. One feels that already she has dreamed her little dreams and had her unsatisfied desires.

And she was only eleven when her parents, realising that a child of that age could bring in money to the family purse, reclaimed her from the Baroness and sent her into the streets to sell gingerbread and flowers.

And the curious thing was that the child seemed to have taken the change naturally, as she would accept the weather. She may have found some sort of interest and satisfaction in this life of the streets, for she never bothered about her old protectress—at least for six years. Then presumably she tired of this wretched life.

She went to the Baroness, who took her in again, gave her clothes and found her a situation. She did more; she found her a husband.

The man from the grocer's called. Jeanne had said she wanted a husband and this man came to suggest the candidate. "There is your husband," said the Baroness.

"Eh bien," replied Jeanne.

The grocer didn't mind. The Baroness, who must have been a generous soul, gave Jeanne a dot of 10,000 francs, which set the couple up in business, and Jeanne Amenaide Brécourt became Madame Gras, wife of a grocer.

It wasn't a happy marriage. Instead of selling the groceries husband and wife began throwing them at each other. That kind of thing could lead neither to happiness nor to prosperity.

And apparently M Gras understood something of his wife. "Your pride will ruin you and prison will get you," he said to her.

"And the hospital will get you," she retorted. They were both right.

Business declined. The Gras shut up shop. Madame Gras, who had known what it was to do business in Paris from very tender years, was not apparently frightened at the prospect. She was only eighteen. Her husband was twenty-five. It was the age when nothing matters, when the young think they know and can do so much and will always be able to set right what goes wrong.

Madame Gras faced life deliberately. She left her husband and changed her name.

As 'Jeanne de la Cour' she became the mistress of an officer.

As is the way of such women she persuaded her 'protector' to set her up in business. Jeanne de la Cour tried a scent shop, but it failed. Then she tried a stationery business and that failed. The life behind a counter, waiting for the lover, was perhaps too dull for her.

She became an actress!

"Hortense, mère du docteur . . . Mlle Jeanne."

"Mlle Jeanne" . . . That was how she was described on the programme. Perhaps she had the dreams of actresses, some of which must be weird. Jeanne was young, pretty, alert and a personality. But she had no success.

And failure burnt into her like an acid. She had need of men. She had no doubt dreamt of a prince of sorts, and as she trailed her bedraggled life along the Paris pavements looking into men's eyes, into one man after another, one after another, she began to hate the whole tribe.

To her sister, Marie, the one creature she really loved, she unbosomed herself. "I'd like to make all these males suffer while I pretended to love them; defile all the females while pretending to defend them; and as one must live in society the men should be my playthings. I know the way of attracting them."

She tried journalism. She tried everything. And she was beaten. She was taken into an asylum in the rue du Faubourg-Saint-Antoine, where they made this note of the twenty-four-year-old patient: "Brunette. Fine dark eyes, very pretty, nervous, very pale. Had attacks of hysteria. Rambles. In speaking of her parents, who were of the working class she said, 'I don't know these people'. She posed as a great lady and was bombastic."

To make her cure complete Jeanne was sent to Vittel, where she had to be somebody and so posed as 'Baroness de la Cour'. She had a successful time, for her, in the Bretagne. She made quite a sensation at Baden.

She wrote to her sister from Vittel : " We have at our *table d'hôte* ten priests and four sisters of charity. As I have told people that I am not a Catholic, two or three married ladies have tried to sow the good seeds into me. . . . How wicked the world is ! These bigots and posing bourgeois are full of these cruelties.

" Also, at the *table d'hôte* are the married women who won't go out with the *cocottes*—and they have perhaps in their lives more shameful things than these girls ; but to keep their places they fancy themselves forced to walk on those who fall. But they won't walk on me, I'll guarantee you that ! I have said a few things and now they are so afraid of me, they bow to me . . ."

She talked of the men ; told of an admiring Baron, of a prefect and retired minister. " But what a pity," she says, " that the fool is young and handsome and the witty man is old and unattractive ! "

At Vittel she had her greatest success. This black-eyed attractive woman would not go about unnoticed, and the men of the place had eyes for eyes that sought theirs.

There occurred the pigeon episode. A wounded pigeon escaped from the guns of the valiant pigeon shooters and came into Jeanne's room. She tended it.

For the moment Jeanne and the wounded pigeon were the topic in Vittel. The prefect or the ex-minister or one of the other of Jeanne's oglers suggested she ought to have a medal from the

Society for the Prevention of Cruelty to Animals.

But Jeanne knew that when the pigeon no longer needed her it would fly away.

It was about this time that Jeanne's husband, the poor grocer died, an event which filled his widow with gladness. She could marry now if she wished . . . At least, she was free. Free. . . . It had an ironically sweet savour in the mouth of a creature like Madame Gras, otherwise "Jeanne de la Cour". She was certainly free. She had one lover after another. Some of them were passionately devoted to her for a time and then they got married, or wearied, or went away. Free. . . . She rejoiced in the feeling all the same.

And then she met René de la Roche, aged twenty, rich, unoccupied, who had an appointment in Paris.

Apparently Jeanne de la Cour could attract the young. She became René's mistress. His youth was the opportunity for her experience. And gradually she won the wholehearted devotion of this young man.

It is not a unique picture; but the comparatively old prostitute capturing the heart of a young man of twenty is happily not too common. For the woman *had* captured the young man's heart. During the three years the *liaison* lasted René de la Roche showed and showered affection on his mistress.

But she knew what life was like. That kind of thing couldn't go on. . . . He was twenty-three; she was . . . Peuh! The row of scents and cosmetics and medicine bottles was enough. . . .

She wasn't happy. She wanted to catch Circumstance and chain it; and couldn't. He was happy now; but how long would it last? That was the thought that haunted her. René's friends would soon be trying to marry him and then . . . A look in the glass . . . She was getting on . . . Those lines . . .

About this time she called on an old friend who had been a ballet dancer and there she saw a touching sight. The retired dancer led to the sofa a young man—blind. Jeanne's friend confided to her. " I love this unfortunate," she said. " I would do anything for him. He is young, rich, with no family and he is going to marry me. I am getting near the forties, as you are, my dear. My hair . . . eh ? . . . Youth has already run on the rocks . . ." She pointed to the blind young man. " There is my spar, my life-belt . . . eh ? "

Jeanne nodded.

"My congratulations," she said, and she added the haunting idea of certain foolish women, " he will never see you grow old."

Never see you grow old. . . . Jeanne of the scents and cosmetics; Jeanne de la Cour approaching the forties with a lover aged twenty-three. . . . Never see you grow old. . . . It was an idea for one who looked keenly in a mirror.

Now Nathalis Mathieu Gaudry is to be introduced. He had been one of Jeanne's playmates when she sold flowers or gingerbread or stood by the *concierge's* stock of vegetables. Jeanne hadn't much use for that ' low down class ' as a rule, but she was on quite friendly terms with Nathalis Gaudry. He had done his military service, fought in Italy sufficiently well to gain a medal, and in 1864 he married. When his wife died eleven years later he came to Paris with his two children and found employment in an oil refinery at St Denis.

Jeanne de la Cour made use of him. He would have married her, but Jeanne wasn't the kind that makes a life-belt of a Nathalis Gaudry, though he was good-looking. But she did her best to find him a wife. She failed; but a working man, living at St Denis, earning five francs a day, wasn't a very favourable proposition. In the meanwhile he was her devoted servant.

To him Jeanne de la Cour would personify the vague notions he had of luxury and the delicate woman. He went to her every Sunday and was her faithful Gibeonite. He would do all sorts of menial jobs for her—hew her wood and draw her water—be rewarded with a smile. He may have hoped for more.

One day he received a letter telling him she had need of him. He was to get leave—she would pay him for his lost time.

By this time Jeanne had doubtless moulded Nathalis Gaudry. Thoroughly unscrupulous, using hashish and cantharides as ordinary folk use common salt, this supple woman had made of Gaudry a creature who would do anything for her.

She told him her story. A man had robbed her. She would be revenged and strike at the man through his son. Nathalis should deliver the blow; he should hit the man so that he would be disabled for life and then she, Jeanne, would kiss him, and marry him. And she gave him a knuckle-duster.

The first appointment failed. The victim did not come. There was another occasion when Nathalis had to call in the rue de la Ferme-des-Mathurins and knock at a door so that he could recognize a man. But Nathalis Gaudry was not really an assassin. At the last moment he turned aside, and when he ought to have been at midnight knocking at a door in the rue de la Ferme-des-Mathurins he was trudging back to St Denis.

But Jeanne de la Cour did not let go her terrible plan.

René was in the country and she gathered a hint of marriage in his letters. It wasn't much of a hint, but it was enough for her. Married. . . . And so she would be left . . . What then ? . . .

She wrote to her lover. He must come to the masked ball at the Opera on the 13th. He was not at all eager to go to this ball, but he agreed to take her if she wished.

Now Jeanne de la Cour wished for Gaudry's help. But he was not an assassin. He had been won once; now he tried to escape. He knew he could never refuse if he saw Jeanne and so he stopped away. But just at this time there was an accident at the works and so he was idle. . . . It is one of those circumstances that can be laid hold of and pointed at. Gaudry, having nothing to do, restless, and scarcely knowing what he did, went to the rue de Boulogne and called on the charmer.

He was lost.

René de la Roche came to Paris to take his mistress to the ball. When he arrived at her rooms she was entertaining Gaudry with details of the plan to make René blind. In the circumstances Gaudry was thrust into an alcove, where there was a stool, which betrays Jeanne's thoughtfulness and attention to detail. She gave René a volume of Montaigne to read, and when René went to fetch the cab Jeanne whispered "Courage" to Gaudry in the alcove.

Till nearly three o'clock they were at the ball. Jeanne de la Cour enjoyed it as much as anybody. She seemed to have no troubles in the world.

Between two and three the carriage drew up before the gate in the rue de Boulogne. No. 5 was at the end of an avenue about twenty-eight yards long. René de la Roche got out of the carriage first and paid the cabman, rang the bell for the *concierge* and went in the alley. Jeanne de la Cour followed him. She saw that the gate was left open and kept half a dozen yards behind her lover.

Suddenly the most agonizing cries rent the air. Agony in the dead of night has a voice of its own.

It tears. Those who heard René de la Roche said it sounded as if his flesh were being plucked from his bones.

Gaudry had thrown the vitriol into René's eyes.

He knocked against the woman as he bolted, and she then called for help for the unfortunate victim.

The *concierges* came. Jeanne cried for water. The doctor was sent for.

Jeanne de la Cour had got her life-belt.

For the police the problem was not an easy one. There was no clear motive. Jeanne de la Cour kept the door closed firmly and refused to admit anybody to see the patient save the doctors. When a cousin of René's grew insistent Jeanne retorted with, "This is my place, and I will throw something in the face of anybody who crosses my threshold when I don't ask them."

"Throw something in the face . . ." It was an incautious statement.

Jeanne de la Cour meant to have René de la Roche for herself. He was young, he had money, he loved her. The sentimental might add, "He would never see her grow old." The police said, "The widow Gras followed the unique passion which has always guided her—money."

Let us take it that to gain security Jeanne de la Cour did not care whom she sacrificed or how she gained her end.

No suspicion attached to her at once. She was reticent. She could only repeat the story of what she saw, which was probably vague.

But René de la Roche's friends were more than impatient: they began to suspect. Why did that woman wish to keep them from René? What was her motive? He was blinded and she wouldn't let them see him.

It was nearly a month after the crime had been committed that M Macé, who subsequently became head of the Detective Department, and was then a police commissionary, visited Jeanne de la Cour in the company of a judge.

She said at first that only doctors were allowed in and she played with a spray.

"Put that down," said Macé, "or we might be sprayed like M de la Roche. . . ."

And M Macé agreed that the eyes of Jeanne de la Cour at that moment signalled battle.

The judge and M Macé gleaned very little. They saw de la Roche, but Jeanne was by his side, and after a few questions she said, "A man must be a barbarian to cause another so much suffering."

Both men agreed they had learnt little from their visit. Yet they had noticed that Jeanne was always ready with something to say whenever her lover was inclined to talk freely.

"We must separate the lover from the mistress," said M Macé sagely.

Jeanne de la Cour was watched.

She went to René de la Roche's room and got hold of his papers. She also went to a cemetery, where she met a man. But the police missed him. Then Jeanne took her lover to apartments in the Boulevard de Sebastopol.

M Macé was on the track. He had had all the details of the affair. René de la Roche had gone ahead . . . walked in front of his mistress . . . H'm . . . H'm . . . Had she arranged it? For him there was a problem to solve, and he set himself the task of solving it.

He came to these considerations:

1. Jeanne had insisted on going with her lover to the ball at the Opera and had fixed the hour of their return at three o'clock in the morning.

2. The position she occupied when they returned

from the ball was in the central alley, and M de la Roche had preceded his mistress by twenty paces, which was altogether contrary to the habits of a man of his breeding.

3. This position allowed Jeanne to leave the gate open, which would facilitate the flight of the vitriol thrower and to receive some vitriol herself on the arm. Now the keeping open of the gate was deliberate because it would otherwise have closed itself. So Jeanne didn't want her accomplice to be caught like a rat in a trap.

4. Jeanne used to be visited every Sunday by someone who was said to be her brother: but he had not been seen since the crime.

They were considerations of a certain value. The case became interesting to the detective.

M Macé was particularly anxious to question the lovers separately and not together; and that was difficult.

The doctor was called in aid. He was informed what was required of him and so he made a report which ended with the phrase that "the care the patient needed was such that it could be given by any competent nurse".

That snatched from Jeanne de la Cour the right to sound the humanitarian cry and allowed Justice to separate Jeanne from her pigeon.

M Macé got power to restore René to his friends. So while Jeanne de la Cour was conducted to M Macé the blinded man was led to his family.

"Then I am arrested?" she said after she had been told she was to be examined by the magistrate.

"Provisionally."

"Who will look after René?"

"His family!"

When she heard those words she raged like a tiger. She cursed everybody. She even threatened.

She was taken back to her rooms. Two police

agents were told to watch her every movement. M Macé superintended the search.

The room told its sinister story. Letters were found. There was the man whom she had blackmailed by pretending she had had a child! There was the final line from a young man who had seen too much and known too little of the world, " Jeanne, in full tide of youth, I die by your fault. But I pardon you. M."

And the row of pots of dye, scents, pastes, creams, pomades, powders, belladonna, of hashish told the hectic tale.

There were some of René de la Roche's things —including letters.

Jeanne said she had found those and had kept them. Perhaps it was not quite right, but René would forgive her.

M Macé was quick. This woman would not readily own to something not right . . . what had she done that was bad ? . . . In all probability it was bad.

M Macé interviewed René de la Roche. He told the young man plainly that his mistress was hard, selfish, ruthless and cruel. And the poor blind man defended her. He swore nothing and nobody would separate him from his adored one.

M Macé played his card. It happened to be merely some half-burnt papers, those same papers Jeanne had admitted she had kept.

Macé gave these to René de la Roche and let him touch them. The young man, with the bandage round his sad and seared eyes, felt the paper, smelt it . . .

" They have been burnt," he said.

" Yes. The pages are covered with a fine aristocratic writing, easy to read——"

" Read it."

M Macé read.

And René de la Roche understood at last.

"It is a revelation," he said. "How did these letters get into Jeanne's hands?"

"Tell me rather how they left yours?"

The young man then said that before coming to this house he had made his will leaving everything to Jeanne, and he desired to obliterate his past. With that object he had all his papers brought to him and he handed them to Jeanne to put on the fire. While they were burning he heard her take the tongs and asked, "What have you taken the tongs for?" "To hold the papers to the flames," she said. And now René de la Roche knew differently. His mistress had taken the letters from the fire. She had got hold of something which she could use for purposes of blackmail if she wished. She cheated him after blinding him.

That cut through René's attachment to his mistress. He could have forgiven her the blinding: he could have forgiven her spoiling his life, but *that* . . . That was infamous.

M Macé dropped a remark that may be useful to all those who would understand the motives that push people to crime. "The dominant note of that woman," he said to René, "is pride mingled with ambition, two incurable vices which thrust to crime."

Pride and ambition are vices. . . . Ambition, we know, should be made of stern stuff. Pride and ambition are like poisons, only useful in proper doses.

When Jeanne was separated from René she wrote him letters—even poems.

But she got no answer. She began to be anxious and her nerves were unsteady. She wrote a letter to Gaudry. She wanted him to confess so that she could go free. She would look after his son if anything happened to him, and leave him one-third of her property.

A ballet dancer, who was being liberated from

prison, took the letter and at once told her lover about Jeanne. "We don't want to bother about a woman who has vitriol thrown at her lover," he said. But the ballet dancer talked, and the talk travelled till the police heard of it.

M Macé interviewed this dancer and there emerged the name of Nathalis, who lived at Saint Denis, and worked in oil.

M Macé went to Saint Denis and there saw Nathalis, who worked in oil, and there also saw clothes burned by acid. Also four letters.

Gaudry, who had not planned the crime and therefore had none of that hard fibre which pushes to such ends crumpled up at once.

"I did it," he said as the tears ran down his face. "I loved her, and she promised to marry me if I would do it."

At last Macé had got the story.

Jeanne de la Cour was growing desperate. She tried to commit suicide with poisoned glass. She tried to make verdigris by pouring lemon-juice on some copper coins. She also tried starving herself.

But on July 23rd, 1877, at the Paris Assize Court, she stood beside Nathalis Gaudry in the dock charged with provoking by gifts and promises the said Gaudry to wound René de la Roche, with having given Gaudry the wherewithal to commit the crime, and with having aided Gaudry.

Two of the greatest advocates of the Paris bar appeared in the case, Madame Gras being represented by Lachaud, the defender of Madame Lafarge, and Gaudry by Demange, the defender of Dreyfus.

When Jeanne and Nathalis met for the first time in prison, before the trial, Jeanne whispered, "Don't accuse me. I beg of you. Save me, and I will save you afterwards."

"It is too late," replied the disillusioned lover.

The trial brought out most of the facts we have

related. As one could imagine, Gaudry, who was a simple soul, losing it in the love of a worthless, unscrupulous woman, had no subtleties. He did his best to answer the questions put to him truthfully and without reserve.

"Gaudry, stand up," said the President. "You know the serious charge that is hanging over you. On the 14th of January, during the night, you were waiting in the courtyard of the house. You had with you some sulphuric acid. There you waited for a young man and threw this corrosive liquid in his face. Are you guilty?"

"Yes, sir."

"Did you know your victim?"

"No, sir."

"You had never seen him?"

"No, sir."

"You have never appeared in court before, Gaudry. You were a good soldier; you got a medal for the Italian campaign; you had a good reputation. How did you come to do this? What was your motive?"

"I had no motive. If I hadn't been pushed I shouldn't have done it."

"What made you do it?"

"I was madly in love with Madame Gras. I would have done anything she asked me."

"It was solely to please her?"

"When I was with her I didn't know what I did."

"But she wasn't near you when you committed the crime?"

"But I could always feel her will."

"What did she want—how did she express it?"

"Revenge me on that man and I will marry you."

The soldier came out later.

"I said to her, 'But it's cowardly to do that. To throw vitriol at night in the eyes of a man who isn't defending himself, and whom I don't know. If you want revenge, I'll provoke him; we'll fight. At least he will have a chance'."

"What did she say?"

"She said it wasn't possible; that he wasn't my class and wouldn't fight a duel with me."

And the woman just before the brutality . . .

"He went to fetch the carriage?"

"Yes."

"At what time?"

"I can't say exactly."

"Then you were alone with her?"

"Yes. She came to me with a candle and said, 'Look how beautiful I am'."

"Weren't you somewhat embarrassed?"

"Yes. She kissed me and said, 'Do what I told you and I swear I will marry you in three months'."

"And the woman Gras and the monsieur went to the ball; what did you do?"

"I went into the dining-room."

"Where you waited till half-past two?"

"Yes."

"And then?"

"I did what had been agreed. I went down into the yard."

"And then?"

"I hid."

"And you threw the acid?"

"Yes, sir."

"And then you ran away?"

"Yes, sir."

"Knocking against the woman Gras as you did so?"

"Yes."

"How did you get away?"

"The gate was open. She told me she would leave it like that."

"Where did you go?"

"To Saint Denis."

"What did you do with the phial?"

"I threw it away in the rue Ventimille. I got to Saint Denis about four o'clock in the morning. I was practically mad. I don't even know what way I went. I changed my clothes, which were spotted with vitriol. At seven o'clock I went to work as usual."

"Did you hide those clothes?"

"Yes."

"At once?"

"No. When I received a letter."

"From whom?"

"From Madame Gras. She wrote me several letters."

Madame Gras was weak at the beginning of her examination. When the judge asked her a question and she was silent, M. Lachaud her counsel, had to say, "Answer! Answer!" And she weakly muttered "I can't."

She was allowed to sit down, and with the questions seemed to come her confidence. She was taken through the details of her early life, and as they did not compromise her she gained ease.

The judge reached the events of the catastrophic night.

"Wasn't Gaudry at your house while you were at the ball?"

"No. No. And he daren't say he was before me."

"What do you say?"

"I say he daren't say it and look me in the face. He's a coward, a wretch——!"

"But he is looking at you."

"No, he isn't. He daren't."

And Gaudry didn't look, according to a writer. This imperious creature, who had sold herself right and left, to old and young, to any national, rich or poor so long as they had enough to pay her, who had led this brave soldier into the dock, dominated him like a lion-tamer, who has the king of beasts crouching in a corner.

The judge continued: "At half-past ten was Gaudry with you?"

"No."

"Gaudry, do you hear?"

"Yes, sir. I was there."

And he stood up to her later and never wavered in his story. But all the time his attitude was one of shame. The woman was quite different. She spoke easily, raised her voice, was ready with gesture, and her black eyes fixed you. She looked forty, said an observer who was present, but not at all like a woman of the street. And he noted her eyes—terrible, the eyes of a tigress.

She turned on M Macé when he gave his evidence. She was telling of her interrogatory when she faced M Macé with, "Don't you squint at me like that; it won't do any good."

M Macé may have thought he was getting in some sort of reply when he mentioned that he had found in the accused woman's room a pot of hashish mixed with cantharides.

And when René de la Roche entered the witness box Madame Gras uttered a smothered, "René!" She followed his every movement with her eyes. Her lips had a Mona Lisa smile, with a latent eagerness. One felt that at any moment she might get up and speak to him. He was wearing large blue glasses and was led in by an attendant.

His appearance was more dramatic than his evidence, which merely confirmed what the court had already heard.

Madame Gras watched him till he was no more to be seen.

The advocate-general had not a difficult task. He made the case lucid when he said, " She (Madame Gras) was determined to keep for herself the blind man and his fortune. He wouldn't be able to marry now. . . . 'He has known me in my beauty; he will not see me grow old. I shall be everything to him.' . . . She would have had the money, for M de la Roche would have been grateful. . . ."

M Lachaud had too big a task for eloquence. He struggled, but all the keys were muted.

M Demange reduced his client to tears and pleaded that Gaudry had been the foolish tool of this terrible woman.

Madame Gras was found guilty and sentenced to fifteen years' imprisonment with hard labour.

Gaudry lost his military medal and was sent to prison for ten years.

A note of brightness. M René de la Roche managed to recover the sight of one eye. He was in the court when the verdict was given.

II

MRS MAYBRICK

MANY have been the marriages due to a sea voyage; some have turned out happily and some have not. Marriages arranged either on land or sea have to run the gamut of human nature, and it is on that voyage the reefs and shoals are encountered and the blessed ones come safe to port.

James Maybrick was a Liverpool cotton-broker, who, at the age of forty-two, was travelling to America. Amongst the passengers were a lady—formerly Mrs Chandler—and her daughter Florence, aged eighteen. The mother had married again, and was no longer a democratic American citizen, but the Baroness Von Roques, wife of a cavalry officer in the German Army. Florence Elizabeth Chandler spent part of her time with her (now) German mother, and part with her American grandmother.

There was a good gap in the ages of James Maybrick and Florence Chandler, so either he was a fascinating man or Miss Chandler was eager to get married, for a marriage was arranged, and shortly took place between James Maybrick of Norfolk, Virginia and Liverpool, England, and Florence Elizabeth Chandler of New York.

We can imagine heads being shaken at the marriage of eighteen to forty-two. We can almost hear what was said. But marriage is a gamble at any age.

James Maybrick and his wife settled down ultimately at Battlecrease House, Aigburth, Liverpool. We have no reason to suppose there was anything but the customary glow and satisfaction in the early years of their married life. A boy and a girl were born to them, hostages to a happiness of a kind, even if they can't guarantee it. Happiness can't be guaranteed by outsiders; it lies within ourselves.

In spite of the fact that the Maybricks were sufficiently well-to-do the ship of content had already struck on a rock. James Maybrick was accused by his wife of paying attention to some woman, and the accuser was herself accused of paying too much attention to a man named Brierly.

We will now quote from the speech by Mr Addison, Q.C.: " On the 16th March, Mrs Maybrick had to telegraph to London to a hotel in Henrietta Street, Cavendish Square, for a sitting-room and bedroom. You will have before you the letters which she wrote, and which will be put in evidence. The effect of them is this: On the 16th March she telegraphed for a sitting-room and bedroom at this private hotel. Having received no answer, she wrote again to the landlord and told him that the rooms were engaged for Mrs Maybrick of Manchester, and she wrote again as to details as to the sort of dinner which ' Mr and Mrs Maybrick ' would like to have, saying that her ' sister-in-law ' was inexperienced in such matters. On the 18th March (Monday) she wrote again to this hotel, saying that Mr and Mrs Maybrick would arrive on the 21st (Thursday), that her sister-in-law would stay there a week—from the 21st to the 28th—and that ' she was not particular as to price '.

" You have her then writing these letters from the 16th to the 18th March, engaging this sitting-room and bedroom for her ' sister-in-law '. On the 21st March (Thursday) she left Battlecrease House to go to London. You will find that in the evidence which occurs later on, and the reason she gave her husband for going to London, was that she had an aunt, who was going to undergo an operation under the care of James Paget, and the aunt wanted her niece — that was herself, Mrs Maybrick — to be present, and she was going to London for a week for this purpose. This she told the nurse Yapp, and her letters were to be directed to the Grand Hotel, London. Having done that, she went straight to London to this place. She arrived there on Thursday, the 21st of last March, at about one o'clock; and at about half-past six a gentleman, whose name we do not know, but who never appears again so far as we know anything about him in this case, came and fetched her. And they went away in a cab, and at eleven at night, when the waiter went to bed, he said they had not returned. That was on the 21st. But, however that may be, the next morning she was undoubtedly at breakfast with a Liverpool gentleman, a cotton-broker, living in Huskisson Street here, whose name cannot be kept out of the case, a gentleman named Brierly. She was found with him on Friday the 22nd, and on Saturday the 23rd. They lived there together as man and wife, slept together, and went out together, and on the Sunday — you will remember she took rooms for a week — about one o'clock they unexpectedly left together, he paying the bill. . . . On the 28th of March (Thursday), exactly a week after she had gone away to London, she returned to Battlecrease House."

That tells us quite clearly that the atmosphere of the Maybrick household was not at 'happiness'. It also shows us that Mrs Maybrick was resolute, was cunning, was daring, and that passion was urging her to the audacious.

On the 29th of March the Grand National was run. The Maybricks were there; but apparently Mrs Maybrick was controlled far more by her passion than by her husband. He had forbidden her to walk about with Brierly, and she took so little notice of his wishes that she walked about the course with her paramour. She said to someone, " I'll give it him hot and strong for speaking to me like that in public." So Mr Maybrick was not a silent sufferer. When they got home the row proper began. In his own house Mr Maybrick turned to violence. He gave his wife a black eye and his upbraiding was torrential.

She had probably denied anything more than trivialities, so her position was not a happy one. But she refused to be beaten and stormed at—particularly when one remembers that Brierly was somewhere in the offing. She dressed to leave home. Her husband tugged at her fur coat and said she wouldn't go in that. A cab was sent for and the servants were all ears listening to this terrible row between master and mistress. " Such a scandal as this will be all over Liverpool to-morrow," he said, echoing that provincial note which rings in us all. " Florence, I never thought it would come to this." And apparently his love of the respectable softened him. " If you once leave this house," he said, using his last threat, " you will never enter it again." He had already seized the children, so they came in as hostages after all.

Alice Yapp, the nurse, put in an appearance. She put an arm round Mrs Maybrick and led her upstairs. And Mrs Maybrick slept at home that night. It would have been far better for her to have crashed the globe of respectability and gone. But to see things in time is not always given us.

Mrs Maybrick went to see an old friend, Mrs Briggs, the next day. She wanted a separation. Mrs Briggs, who was separated from her husband and therefore knew something about such things, played for pacification. But Mrs Maybrick now had a repugnance for her husband. It wasn't a question of forgiveness or a black eye: it was a question of passion. She was in love with Brierly; she couldn't stand this husband of hers, who was twenty-four years her senior. She told Dr Hopper of the repugnance she felt for her husband. But Dr Hopper tried to patch things up. In fact, he succeeded to all outward seeming. Mrs Maybrick's debts—£1,200 —were mentioned and Mr Maybrick agreed to pay them.

About a fortnight after the Grand National Mr Maybrick went to London. One of the debts he had agreed to pay for his wife was with a London money-lender, and that was the principal reason for the visit; another was that Michael Maybrick had suggested that his brother James should come and see Dr Fuller, who practised at Alwyn Street, near Wellington Mansions, Regent's Park.

James Maybrick went to London and had an hour's consultation with Dr Fuller. Nothing particularly the matter, said the doctor. Indigestion —no fear of paralysis at all. He gave him a tonic, and he prescribed nothing with arsenic in it. Neither did he think for a moment that Mr Maybrick was at that time taking arsenic.

About the 20th of April Mrs Maybrick went to a chemist in the neighbourhood and asked him for one dozen fly-papers, alleging that the flies had begun to be troublesome in the kitchen.

When Célestine Doudet had *caleçons de chasteté* she didn't use them. When Madame Lafarge bought arsenic to kill rats, she didn't put down arsenic, but bi-carbonate of soda. If Mrs Maybrick found the flies troublesome in the kitchen, why didn't she put the fly-papers, there? The answer is that, according to Mary Cadwallader, the maid, the flies were not troublesome at that time. And the more pertinent answer is that Mrs Maybrick never bought these fly-papers with the idea of letting the flies blow themselves out on them. She confessed so much herself. She said she got them to use as a cosmetic.

The atmosphere of the Maybrick household was sensitive to fly-papers. Elizabeth Brierley (no connection of the man Brierly), a housemaid, saw in the bedroom, in a small sponge basin on the washstand, some fly-papers. She did what the average housemaid would do in similar circumstances—she called in someone to look at the fly-papers with her. Brierley beckoned Yapp, who lifted up the towel and saw the soaking fly-papers.

What we want to ask is: "What did you think?" We get not a word of that. But their thoughts interest us, and just as we wish to be satisfied we find these two servants are dragged to some other incident.

This is from the evidence of Alice Yapp:

"What did you find?"

"I found the wash-basin covered with a towel, and I took the towel off. There was another towel on a plate, and I lifted the plate and saw a basin containing some fly-papers."

"About how many?"

"I cannot say."

"How do you know they were fly-papers?"

"I saw 'fly-paper' written on them."

"Was there anything else?"

"They were in a basin and there was a small quantity of liquid."

"What did you do?"

"I did not meddle with them and put back the things as I found them."

"Did you ever, up to that time, see any fly-papers in the house at all for killing flies, or anything of that kind?"

"No, sir."

"So far as you know, were there any flies giving trouble?"

"No, sir."

"Did you ever see the fly-papers again?"

"No, sir."

"Do you know what became of them?"

"No, sir."

Elizabeth Brierley said, "I remember seeing some fly-papers in one of the rooms about twelve o'clock one day. They were in the bedroom. That was one day after the Grand National. They were in a small sponge basin on the washstand in my master and mistress's bedroom. I did not see how many fly-papers there were, but I called the attention of Alice Yapp to them. I never mentioned the matter to Mrs Maybrick again. At that time Mrs Maybrick was in the house; I found some traces of the fly-papers afterwards in the slop-pail next morning. There were no fly-papers in use in the house for killing flies; either before or immediately after I saw them in steep in the room. The flies were not troublesome at the time."

The jury subsequently came to a conclusion why those fly-papers had been bought for flies that weren't troublesome and were in 'steep' in the bedroom occupied by Mrs Maybrick. But what did the servants think? There must have been some gossip in the servants' hall. Didn't they know that arsenic could be extracted from fly-papers? They were obviously curious, so they must have talked. . . .

It was about the 27th of April, so the theory ran, that James Maybrick set out on his fatal illness. It was the day of the Wirral Races. Mr Maybrick rode there and it was a very wet day. That might suggest a reason why he should complain the next day of a feeling of numbness up to the knees. But he had complained to Humphreys the cook, before going out that morning, and had felt somewhat seedy all day. At dinner he behaved almost as if he were drunk.

Mrs. Maybrick told Alice Yapp, the nurse, that her master was ill because he had taken an overdose of medicine. Medicines are not beverages and should only be consumed according to orders, but an overdose of this medicine, that Mr Maybrick took, should not in the ordinary way have made him ill; only somehow some arsenic had crept into it!

Naturally, the doctor did not know this at the time, and made the usual diagnosis when he was called to see Mr Maybrick on Sunday, for on that day Mr Maybrick was very ill indeed.

What followed was a sick man's travail.

Every day's doings became of tremendous importance subsequently.

Dr Humphreys was called in on Sunday the 28th of April and visited Mr Maybrick again on the Monday, when he found him better. He came to the conclusion that his patient was suffering from chronic dyspepsia and so prescribed a diet for him—coffee, toast and some bacon for breakfast; some Revalenta food and tea for luncheon, and for dinner he was to have alternate meals of fish and bacon.

But James Maybrick did not get better, though he fancied he was on the right road, for on the Wednesday he told the doctor not to call again. It was a brave message, for on Friday Dr Humphreys was sent for.

Mr Maybrick shook his head over the medicine; he didn't think it was doing him any good. Mrs Maybrick, who was present, said he always complained that medicine did him no good after he had taken it for two or three days. But the curious thing was that the doctor was baffled. He actually said to Mr Maybrick, " I really cannot see anything the matter with you. Your tongue is certainly not so clean as it ought to be, but otherwise I cannot see any difference with you. My advice is to go on the same for two or three weeks; the medicine cannot disagree with you, as it tends more to assist your digestion than anything else."

And there was no arsenic in the prescription given by Dr Humphreys.

But on Monday the 28th inst Mrs Maybrick went to another chemist in Cressington and bought two dozen fly-papers, each paper containing $1\frac{1}{2}$ grains of arsenic. Nobody but Mrs Maybrick knew these arsenical fly-papers were in the house. For flies? Or cosmetic? Or what? . . .

Mr Maybrick had a Turkish bath and was so ill after it that Dr Humphreys was sent for at midnight. The doctor found his patient suffering great pain from the hips to the knees. Some of these shampooers in the baths are occasionally rough, and Dr Humphreys thought one of them might have overdone the rubbing and towelling.

But Mr Maybrick also mentioned that he had been sick, and promptly found a reason for it, as sick men will—it was because some inferior sherry had been put into Du Barry's Revalenta food.

One sees the doctor nodding like a young Jove. "H'm . . . H'm! . . . ."

However, to relieve the pain the doctor ordered injections of morphia.

But Mr Maybrick's sickness would not leave him. He could retain nothing in his stomach and had been vomiting, when Dr Humphreys saw him on the 4th. Still, morphia did play havoc with the stomach. . . . He ordered ipecacuanha wine to allay the vomiting. But the ipecacuanha wine was ineffectual. On the Sunday Mr Maybrick was vomiting and hawking. His mouth was dirty and his throat was troublesome. "Don't quite like this somehow," one can hear the doctor saying, for he suggested to Mrs Maybrick that another doctor should be called in. Mrs Maybrick wouldn't hear of that.

The doctor ordered Valentine's meat juice, but it had no better luck than the ipecacuanha wine, so that was stopped. Also the medicine. And Dr Humphreys gave his patient some arsenic. He mixed it himself. It was Fowler's solution, which is a mixture of arsenic, carbonate of potash and lavender water. There were sixty or eighty doses and the whole of them contained about 1-25th of a grain. Mr Maybrick took three doses of that medicine, by which he consumed 1-250th of a grain of arsenic.

The doctor saw samples of the vomit—one greenish, the other yellowish.

On Monday the patient had a blister, and on Tuesday he spoke most cheerfully to the doctor, "Humphreys, I am quite a different man altogether to-day, after you put on that blister last night."

Dr Humphreys threw away the remainder of Fowler's solution of arsenic, poured it away himself down the slop basin.

A Dr Carter was called in by Mr Edwin Maybrick, and the two doctors after consultation came to the opinion Mr Maybrick would soon recover.

Friends called at Battlecrease House naturally, and amongst the callers was Mrs Briggs, who had been Mrs Maybrick's confidante after the trouble following the Grand National row. And it was to Mrs Briggs and Mrs Hughes, her sister, that the servants, who had gossiped about those fly-papers, poured their hints and suspicions. After all, if you go to visitors with a tale about the mistress there is probably something in the nature of a suspicion.

"Fly-papers soaking . . ." And Mrs Briggs knew that Florence Maybrick had been "carrying on" with the man, Brierly, for she had also been to the post office to get a letter for Mrs Maybrick, who didn't apparently wish it to be addressed to the house where her husband lived.

A telegram was sent to Michael Maybrick in London:

"Come at once. Strange things going on here."

A nurse was sent for, and when Nurse Gore arrived, Mr Edwin Maybrick told her that no one was to be allowed to attend on his brother, except the nurses.

Suspicion was markedly flapping his wings in Battlecrease House on that day. And on that day Mrs Maybrick gave Alice Yapp a letter to post. But Alice Yapp didn't post it. It was addressed to "A. Brierly, Esq.", and Alice Yapp opened it and gave it to Mr Edwin Maybrick.

As Alice Yapp's cross-examination by Sir Charles Russell was of tense, dramatic character, we will quote it.

"Now with regard to this letter, you had heard the name of your mistress coupled with the name of Brierly before you got the letter?"

"Never."

"Why did you open that letter?"

"Because Mrs Maybrick wished that it should go by that post."

"Why did you open that letter?"

(No reply.)

The Judge: "Did anything happen to the letter?"

"Yes, it fell in the dirt, my lord."

Sir Charles Russell: "Why did you open that letter?"

"I have answered you, sir."

The Judge: "She said because it fell in the dirt."

Sir Charles Russell: "I think with great deference to your lordship, she did not say so; your lordship is referring to something before."

The Judge: "She has said so just now."

Sir Charles Russell: "Well, I did not catch it;

anyhow I want to have it out again." (To witness), "Why did you open that letter?"

"I opened the letter to put it in a clean envelope."

"Why didn't you put it in a clean envelope without opening it?"

(No reply.)

"Was it a wet day?"

"It was showery."

"Are you sure of that?"

"Yes."

"Will you undertake to say that? I ask you to consider. Was it a wet day?"

(No reply.)

"Aye or no?"

(No reply.)

"Was it a wet or a dry day?"

(No reply.)

"Had the day before been a dry day?"

"It was showery."

"Will you swear that on Wednesday it was showery?"

"I cannot say positively."

"Was the child in a perambulator?"

"No, sir."

"Was the child able to walk?"

"Yes, sir."

"What did you do with the letter?"

"I gave it to Mr Edwin Maybrick."

"No. No. I mean when you got it from Mrs Maybrick?"

"I gave it to the child to post."

"Did you ever do that before?"

"Always. And Mrs Maybrick always gave letters to the baby to carry to the post."

"I was asking what you did with it?"

"I gave it to the baby."

"Always did?"

"Yes."

"Did this incident ever happen, or anything like it before?"

"No, sir."

"Let me see the letter. Have you got the envelope? Where did the child drop it?"

"Right by the post office in crossing the road."

"Which side?"

"Near the post office."

"Then you had securely passed the road and were stepping on to the kerbstone?"

"Yes."

"And saw this mark upon it, did you?"

"Yes."

"Just take it in your hand. Is the direction clear enough?"

"It was much dirtier at the time."

"It hasn't obscured the direction, which is plain enough?"

"No."

"You didn't rub the mud off. What did you do?"

"I went into the post office and asked for a clean envelope to readdress it. I opened it as I was going into the post office."

"Did it never occur to you that you could get a clean envelope, if you were particular about cleanliness, and put it unopened into that?"

"Oh, I never thought of that."

"Then between the picking of it up on the post office side of the pathway, and your going into the shop you had formed the design of opening it, and did, in fact, open it as you were going in?"

"Yes."

"If, as you suggest, this fell in the mud and was wet there is no running of the ink in that direction. Look at it?"

"No, sir."

"Can you suggest how there can be any damp

or wet in connection with it without causing some running of the ink ? "

" I cannot."

" On your oath, girl, did you not manufacture that stain as an excuse for opening your mistress's letter ? "

" I did not."

" Have you any explanation to offer about the running of the ink ? "

" I have not."

" I put it to you for the last time. Did you not open the letter deliberately because you suspected your mistress ? "

" No, sir. I did not."

And when Mr Addison re-examined her she still protested she had no suspicions.

Curious. She and the other servants talk about fly-papers. There are probably to-day and there certainly were then many people, including cooks and housemaids, who did not know that arsenic could be extracted from fly-papers. In that case why did Brierley and Yapp look seriously at the fly-papers in the basin ? Why was Mrs Briggs told about the fly-papers ?

All people must betray themselves. The nurse girl has a certain pride; she flatters herself she can boast of certain qualities. The reading of a letter out of pure curiosity, or of curiosity tinged with suspicion, doesn't sound a nice action. . . . It is better to suggest a clean envelope. And the child may have dropped the letter. But no suspicion ? One is inclined to shake one's head over that.

A contemporary writer at the time thus described this scene. " The calling of the name of ' Alice Yapp ' by Mr Addison created a murmur of excitement in court. This young nurse, who was in the Maybrick household, and who distinguished herself by opening her mistress's letter to Mr Brierly, is a good-looking girl of about two-and-twenty with a painfully diffident manner—somewhat in contrast with her demeanour at the inquest, when the whole affair seemed to be treated in a light-hearted and somewhat frivolous humour. She was dressed in sober black, with a high black hat with ribbon trimmings and a bunch of pink flowers. . . .

"At this point a slight incident showed that the great cross-examiner had a claw under the velvet paw with which he played with the witness. Mr Addison whispered a correction of something the girl said. Sir Charles promptly sat down and snapped, 'Make your objection'. Mr Addison had to rise somewhat lugubriously, and after the 'objection' was taken and the Judge had muttered something, Sir Charles rose and went on with his examination with the most supreme indifference. He had shown his teeth however, and the next series of questions made the girl in the witness-box visibly tremble.

"'Why did you open the letter?' The girl faltered the old explanation about dropping it in the mud and her intention to get a clean envelope.

"'*Why* did you open the letter?' thundered the counsel, as if no explanation had been given.

"Three times over he repeated the question. The Judge came to the rescue of the trembling girl and repeated her explanation. Sir Charles impetuously interrupted his lordship with, 'You are thinking of something you have before you, or that she has said before. I want it *now*'.

"Several of the counsel round Sir Charles assured him that the girl had explained, and the Judge was again going to help the witness out of her trouble when the defending counsel cut it all short by, 'Never mind if she has: I want it again. Why— did — you— open — that — letter?' Mrs Maybrick looked up slightly and everybody in the court, amid the dead silence that followed the five times repeated question, must have felt a palpitation similar to the witness. She admitted in re-examination that her suspicions had been originally aroused by talk in the house about the taste of the food."

So we get the great cross-examiner baffled by the nurse-maid because she won't admit she suspected her mistress. But why this breaking of a butterfly on a wheel? What Sir Charles Russell did not get, by this thunder, Mr Addison drew by his suavity. When Sir Charles sat down Mr Addison rose.

"When you opened the letter you still thought nothing of it?" (The 'it' refers to the fly-papers.)

"Yes, when I saw what was in that letter."

This presumably means: I hadn't been suspicious before, but when I saw what was in the letter I was.

But this followed: "Was that the first time you had any suspicion about it?"

"No, sir. I had been told of the soup, and bread and milk and things tasting differently."

"That was before you opened the letter?"

"Yes."

From which we gather that there *was* gossip in the kitchen, and the servants had wagged their heads over the discovery of the fly-papers, and they had also talked about food "tasting differently". That came from the cook. So we venture to suggest that Alice Yapp did not paint the intellectual and emotional situation exactly when representing herself as going suspicionless with a letter from her mistress addressed to A. Brierly, Esq., about whom all the servants knew there had been a terrible row between the master and mistress after the Grand National.

Sir Charles Russell in his final speech for the defence had to refer to this letter, and this is what he said, "On that Wednesday occurred an event, the importance of which I do not seek for one moment to conceal from myself—for so important do I regard it as even to suggest to you that if it had not taken place you never would have heard of this charge. I mean the intercepted letter on the Wednesday to the man Brierly. Mr Addison, in opening his case, referred to that letter. I don't at all complain of the way in which he referred to it. But that letter discloses clearly this, that she was addressing the man, Brierly, even then in terms in the highest degree improper, that she was betraying an anxiety to keep on close and affectionate terms with him as long as there was any chance of discovery of the guilty visit she had paid to London, and that she was speaking, aye, and if you wish, speaking in exaggerated language of the illness of her husband as it then appeared, and of the serious character of the illness. In that letter she also speaks of the presence of his relatives, and of the anxiety which she shows, and when you come to recollect the story of Mrs Briggs and her sister and the statement of Nurse Gore you cannot have any doubt how it came that that illness presented so serious an aspect to her, and how she came to describe the feelings of herself and of her husband's relatives as feelings of terrible anxiety. Why do I say this? Because Mrs Briggs and her sister came, and they both tell you in the box they at once came to the conclusion that he was—I will not say in mortal peril—but in peril, and that it was a most serious state of things —far more serious than the doctors thought it was—and they said so to Mrs Maybrick. When Nurse Gore came she thought it a very serious case. The servant in the house, Yapp, speaks to the same effect. The letter was written and given to be posted, but it never was conveyed to the post office under the circumstances which you have heard. You may recollect my cross-examination of Nurse Yapp. That cross-examination was not directed to throwing any doubt upon the fact that the letter was written and was given to her to be posted, because there has been no contest about that at all, but in order that you might see how rapidly and how strongly suspicion had been generated in the minds of the servants in that house. Suspicion being generated, how probable it was that every act of this woman would, as far as they could scan it, be scanned by jealous and even suspicious eyes; and while it is not material to my purpose to do more than this, I do suggest that the story as to the reason why that letter was opened has not been truly and fully given you by the nurse—that, if it fell, it fell as a contrivance to supply an excuse for opening it, for it is obvious that in the case of an intelligent person like that, even if it was the case that the address had been so smeared as not to be perfectly legible, the obvious course which a trustworthy servant would pursue, if there were not any motive to the contrary, would have been merely to enclose that letter unopened in another envelope. Even that letter—take it, read it, scan it as you will, with all its exaggerations—for exaggeration there is—read it, and ask yourselves is it the letter of a guilty woman who is then planning the murder of her husband?"

Very well, let us take and read and scan that letter.

First we will read Brierly's to her.

My dear Florrie,

I suppose now you have gone I am safe in writing to you. I don't quite understand what you mean in your last about explaining my line of action. You know I could not write, and was willing to meet you, although it would have been very dangerous. Most certainly your telegram yesterday was a staggerer, and it looks as if the result was certain, but as yet I cannot find an advertisement in any London paper.

(Obviously they were afraid that if their London visit had not been discovered, it was the object of suspicion.)

I should like to see you, but at present dare not move, and we had better perhaps not meet until late in the autumn. I am going to try and get away in about a fortnight. I think I shall take a round trip to the Mediterranean, which will take six or seven weeks, unless *you wish me to stay in England*. Supposing the rooms are found, I think both you and I would be better away, as the man's memory would be doubted after three months. I will write and tell you when I go. I cannot trust myself at present to write about my feelings on this unhappy business, but I do hope that sometime hence I shall be able to show you that I do not quite deserve the strictures contained in your last two letters. I went to the D. and D. and of course heard some tales, but myself knew nothing about anything. And now dear, good-bye, hoping we shall meet again in the autumn. I will write to you about sending letters just before I go.

A. B.

It was in answer to that letter that Mrs Maybrick wrote what follows:

Wednesday.

DEAREST,

Your letter under cover to John K. came to hand just after I had written to you on Monday. I did not expect to hear from you so soon, and had delayed in giving him the necessary instructions. Since my return I have been nursing M. day and night. *He is sick unto death.* The doctors held a consultation yesterday, and now all depends upon how long his strength will hold out. Both my brothers-in-law are here and we are terribly anxious. I cannot answer your letter fully to-day, my darling, but relieve your mind of *all fear of discovery now and in the future.* M. has been delirious since Sunday, and I know now that *he is perfectly ignorant of everything, even of the name of the street, and also that he has not been making any enquiries whatever.* The tale he told me was a pure fabrication, and only intended to frighten the truth out of me. In fact he *believes* my statement, although he will not *admit it.* You need not therefore go abroad on that account, dearest; but, in any case, please don't leave England, until *I have seen you once again.* You must feel that those two letters of mine were written under circumstances which must even excuse their injustice in your eyes. Do you suppose I could act as I am doing if I really felt and meant what I inferred then ? If you wish to write to me about anything do *so now,* as all the letters pass through my hands at present. Excuse this scrawl, my own darling, but I dare not leave the room for a moment, and I do not know when I shall be able to write to you again. In haste.

Yours ever,
FLORRIE.

Mrs Maybrick's diagnosis of her husband's disease was not that of the doctors'. Dr Carter had been called in for a consultation with Dr Humphreys on Tuesday, the day before Mrs Maybrick's letter to Brierly was written, and Dr Carter suggested Mr Maybrick was suffering from acute dyspepsia and acute inflammation of the stomach. Dr Humphreys said he formed a hopeful prognosis and thought Mr Maybrick would soon recover. Mrs Maybrick's reading of the case the day after the consultation between the doctors after a hopeful prognosis had been formed was that her husband was *sick unto death,* and so she wrote to " dearest " not to go away yet. As if to emphasize the staring fatality of his illness, Mrs Maybrick, it will be noticed, said, " M. (that is Maybrick) has been delirious since Sunday ". Dr Humphreys, who was attending Mr Maybrick, had not noticed that delirium. He was asked in the box, " Had he been in any way delirious since Sunday or did you say so ? " " No," he answered.

Nurse Yapp, having heard the quarrel between

her master and mistress after the Grand National, having seen fly-papers in soak, and knowing her master is very seriously ill, had also read a letter from her mistress to someone she addressed as "Dearest," in which it was said . . . "He is sick unto death. . . ."

Mr Edwin Maybrick had had a telegram from Mrs Maybrick that day, saying, " Jim worse again ; have wired for a nurse". So he went to Battlecrease and also telegraphed to his brother Michael Maybrick in London.

And at about half-past five Nurse Yapp, who had something on her mind, asked Mr Maybrick if she could speak to him. They went into the garden, to a seat, out of sight of the house, and there Nurse Yapp gave him the letter beginning, "Dearest", signed "Florrie", and addressed to A. Brierly, Esq.

It is easy to picture the scene of the nurse handing that terrible letter to her master's brother on that May afternoon in the garden of Battlecrease House.

Mr Edwin Maybrick did not say in the box what he thought, but we can imagine it. We know that he waited eagerly for the arrival of his brother, and the two of them read once more the letter addressed to A. Brierly beginning "Dearest . . ."

A new nurse, named Gore, had arrived that day, and the brothers of the sick man—there was no nonsense about suspicions now—gave orders that no food, nothing was to be given to the invalid, except by the nurses.

At half-past six that night Nurse Gore remarked that a tumbler was missing. Mrs Maybrick put some medicine in it and said water must be added, or it would burn the patient's throat. Nurse Gore had no intention of letting her patient burn his throat with that medicine, so she threw it in the sink in the housemaid's closet. And afterwards traces of arsenic were found in the closet, without anybody being able to suggest how they got there except on the assumption that there was arsenic in the medicine which Mrs Maybrick poured in the glass which Nurse Gore poured in the closet.

The progress of the disease was thus described by Mr Addison: "The 9th of May was Thursday. Nurse Gore had been on duty a long time on Thursday, and at eleven o'clock the institution sent another nurse named Callery, who relieved Nurse Gore. Dr Carter, head physician, came on the afternoon of the 9th, when Nurse Callery was there. On Tuesday both doctors could only attribute the symptoms of Mr Maybrick to acute dyspepsia, but on Thursday there came on with increased violence during the night a symptom which at once attracted the marked attention of Dr Carter. He found this tenesmus, this straining and retching, was very painful and persistent; and he then for the first time seems to have come to the conclusion that they showed a symptom which an acute dyspepsia would not account for, and there was then a strong presumption that the symptoms were those, and those only, of an irritant poison."

In examination the doctor was asked, "But did you not suspect the presence of any poison?"

"No, certainly not."

"As a doctor you would not do so?"

"No, decidedly not. It is the last thing—the very last thing—we would think of."

Which seems a pity.

Nurse Gore returned at eleven o'clock on Thursday night, and to us it is clear there was an atmosphere of suspicion in that house. The wife of the sick man was not allowed to give him any food or drink —not even a bit of ice. Her nursemaid and her brothers-in-law had read her letter to Brierly, though of this she was ignorant. The nurses had to watch her as if they were spies. . . .

Nurse Gore on returning to duty opened a bottle of Valentine's meat juice. And now let us quote from the actual evidence given by Nurse Gore.

"Did anyone else come in?" (this was on Thursday night).

"Yes, Mrs Maybrick came in."

"Now, tell us in your own way what happened at that time, between the Thursday night and the Friday morning?"

"Mrs Maybrick passed through the bedroom, and in doing so she took the bottle from the chest of drawers."

"Is that the same bottle you opened and made the extract for Mr Maybrick?"

"Yes."

"Now what happened after that?"

"She went into the dressing-room and remained there about two minutes."

"What did she do then?"

"She brought it back into the room and wished me to go for some ice."

"How do you know she wished you to do so?"

"She expressed it."

"What did she say?"

"She told me to get some ice to put in the water to bathe Mr Maybrick's head."

"Did you see what she did with the bottle?"

"She raised her hand and put it on the table."

"How did she do it?"

"She had her hand by her side, and while speaking to me raised it and put the bottle on the table."

"She asked you to get some ice—you had to go out of the room to get it?"

"Yes."

"What did you say to that?"

"I said to her that the patient was asleep; I could go when he awoke."

"What happened next?"

"She went to lie down in the dressing-room."

Nurse Gore explained how she had opened this new bottle of meat juice and put it in water to reduce it to its proper strength, and that it was this bottle Mrs Maybrick had taken out of the room.

"It was afterwards moved to the washstand?"

"Yes."

"Your attention was directed to it?"

"Yes."

"And it perhaps would not be too much to say that your suspicions were aroused?"

"Yes."

"Very well. Your suspicions being aroused you took care not to give it to the patient?"

"Yes."

"So it stands thus—you are positive that during your watch nothing was given from this bottle?"

"No."

"Is it not a fact that before you left your watch after that incident, you mentioned the circumstance to the nurse who succeeded you so as to put her on her guard?"

"Yes."

And Nurse Callery also kept her eye on that meat juice which Mrs Maybrick had carried out of the bedroom and then removed from a table to the washstand. It was subsequently handed to Mr Michael Maybrick, who handed it to Dr Carter, who found arsenic in it.

On Friday the 10th Mr Maybrick was in a very exhausted condition. Nurse Callery heard him say to Mrs Maybrick, "You have given me the wrong medicine again." She retorted with, "What are you talking about? You never had wrong medicine." And on the evening of that day the patient said to Mrs Maybrick, "Oh, Bunny, Bunny, how could you do it? I did not think it of you." Three times he said it, and we can only conjecture what he meant.

Her reply was, " You silly old darling, don't trouble your head about things."

Dr Carter didn't diagnose the patient's illness as acute dyspepsia now. But the knowledge had lingered too long. James Maybrick died.

After what had happened it was obvious that Mrs Maybrick would be arrested and charged with poisoning her husband.

A search was made in the house, and in a closet was found a chocolate box in which was a parcel labelled " Arsenic Poison," and written after it the words, " for cats ". In a hat-box there was a bottle of Valentine's meat essence, containing arsenic, and some other bottles containing arsenic in process of solution. One bottle contained a strong solution of arsenic, with several grains in a solid form in the bottle; another bottle contained several grains solid and also a strong solution; and a third bottle contained fifteen or twenty grains solid arsenic, but only two drops of the solution. In the other hat-box there was a tumbler, which contained a fluid resembling milk, and in that tumbler was a piece of a handkerchief soaking. In this tumbler were twenty grains of arsenic. Later, Mrs Maybrick's dressing-gown was examined; it was the dressing-gown she had worn when her husband was in his last illness. A handkerchief was found in one of the pockets containing traces of arsenic.

There was a post-mortem, and the doctors who conducted it came to the conclusion that James Maybrick died from the administration of arsenic.

Mrs Maybrick in her trouble turned to Brierly.

Battlecrease House,
Aigburth.

The " dearest " has gone. It doesn't do to write that now. So she begins curtly:

> I am writing to you to give me every assistance in your power in my present fearful trouble. I am in custody,

without any of my family with me and without money. I have cabled to my solicitor in New York to come here at once. In the meantime, send some money for present needs. The truth is known about my visit to London. Your last letter is in the hands of the police. Appearances may be against me, but before God I swear I am innocent.

     FLORENCE E. MAYBRICK.

It was a sensational case. Almost all such cases are when they are lit with passion, which casts over them a brilliant if sickly hue.

Mr Brierly was present at the inquest, and the curious may be interested to know that he was very ordinary looking—scarcely even that. He was not called as a witness, but he was at hand both during the inquest and the trial. The public got its thrills from the bits of evidence—the buying of fly-papers, Alice Yapp's story of the dropped letter, Mrs Maybrick's declaration to a Mrs Samuelson that she hated her husband, the presence of " Stephen Adams ", the singer, who was Mr Michael Maybrick.

The coroner's jury returned a verdict of wilful murder against Mrs Maybrick.

The trial took place at Liverpool on July 31st, 1889, before Sir James Fitzjames Stephen. Mr Addison, Q.C., Mr W. R. McConnell and Mr Thomas Swift prosecuted, and the prisoner was defended by Sir Charles Russell Q.C., and Mr William Pickford.

The indictment was : that Florence Elizabeth Maybrick, aged twenty-six, did feloniously, wilfully and of malice aforethought, kill and murder one James Maybrick.

The outline of the case we have already given. The facts mentioned were elicited in the course of the trial. The battle took place on the plain ground of poison. " The deceased," said the defence, " was a regular drug-taker, and if he died of poison it was not administered by the prisoner. In any case we do not agree that Mr Maybrick died of arsenic poisoning. We say it was gastro-enteritis."

The defence, taking that line, had practically to let the *liaison* with Brierly go by default. Sir Charles Russell's dramatic cross-examination of Alice Yapp was done to discredit that witness and, as he said, to suggest there was an atmosphere of suspicion at Battlecrease House.

This case has been discussed almost as much as the trial of Charles I. It has a peculiar fascination for lawyers. Their legal minds alight with gladness on the forensic hillocks of the Maybrick case where they crow and sharpen their beaks; and those who are flustered by wig and gown and the meticulous, ask with the expression of fledglings, " Was Mrs Maybrick *really* guilty ? "

There was no question of the fact that Mrs Maybrick had been carrying on an illicit intercourse with Brierly, that she had written a letter to her lover at the time her husband was ill, but also at a time when the doctors thought he was progressing favourably, saying, ' he was sick unto death ', that she had bought a great number of fly-papers from which she had undoubtedly got arsenic, that she had been seen handling Mr Maybrick's medicine and food suspiciously and that after she had taken some meat juice out of the room and brought it back it contained arsenic. And from the dock she confessed to putting some " white powder " in it. Arsenic is a white powder.

Did James Maybrick die of arsenical poisoning ?

Dr Humphreys, who with Dr Carter and Dr Barron conducted the post-mortem in the course of his evidence, had to answer this question :

" From what you saw during his life and from the post-mortem examination, what do you say was the cause of death ? "

His answer was, " Arsenic. Arsenical poisoning."

Subsequently he added, ". . . I said arsenical poisoning. I said that knowing as I do that an examination has been made of the contents of the stomach; but, asking me what conclusion I came to after having made the post-mortem, recollecting the symptoms that he died of, I could only say that it was due to some irritant poison, most probably arsenic, but I should not like to swear that it was."

Sir Charles Russell cross-examined Dr Humphreys principally with the view to showing that other causes, other than arsenic, might not only have contributed to but actually caused Mr Maybrick's death.

And this is interesting.

Sir Charles Russell is cross-examining.

"I wish to ask you this, you have said, have you not, that but for the suggestion of arsenic, you would have been prepared to give a certificate of the cause of death?"

"No, I did not say so. I said the suggestion was made before I conceived it, before I thought of it on Wednesday or Thursday."

"I think you said so yesterday, Dr Humphreys —that the idea of arsenic did not occur to your mind until it was suggested to you? Had it not been for the suggestion of arsenic, were you prepared to give a certificate of death if he had died on Wednesday?"

"Yes."

"And in your judgment what was the cause of death?"

"Acute congestion of the stomach."

"Do you call that gastritis or gastro-enteritis?"

"Yes, gastritis or gastro-enteritis."

Mr Justice Stephen asked, "Then if nothing about poisoning had been suggested to you, you would have certified that he had died of gastritis or gastro-enteritis?"

"Yes, my lord."

Sir Charles Russell: " Now, Dr Humphreys, I wish to ask you this question, and just consider, please, before you answer it. Mention any post-mortem symptom—never mind the analysis for the moment—but mention any post-mortem symptom which is distinctive of arsenical poisoning and which is not also distinctive of gastritis or gastro-enteritis ? "

" I can't give you any."

Dr Humphreys was subsequently asked by Mr Addison :

" Can you in some of its stages distinguish it (an irritant poison) from irritability caused by dyspepsia ? "

" No, I could not."

In other words the symptoms that distinguish irritability of the stomach caused by acute dyspepsia and that caused by arsenic are very similar.

The reader might like to know what the symptoms from arsenical poisoning are. This is from the *Encyclopaedia Britannica*, " In a typical case a sensation of heat developing into a burning pain is felt in the throat and stomach. This is soon followed by uncontrolled vomiting and a little later by severe purging, the stools being first of all falcal but later assuming a rice-water appearance and often containing blood. The patient suffers from intense thirst, which cannot be relieved as drinking is immediately followed by rejection of the swallowed fluid. There is profound collapse, the features are sunken and respiration is difficult. The pain in the stomach is persistent, and cramps in the calves of the legs add to the torture. . . . In criminal poisoning repeated doses are usually given, so that such cases may not be typical, but will present some of the aspects of acute and some of chronic arsenical poisoning. . . ."

Mr Maybrick vomited and hawked. His throat was dry and he had a burning thirst. He had pains in his legs. His bowels were loose and the purging

was so violent he was sore. He suffered from tenesmus
—which is a terrible straining of the bowels—without
any result.

Dr Humphreys was asked this question about
tenesmus.

" Have you attended cases of dyspepsia very
often and have you ever known it accompanied by
tenesmus ? "

" Never."

" Have you ever seen a case of tenesmus to the
same degree as this ? "

" I never recollect having seen it to this degree."

And at the end of his cross-examination and re-
examination Dr Humphreys was asked this :

" Have you any doubt from the symptoms, the
post-mortem, and the analysis made by Mr Davies,
and the case altogether—have you any doubt of the
cause of death ? "

" No, I have no doubt whatever."

By Mr Justice Stephen. " I want your last
sentence explained. When you say, ' I have no
doubt whatever ', do I understand you to include
in that opinion your knowledge of the result of the
chemical analysis ? "

" It includes everything collectively, with all the
symptoms during life, all the appearance after
death, and the result of the analysis of the contents
of the stomach."

Recall it. " From what you saw during his life
and from the post-mortem examination, what do
you say was the cause of death ? "

" Arsenic. Arsenical poisoning."

Dr Carter in his evidence said, " Dr Humphreys
said deceased had been suffering for some days from
vomiting. I must make a slight correction in the
sequence of the symptoms. Diarrhoea was just
appearing. His principal complaint was of extreme
dryness and irritability in the throat ; of a sensation

as if a hair was in it, and the extremely foul taste which he had in his mouth. He said he had been vomiting for several days. . . . I concluded that deceased was suffering from acute dyspepsia. . . ."

The pregnant questions : " Now taking the whole of the history of the case, your conclusion is ? "

" I can have no doubt about it."

" Excuse me, you can't have any doubt about what, doctor ? "

" That it was arsenical poisoning."

Dr Alexander Barron, Professor of Pathology at University College, Liverpool, and a practising physician said, " I did not attend the late Mr James Maybrick during his life-time, but I assisted at the post-mortem examination of the body on the 13th of May. I understood that I attended the post-mortem on Mrs Maybrick's behalf, and I assisted at it with Dr Carter and Dr Humphreys. I came to the conclusion that death was due to acute inflammation of the stomach, probably caused by some irritant poison."

Mr Edward Davies, an analytical and consulting chemist of Liverpool, Fellow of the Pharmaceutical Society, and of the Institute of Chemists, said he had analyzed a bottle of meat juice given him by Dr Carter.

" With what result ? "

" I found presence of arsenic."

" Can you tell me whether that arsenic had been put in in solution or solid ? "

" It had been put in, I believe, in solution, because there was no solid arsenic in it."

The witness also analyzed the intestines and found arsenic there.

" What is the next that contained arsenic ? "

" Three glass jars, 1, 2, and 3. They contain arsenic."

"What are they?"

"The stomach, no arsenic; the liver, arsenic distinctly."

There was a fourth glass covered with white paper and sealed No. 2 and 4, containing arsenic. They are deposits. They were taken from the sinks or from the lavatory of the house. No. 8, containing arsenic, was a bottle with a black powder and a handkerchief. There was no arsenic in the bottle, but there was in the handkerchief.

"What is this bottle?"

"It is a bottle with liquid and black powder found in Mrs Maybrick's bedroom."

"How do you describe the bottle?"

"It contains liquid up to the top of this paper and in it I found some twelve to fifteen grains of solid arsenic."

"What did you find in No. 10?"

These numbers referred to the exhibits. The parts of the body and other articles that had been analyzed and found to contain arsenic were numbered and, where possible, put into bottles. The reference to the number made it easy for witnesses and counsel to follow.

"It contained a saturated solution of arsenic with a small portion of solid arsenic at the bottom."

"What do you find in No. 11?"

"I found several grains of solid arsenic and a small quantity of fluid. . . . There would be ten to twelve grains in the bottle."

No. 12 was a tumbler.

"It contained a liquid evidently milk, and there was a handkerchief in it thoroughly soaked. I squeezed the handkerchief, and took a portion of it and some of the liquid and tested it for arsenic. I found a very large quantity, so I took the remainder semi-fluid, a portion of which I had used, and would be about one half, and found that what still remained in the handkerchief would be 4.50 grains. That contained 2.94 or practically three grains of arsenic. That would be altogether in the portion that remained between thirty and forty grains in the whole lot. . . .

"The next article is No. 17. This is a box described as a chocolate-box, and it contained a package marked 'Arsenic, poison for cats'. This now contains, with what was taken for analysis, 71 grains. Of these 65.2 were arsenic, the remainder being charcoal in a fine powder. . . . No. 27 of the list was the pan, basin and jug, which I received for examination. Pan and basin, when first examined, were apparently clean, but under the ledge of the jug were two little drops of dried skim, rather less than a quarter of an inch long, such as might have come from gruel. I boiled the water in the pan and poured it into the basin, thence back to the pan, and then into the jug, after having made the water boiling hot again. I then rinsed them out with distilled water and reduced the bulk, which I tested for arsenic. . . . I got distinct stain in the first instance, and with Reinsch's test afterwards I got very marked and distinct crystals of arsenic. I then bought a new pan of the same kind as the other, and boiled distilled water in it for two or three hours and reduced it to a small bulk, and tested it for arsenic. . . . The only possible thing from which it could have come was the substance adhering to the jug. . . . I examined the dressing-gown, and in the pocket I found some stains, not very much. I cut the pocket out, and testing it, found distinct traces of arsenic. From subsequent tests I found there was no arsenic in the material or dye of the dress. There was a handkerchief found in the dressing gown, which bore Mrs Maybrick's name. . . . I found 2-100ths of a grain of arsenic in the whole handkerchief. . . . After Mr Maybrick's body was disinterred I made a determination of the amount of arsenic in the liver. That was on June 3rd. I received a large stone jar containing the kidney and part of the liver, part of the heart, the scrotum, the femur, the sternum, the lungs and part of the pelvic bones. . . . I distributed the contents of this jar into six other jars. Then I tested the kidneys. I took four ounces and found arsenic, but did not get it sufficiently pure to enable me to weigh it. I estimated the amount at about 1-100th part of a grain. I took six ounces of liver, but owing to the presence of a large quantity of bismuth I found it difficult to get the article sufficiently pure to weigh. In purifying I lost a considerable part. I weighed 2-100ths of a grain, which in the whole liver would be equal to about one-eighth of a grain. This was a minimum quantity. There was certainly that; I believe more. The liver weighed about three pounds. I analyzed the pelvic bone, but could not detect any arsenic, nor could I do so in the lungs and heart. . . . I sent what remained of all samples to Dr Stevenson in London. . . . I have been an analyst for thirty-six years."

Dr Stevenson, the next witness, whose evidence we shall quote, edited an edition of Taylor's *Medical Jurisprudence*. This quotation from that book will be found interesting.

"It need hardly be observed that the quantity of arsenic found in the stomach or other organs can convey no accurate idea of the quantity actually taken by the deceased, since more or less of the poison may have been removed by violent vomiting or purging, as well as by absorption and elimination."

In other words, be sure there is arsenic in the body: the quantity is not all important.

Dr Stevenson had, as we have seen, samples of the viscera of the deceased to analzye.

His view on the case was put tersely.

"What does that result in in your mind?" he was asked.

"That the body at the time of death probably contained a fatal dose of arsenic. I have found a little more or a little less than the quantity I did find here in undoubtedly fatal cases of arsenical poisoning."

"What do you say, doctor?"

"I have no doubt that this man died from the effects of arsenic."

"Tell us the general grounds of that opinion."

"His main symptoms were those attributable to irritant poisoning; and during his more serious illness, I think all his symptoms might be attributed to that. The symptoms of irritant poisoning more closely resemble those of arsenic than those of any other irritant of which I know."

"In what respect is that so?"

"Well, the dryness of the throat, glazed appearance, the whole character of the sickness, and, taking the whole of it, the anomalies—if I might use the term—of the symptoms, are more marked in arsenic than in any other form of irritant poisoning. . . . The general symptoms of arsenical poison which usually appear within half an hour to an hour of taking some article of food or medicine are nausea, with a sinking sensation at the stomach; vomiting, and unlike vomiting produced by any ordinary article of food or drink that disagrees, the vomiting affords no relief, as a rule, and often comes on again. Then there is most commonly pain in the stomach and diarrhoea. After a time the region of the stomach becomes tender to pressure; the patient becomes restless; often bathed in perspiration. The throat is complained of; there is pain in the throat extending down to the stomach. The tongue is very foul in appearance and furred. There is not the bad smell as in the ordinary dyspeptic tongue. The patient goes on getting collapsed, gets a rapid and feeble pulse, a thirst; there is great straining at stool; vomits and evacuations are frequently stained with blood, and the patient dies."

Sir Charles Russell's defence of Mrs Maybrick was able. His line was this: James Maybrick died of something that set up irritation in the stomach. Call it gastritis or gastro-enteritis. It is not an uncommon complaint. It can be caused by food. All the doctors agreed to that. And as a matter of fact, doctors will be called as witness who will say that the deceased died of gastro-enteritis and that there is no reason to suggest he died of arsenical poisoning. Even Dr Stevenson has admitted that the finding of arsenic in the body makes him say Mr Maybrick died of arsenic and not of gastro-enteritis. But what if I show you that the deceased took arsenic? That he was a drug-taker? That would account for the arsenic in the body.

Evidence was called that Mr Maybrick had at one time suffered from malaria and took arsenic as a periodic. This witness only testified to the years from 1877 to 1881. The trial took place in 1889.

A ship's captain gave similar evidence to something that related to the year 1880.

A waiter from a hotel in Norfolk, Virginia, spoke to buying arsenic for Mr Maybrick—up to 1880.

A Mr Heaton, a retired chemist, said he used to supply Mr Maybrick with liquor arsenicalis up to —the end of 1887. This was in a tonic which he used to supply to city men. As many as sixteen men had been in his shop in the morning for a tonic, but they did not all get liquor arsenicalis, of course.

Dr Drysdale, who had been consulted by Mr Maybrick, said the deceased took a deal of medicine, but he couldn't remember ever giving him arsenic.

Mr Wm. J. Thomson was called to say that Mr

Maybrick said he had taken a double dose of medicine on the day of the Wirral Races.

Dr Tidy, Examiner of Forensic Medicine at the London Hospital, was asked if he had followed the description of the sickness of the deceased.

"Yes, I have followed every detail in the case so far as I could, and I have read all the depositions both before the Coroner and before the magistrate."

"I will ask you first whether the account of the vomiting agrees with your description of excessive and persistent vomiting?"

"Certainly not; it is not that kind of vomiting that is described as taking place in a typical case of arsenical poisoning."

"Why?"

"Why—the vomiting is persistent, incessant, and violent. The peculiarity of the vomiting in arsenic cases is that it does not relieve; but the patient, as soon as he has vomited, begins to vomit again immediately."

"Taking the whole of the symptoms which have been before the post-mortem and analysis, could any one in your judgment safely suggest to us arsenical poisoning?"

"I can only speak for myself in the case."

"And you say undoubtedly that these are not the symptoms of arsenical poisoning, nor do they point to such?"

"Certainly not."

"When you find that a person has undoubtedly died from some irritant poison—when you find the arsenic there, does it lead you to suppose that this was arsenic?"

"No, it does not."

Dr Macnamara, Professor of Materia Medica at the Royal College and Senior Surgeon at the Lock Hospital, Dublin, was asked this:

"Now bringing your best judgment to bear upon the matter, you have been present at the whole of this trial, and heard the evidence, in your opinion was this a death from arsenical poisoning?"

"Certainly not."

Dr Paul, Professor of Medical Jurisprudence at University College, Liverpool, and Examiner in Forensic Medicine and Toxicology at Victoria University, said this was a case of gastro-enteritis. "The post-mortem appearances did not show that it was set up by arsenic."

The evidence was ended.

And then Mrs Maybrick herself made a statement. She had to struggle to stand up to face the court —it can have been no mean ordeal. Nothing but circumstance could have thrust that woman to speak from the rail of the dock.

She told how she used to make her face-wash and then she dealt with the incident of the beef juice.

"My lord," she said, "I now wish to refer to the bottle of meat essence. On Thursday night, the 9th of May, after Nurse Gore had given my husband beef tea, I went and sat on the bed beside him. He complained to me of being very sick and very depressed, and he implored me then to give him this powder, which he had referred to early in the evening, and which I had declined to give him. I was overwrought, terribly anxious, miserably unhappy, and his evident distress utterly unnerved me. He had told me that the powder would not harm him, and that I could put it in his food. I then consented. My lord, I had not one true or honest friend in that house. I had no one to consult and no one to advise me. . . . When I found the powder I took it into the inner room, with the beef juice, and in pushing through the door I upset the bottle, and, in order to make up the quantity of fluid spilled, I added a considerable quantity of water. On returning to the room, I found my husband asleep and I placed the bottle on the table by the window. When he woke he had a choking sensation in his throat and vomited...."

What effect that speech had on the jury we can't say. The public were all ready to cheer the beautiful lady in the dock. A group of devoted wives had got a bouquet to present to her when the verdict was delivered, while other reputable citizens chased the witnesses for the prosecution whenever they saw them in the street. And the jury were, oddly enough, allowed to mix with the crowd that was so blatantly sympathetic towards the prisoner.

Counsel delivered their speeches. The Judge summed up. The jury took less than three quarters of an hour to consider their verdict and when the foreman had pronounced the word 'Guilty' there was an " instant's hush and then a loud murmur —half a groan and half an ejaculation of astonishment...."

Mrs Briggs and Mr William Swift, who had been engaged in the case, had to run for safety. A huge crowd waited for the judge and groaned as he drove away. Mr Brierly got away in a hansom.

Sober journalists lost their heads over the verdict. Petitions for a reprieve were scattered broadcast and signed with as little thought as go to the scribbling of a name on such things.

A Liverpool paper struck a note that one feels interpreted the emotion of the hour: " With the unreflecting mob outside the prisoner has been from the outset an object of sympathy. Her youth and comeliness, coupled with the pathetic, not to say, dramatic, appeal which she made to the jury, excited their compassion deeply. And taken in conjunction with the humane sentiment there was a rooted feeling that with so brilliant an advocate as Sir Charles Russell defending her, she ought to have got off."

The newspapers devoted columns to explanations, recriminations, descriptions, criticisms, arguments. Petitions for a reprieve were signed by thousands of hysterical and some sagacious people. Certain very distinguished men said the verdict was not a true one because it had not been absolutely proved (*a*) that Mr Maybrick had died of arsenic and (*b*) if he had, that Mrs Maybrick had feloniously, wilfully, and of malice aforethought administered that poison.

Tomes have been written on the case—usually by lawyers, who love fine distinctions.

The jury were not merely hooted, they were subsequently sneered at. Their professions were set down as if the person held his nose as he mentioned them: plumber, turner, provision-dealer, plumber, farmer, plumber and glazier, grocer, ironmonger, milliner, printer, farmer, baker.

The theory may be held that a jury composed of doctors or lawyers or professional men would be superior to one made up of farmers, plumbers, grocers and suchlike people. We don't know why. We believe that twelve honest ordinary men, who are shut up in a room till they thresh out a matter that is within the grasp of ordinary people, will find by good common sense and argument the truth of the thing. Technical matters have to be made clear, but the gift of common sense is just as likely to be with farmers and plumbers as with doctors and lawyers or judges.

One can imagine the jury saying, there has been a post-mortem on the body of the late James Maybrick and the three doctors who conducted it agree he died from an irritant poison; two of them clearly say the poison was arsenic. An analysis has been made of certain parts of the body and we have had expert witnesses to tell us that arsenic was found there, and in sufficient quantity to make a fatal dose. Who gave Mr Maybrick that arsenic? The defence say he was a drug-taker and took it himself. But they call witnesses who speak to a long time ago, when Mr Maybrick may have taken arsenic as a periodic against malaria; the evidence that relates to the present day is practically nil. A retired chemist said Mr Maybrick used to have a pick-me-up at his shop. But great numbers of people do that. They perhaps eat too much (probably too badly) or drink too much and have indigestion, and so go to the chemist, who puts a little liquor arsenicalis in the pick-me-up. And probably some juryman said, 'We're all drug-takers at fifty. I take cascara sagrada'. Another says, 'I take Easton's Syrup'. 'I take Epsom salts'. 'I take such and such'. 'And I take them all if I feel that way inclined,' says a fifth. When someone said to Mr Maybrick that he was a drug-taker he said it was a "damned lie". The jury couldn't persuade themselves that Mr Maybrick had given himself the arsenic that was making him ill. Did Mrs Maybrick give it him? She got arsenic from fly-papers. She had quarrelled with her husband and said she hated him! She was in love with a man called Brierly. When her husband was ill, but not so ill as to cause anxiety to the doctors, she wrote to her lover, telling him not to go away as her husband was going to die—'was sick unto death'. If she were giving him arsenic she would know that. She was seen tampering with the sick man's food, and when that food was analyzed it was found to contain arsenic. Moreover, when she made her final speech from the dock she admitted putting a white powder in his food! And arsenic was found in the pocket of her dressing-gown, in her handkerchief.

Mrs Maybrick was not hanged.

"The Home Secretary, after fullest consideration, and after taking the best legal and medical advice that could be obtained, has advised Her Majesty to respite the capital sentence on Florence Maybrick and to commute the punishment to penal servitude for life, inasmuch as, although the evidence leads clearly to the conclusion that the prisoner administered and attempted to administer arsenic to her husband with intent to murder, yet it does not wholly exclude a reasonable doubt whether his death was in fact caused by the administration of arsenic.

"This decision is understood not to imply the slightest reflection on the able and experienced practitioners who gave evidence, or on the tribunal by which the prisoner was tried.

"We understand the course adopted has the concurrence of the learned judge."

So ran the official notice.

After being imprisoned for fifteen years Mrs Maybrick was released on January 25th, 1904.

This case captured the public. There was the young, pretty wife of fair social standing, and the old husband. Once Mrs Maybrick had let her passion for Brierly get the upper hand she was determined to satisfy it at any cost. She was of that type that does not hesitate at murder. She was hard, ruthless, resolute, sheer.

III

MADAME LAFARGE

MARRIAGES are almost a commercial matter in France. The *dot* is all important. No *dot*, no marriage—though there must be some people who bring little to the matrimonial contract.

One is inclined to wonder how it was that Marie Cappelle's friends had any need to go to a marriage broker. She was striking and attractive, though from her portraits we should not describe her as beautiful. Arresting certainly. She had well-marked features, a forehead suggesting the imaginative and a mouth hinting at executive capacity.

Marie Cappelle's father was an artillery Colonel of good family. Marie's grandmother shared the lessons given by Madame de Genlis to Mademoiselle d'Orléans. One of her uncles was Baron de Martens, a Prussian diplomatist, and another, Baron Paul Garat, Secretary-General of the Bank of France.

One can imagine that some sequestered girl, with few opportunities of meeting people, might be forced to find a husband from the marriage broker's; but Marie Cappelle aged twenty-three, had a *dot* of about eighty thousand francs (£3,200), was well connected, which counts for much in France—as elsewhere—and moved in pleasant circles in Paris where eligible men were surely to be met. It was doubtless for some good reasons that her relatives consulted M Defoy, a well-known matrimonial agent, and the result was Marie Cappelle married Charles Joseph Pouch Lafarge.

Madame Lafarge

This M Lafarge was twenty-eight years of age, far from handsome, a widower, of respectable *bourgeois* family, an ironmaster with his works and chateau. He must have made an impression on Marie Cappelle's friends, and one is inclined to think that the Limousin ironmaster, with his chateau and park, suggested more pecuniary resources than he actually possessed. He had a picture of Le Glandier with him to show his destined wife; and a fine house, set in the middle of a noble park, can be alluring to a girl, who has got the idea of marriage in her head and desires the *beau parti*.

The marriage took place very quickly, and Marie Cappelle, now Marie Lafarge, left with her husband for Le Glandier. With them was Marie's maid, Clémentine Servat, a devoted companion from childhood, who looked so smart that the people in the Limousin country thought she must be paid as much as 90 francs a year!

Most women know—or should know—that there are things to be realized concerning their husbands that have not been markedly apparent before the marriage.

Charles Lafarge had rough country manners. As the carriage jolted its way along he lay in a corner and snored. When he was awake he would take his wife in his arms and caress her loudly, violently and with frank relish. The blue-blooded wife shrank from his boisterous ways. At Orleans she had a bath, and because she locked the door her husband was furious. He was her husband, *parbleu!* What did she want to shut him out for? He would show her when they got to Le Glandier. . . . 'Locking the door because she has a bath!'

And probably after the bath he was showering kisses on her.

One sees him, the physical man, perfectly satisfied with the wife he was taking home.

When they arrived home, however, Marie Lafarge realized the misleading nature of pictures, actual and dreamed. The chateau of Le Glandier was a solid, unpretentious, unlovely building, set in the middle of grounds very much neglected. The long, bare corridors of the house must have chilled this already chilled bride.

That she was capable of acting strangely when she was chilled was shown by the sequence.

M Lafarge's mother, sister and brother-in-law were in the house waiting to welcome the bride, and Marie Lafarge went to her room and locked herself in!

Her conduct is comprehensible if one thinks of the romantic brooding girl, who has dreamed many dreams no doubt of a very exalted kind, who has (say half) persuaded herself that *the* dream has at last come true and clearly and indubitably between Paris and Limousin sees the glamour fade away. To comprehend is not to endorse.

Marie Lafarge behaved foolishly as well as oddly. She was certainly a neurotic. How else can one account for her conduct? While she was locked in that room she penned this letter:

CHARLES,
On my knees I beg your pardon. I don't love you. I love another. O God! How I have suffered. Let me die. My head is bursting. Will you help me?

For pity's sake listen to me. He is called Charles too. He is handsome; he is noble; he was brought up near me; we have loved each other ever since we could love. A year ago another woman captured him. I thought I was going to die.

It was from spite that I wanted to get married. Alas! I saw you. I ignored all the mysteries of marriage. I trembled when I took your hand. I imagined you like a father to whom a kiss on the forehead would suffice. Do you understand what I have suffered these last five days? If you don't save me I shall die.

I esteem you enormously; I venerate you. But my habits and education have put a barrier between us. . . .

And he repents. I have seen him again. I saw him at Orleans when you were dining. He was on a balcony opposite mine. He is here—hidden at Uzerches. I shall be an adultress in spite of myself, in spite of you if you don't save me.

Tell me, Charles, that this evening you will agree. Set two horses on the road to Brives; I will take the courier to Bordeaux and leave for Smyrna. I will leave you all my fortune. . . . Don't let anybody know that I live. If you like I will throw my cloak over one of your precipices and all will be over; or I will take arsenic. I have some. For the honour of your mother don't refuse me. In the name of God forgive me. I am waiting your reply like a criminal waits the verdict. Alas! If I didn't love him more than life I could have loved you because I respect you. As it is, your caresses disgust me. Kill me: I deserve it. And yet I hope. Put a note under my door this evening; otherwise I shall be dead. Don't bother about me. I will walk to Brives. Your mother so tender; your sister, so sweet—they crush me. I am horrible to myself. Oh! Be generous. Save me from suicide. I must trust in you. I can't write to him. Be a man. You don't love me any more. Horses won't betray us; find me two old costumes belonging to your peasants. Pardon! And God recompense you for the evil I do you.

I shall only take a few personal jewels. You can send what you think fit to Smyrna. Don't accuse me of treachery. Since Monday, since I learned that I was to be something more than a sister, when my aunts told me what it was to give myself to a man, I swore I would die. I took poison, but the dose was too small. I had a pistol at my temple yesterday—and was afraid. To-day everything depends on you.

Save me. Be the good angel to the poor orphan; or else kill her—or tell her to kill herself. Write, for without your word of honour I won't open my door.

(Signed) MARIE.

What a letter! Hysteria is stamped in it. Many women have experienced shocks on the honeymoon, but the well-connected lady of Paris, however secluded she may have been, hardly suggests such chaste terror as this letter would in places suggest. Poison . . . Pistol . . . Smyrna. And the other Charles is dragged in. He was clearly an invention: solid as a ghost. Pure hysteria.

The woman was out of the normal, and this letter was its expression. It was the outburst of many crushed dreams and many repressions. Marie Lafarge was 'wound up'. Some women would merely have wept; some might have screamed and stamped a little. After all, emotion should have a safe outlet. This . . . after the dreams ! . . .

And Marie Lafarge, instead of being content with tears, wrote that letter!

One can easily imagine the consternation in the Lafarge household. There was Madame Lafarge *mère*, the typical French country-women; Madame Buffières, the sister of Charles, and her husband.

Charles, the husband, has the letter first; and any husband can film his feelings on reading it. His language could not have been choice. Then Madame Lafarge *mère* takes the letter as he shrieks in his rage and hammers on the locked door. And then the sister reads . . . and the brother . . . and they all speak at once, gestures intermingling.

The mother has enough knowledge of her sex to know the letter is pure nonsense. She sees the letter doesn't ring true. And she pacifies her son. A friend is called in and he preaches patience. So, finally, Marie is pacified too. Charles talks to her kindly through the door, and at last the door is opened.

Peace descends on the Lafarge household. After the storm, calm. Domesticity is familiar with these stormy and set-fair scenes.

But Marie Lafarge was no harmonious part of Limousin society; she felt a contempt for these very countrified people. That she was, however, 'settling down' is suggested by a letter she wrote to M. Garat. "I have accepted my position, though it is outwardly trying. But with will, patience and the love of my husband I shall manage. Charles adores me, and I am deeply touched. . . ."

To Madame de Montbreton she wrote:

"The misfortune of life is that one dreams before living, and nothing is so sad as deception. . . . When I feel a tear running cold on my cheek, then, in the middle of the big empty room, I think of those I love, I put on a hat and I go out and admire the lovely countryside. . . .

"Charles fits in with the surroundings; hiding under a rough exterior a noble heart, he loves me above everything. He adores me, reveres me. His mother is an excellent woman. . . ."

Not the letters of a crushed woman or even an unhappy one.

Fate strode.

M Lafarge was ambitious for his business. He wished to take out a patent, and his wife was greatly interested in the idea. To effect what he wanted M Lafarge had need of his wife's *dot*, and she was quite willing that her money should be used to further the prosperity of the business.

They exchanged wills. He was to leave her everything, she to bequeath all to him. In view of what happened this could not be ignored. Particularly as she took care to send his will to a confidential friend at Soissons, though she left her other papers in the house. In the light of subsequent events this became an incident of importance. She had said she was ill, and her husband had nursed her. It was then she suggested the idea of the will. But was she really ill? Did the illness provide a setting,

appropriate time and scenery for the suggestion ? . . .
She was soon well. . . .

Lafarge went to Paris, and the letters that passed between husband and wife were warmly affectionate. When the matter of the patent was settled Lafarge had still the loan to contract, and for that his wife sent him a power of attorney so that he could sell or mortgage what he wished of her belongings. Lafarge had called to Paris from his works a clerk of the name of Denis, who was the kind of man to be useful in borrowing money by means that were not necessarily scrupulous.

How had Marie Lafarge settled down by this time ? In view of the letters to her husband it might be said she was a fairly happy married woman. In view of what subsequently happened it is just as well to see—hypothetically if one chooses—the woman who had accepted certain facts, who had been won in some measure by a devoted husband, but who could not accept certain other facts, and wondered . . . and planned how to escape. We are dealing with a woman out of the common. Marie Lafarge may well have said to herself, 'I will get out of this . . .' The question arises: When did she decide to endeavour to escape from what she might have described as her prison in the way she was charged with adopting ?

It must have been before Charles went to Paris or while he was there. It was during his absence that she had engaged a Mademoiselle Brun to paint her portrait, which was to be sent to Paris. But we can imagine the fanciful, romantic brooding woman being jarred in the country home, with all the fragments of her shed dreams about her.

When the portrait was finished, Marie Lafarge sent it to her husband with a cake. She had asked Madame Lafarge *mère* to make some *choux*, little cakes for which she was famous, and Marie Lafarge had a pretty notion: she would ask Charles to eat one in the evening of December 18th, and she would eat one like it at the same time.

Charles Lafarge ate but a small portion of the cake, but it was enough to make him ill and vomit. Moreover, what Charles Lafarge received was not a *choux*; it was not a small but a large cake!

Dates are important.

On the 12th of December Marie Lafarge had written to the local druggist:

> "I am eaten out with rats, monsieur. I have already tried plaster and nux vomica to get rid of them; but they are still here. Will you or can you let me have some arsenic? You can rely on my prudence. It is to put in a linen cupboard."

It was signed "Marie Lafarge du Glandier".

That was six days before the date fixed by Marie Lafarge on which her husband was to eat the famous cake in Paris.

M Lafarge returned to Le Glandier on January 5th.

And on January 5th Marie Lafarge wrote again to the druggist for arsenic. She never denied she had arsenic; she pleaded she had got it to kill the rats.

Charles Lafarge went almost at once to bed when he arrived home. He had some supper with his wife—cold truffled fowl—and he was very ill after it, suffering from a burning in the throat, pains in the stomach and a feeling of cold.

There were plenty of women in the house to look after the sick man. Besides his wife there was his mother, his sister, Clémentine, Mademoiselle Brun as well as the domestics. In spite of nursing, Charles Lafarge got worse. The wife wished to prepare most of his dishes or, at least, take them to him. The mother began to be anxious . . . suspicious. . . . Perhaps the suspicions did not come till it was too late.

Dr Bardou had been treating the patient for gastritis—there was so much pain and vomiting; besides, what did Dr Bardou, this country practitioner know of arsenic?

On the 10th of January Marie Lafarge got another supply of arsenic—64 grammes!

And she was seen to put a white powder in various dishes for the sick man. On the 11th of January, for instance, some egg and milk was placed near Lafarge's bed as he was asleep. Marie Lafarge, who was in bed, told her maid to put the egg and milk near her. And Mademoiselle Brun, who slept in the same room, saw Marie Lafarge get up and put some white powder in the egg and milk.

Madame Lafarge came in the room at that moment, and Mademoiselle Brun asked Marie Lafarge what she had put in the egg and milk. She said it was "*Fleur d'orange*".

When the egg and milk broth was shown to the doctor he suggested the powder might be chalk or perhaps the white of an egg.

So they made more egg and milk and tried chalk and white of egg and got no result similar to the one Marie Lafarge had had with her 'gum' or '*fleur d'orange*'.

The same day, when Lafarge had drunk some sweetened wine, he cried out, "What have you given me? It burns!" Marie Lafarge didn't answer her husband, but said calmly to Mademoiselle Brun, "That isn't surprising if he is inflamed and takes wine". She went straight away, according to Mademoiselle Brun, towards a commode, opened the top drawer, took from a fancy pot a little white powder and stirred it with her finger in the glass.

Marie Lafarge then said she had put 'gum' into the glass. But when gum was tried it dissolved, and the powder had not dissolved.

So some of the egg and milk was sent to a chemist

at Uzerches for analysis. He told them to let the sick man have nothing to eat or drink that was not prepared by trusted hands!

Lafarge, as he lay in bed, heard the rats and complained. "Don't worry," said his wife. "I have something in my pocket that will destroy a whole army of rats."

She had sixty-four grammes of arsenic in her pocket.

Lafarge told her she ought not to have such dangerous stuff so near his handkerchief, and sent the packet to Clémentine to make a paste for the rats. It may be appropriate now to follow the history of this packet.

Clémentine Servat confessed afterwards that she was so afraid of handling the poison that she buried it in the garden. The packet was dug up and found to contain bicarbonate of soda!

The question arose: what happened to the arsenic obtained by Marie Lafarge?

Each day the sick man grew worse.

By Sunday the 12th of January suspicions were crystallizing. Mademoiselle Brun took to Madame Lafarge *mère* and Madame Buffières some of the powder she had seen in the pot in the drawer. They burnt it. It smelt like garlic. It smelt very like the white sediment that lay at the bottom of the pot from which Charles had drunk.

On the 13th Denis was sent to Lubersac to fetch another doctor, M Jules Lespinasse, who was informed of the purchases of arsenic by Lafarge's wife. He tried peroxide of iron. But it was too late. Charles Lafarge would not have his wife near him at the last, and he died after having suffered great agony on January 14th at 6 o'clock in the morning.

It is not difficult to imagine the minds of the mother, sister and wife of the late Charles Lafarge. The mother, grief stricken, full of the desire to avenge the death of her son ; the sister sharing those feelings. But what of the wife ? ...

Madame Lafarge *mère* locked her daughter-in-law in a room and then took possession of all her papers. And the police took possession of Marie Lafarge.

But before the trial of Marie Lafarge on a charge of poisoning her husband took place, the public were astounded to hear that she was accused of having stolen jewels from her friend, Madame la Vicomtesse de Leautaud.

This trial took place first.

Madame de Leautaud, who had been a Mademoisell de Nicolai, explained that she had known Madame Lafarge for about five years, when she was staying with Madame de Montbreton, her (Madame de Leautaud's) sister. And this was how the jewels disappeared, according to Madame de Leautaud.

At the close of 1839, Marie Cappelle, as Madame Marie Lafarge was then, went to visit Madame de Leautaud, who had been married nearly two years. During the first week of Marie Cappelle's visit a diamond necklace disappeared. The jewels had been examined in the salon—for the talk had turned on diamonds—and the case left there while Madame de Leautaud, Mademoiselle Cappelle and M Delvaut went a walk. The case was there when they returned and Madame de Leautaud took it up to the drawer in her room.

The diamonds were quite safe the next day, because they were shown to another visitor—a Madame de Nieuwerkerque.

Six days later, noticing a velvet bag, belonging to Mademoiselle Cappelle, was fastened with imitation stones, Madame de Leautaud wanted to compare with them some imitation stones that she had. It was easy to get from the false to the true. How did the sham look beside the real ? So the genuine diamonds were sought for—and sought for in vain; the case was empty.

When the talk had turned on real stones, Marie Cappelle had left the room, M de Leautaud and Madame de Nieuwerkerque being the other people present.

At first it was thought the diamonds had been taken as a joke by some relative. But it was no joke. Then a servant was suspected. Then Marie Cappelle was suspected. Madame de Leautaud was precise. She said they discovered that Mademoiselle Cappelle had told them a number of lies about small affairs, and had also made herself very friendly to the maid who had been suspected. In fact, she had gone so far as to tell the girl that, if she were discharged on account of the suspicions that had been flung at her, she, Marie Cappelle, would find her a place.

Then there was a mesmeric incident, which reminds one of *Le Juif Polonais* or " The Bells " which the late Henry Irving made famous. Madame de Montbreton sent Marie Cappelle to sleep. (Our view is that the young lady was very wide awake.) During the presumed sleep Marie Cappelle was asked what had happened to the diamonds stolen from Madame de Leautaud. She was not suspected by Madame de Montbreton, and she replied, as if from the depths of a truthful sleep, that the diamonds had been stolen by a man, not exactly of the house, who had sold them to a Jew and that they were now abroad. The mountings had been thrown in ditches near the chateau.

Monsieur de Leautaud told M Allard, *chef de la police de Sureté* about this, and M Allard at once wished to know more about Marie Cappelle. He knew there had been thefts from M Garat, Marie Cappelle's uncle. And slowly other things came to light. When

Marie Cappelle was about to be married she was told by her godfather, M de Braque, to buy something. She told him she had bought some pearls. But she had taken five pearls to a jeweller in the rue de Richelieu, and got him to mount them in a pair of earrings and a ring. She said the ring had been given her by Madame de Leautaud! "Come from" would have been a more appropriate description. Madame Garat furnished these details.

But there was no need for Madame de Leautaud to identify her jewels. Madame Lafarge admitted the jewels were Madame de Leautaud's; but. . . . And this was her story.

When Madame de Leautaud was Mademoiselle de Nicolai she told Marie Cappelle she was followed everywhere by a young man she had seen in an omnibus. This young man, being something of a writer, had naturally precious little money, but was well connected and called Clavet. With Marie Cappelle as go-between the two young people corresponded.

Then Mademoiselle de Nicolai married, and one day, as 'Madame de Leautaud', she told Marie Cappelle that the silence of Monsieur Clavet must be bought. . . . She would raise money. . . . She would sell her diamonds and pretend they had been stolen.

"It was all a trick," said Marie Lafarge. "The disappearance of the diamonds was arranged between us. Madame de Leautaud begged me to get rid of them, and I only agreed on condition that she helped me to take them out of their settings, so that I could hide them safely. . . ."

Apparently there was a man named Clavet, who had admired Mademoiselle de Nicolai from afar. He had gone to Algeria, and was in Mexico at the time of the trial. A friend of his said that Clavet wished he had nothing to do with Mademoiselle Cappelle, for he thought she was in love with him!

Madame Lafarge

But when Lafarge died, and there was a perquisition at Glandier, the diamonds were discovered in a small box and identified by M and Madame de Leautaud.

Marie Lafarge, being asked at that time how the diamonds came into her possession, said they had been sent to Uzerches by one of her great uncles of Toulouse, on the part of an aunt, whose name she didn't know. And she couldn't remember how she had got hold of the pearls; she had had them so long. . . .

And the prosecution said there was still another explanation given by Madame Marie Lafarge about her possession of these diamonds.

One day M Lafarge wanted to cut some glass, and his wife said she had a diamond. She produces the diamond, in fact several diamonds—a handful.

Her husband stands amazed. The whole family is amazed. " Why, there are jewels there for 30,000 francs. . . ."

" I have had them since I was eight years old," said Marie Lafarge to the astonished members of the family : " they were confided to an old nurse by my grandfather. When I came of age they were given to me."

" Why didn't you show them before ? "

There were a number of witnesses. Jewellers identified the diamonds. M and Madame de Leautaud gave evidence. Marie Lafarge refused to go in the box and remained in the dock.

If one had to choose between the tales told by Madame de Leautaud and Marie Lafarge, one accepts Madame de Leautaud's. Marie Lafarge says the jewels are given to her to sell so that she can give money to a man to keep his tongue still. But she doesn't sell—says she hasn't time. Yet she takes some of the jewels and has them made into earrings for herself.

And apparently she never tries to sell the jewels. Moreover, she doesn't tell the same tale twice when she is asked how she came in possession of these precious stones. One can't believe a witness like this.

Marie Lafarge had jewels in her possession to which she had no right and, after hearing all the evidence, the Court came to the conclusion that Marie Lafarge had stolen those jewels from her friend, Madame de Leautaud, and the sentence was 'Two years' imprisonment'.

As everybody realized, that case prejudiced the other and more terrible one. 'If this woman can steal and lie like that what can't she do?' People will talk.

The court at Tulle was crowded. There wasn't a room to be had in the town. Witnesses and others were hunting on the high roads for places to lay their heads.

What it was like in the court one can imagine. The Leautauds are here again as witnesses. Also the Garats and the Lafarges and a crowd of others.

The prisoner was in black. She must have been a striking figure, with the strong features, pale skin, ebony black hair, and clothed in that depressing, overloaded crepe that widows in France seem to wallow in. She wasn't beautiful. One frequently hears her referred to as if she were a beauty: but no artist would ever have taken Marie Lafarge as a model. Guilty of theft, now accused of murder, and only twenty-four!

M Lachaud, who was to be so distinguished a member of the Paris bar, was one of her defenders at the chivalrous age of twenty-three. M Paillet was the 'leader' and 'with him' were M Lachaud of Tulle and M Bac of Limoges. M Decous, avocat-général a la Cour royale de Limoges, was the prosecuting counsel.

Like most notable prisoners Marie Lafarge was quite cool and ready under examination. One or two damaging details came out when M Decous examined her.

"In your room there was a bed occupied by Mademoiselle Brun; she saw you put some white powder in the egg and milk; you were asked what you had put in and you replied, '*On y a mis, et non j'y ai mis, de la fleur d'orange*'. On which the other person said, 'There is nothing in common between orange flower and a white powder'. Then you said nothing.

"In finishing on this point I will recall to you that the chemical tests have shown the presence of poison in almost all the potions which you touched, especially on the 11th of January. There was some in the egg and milk, in the toast and water, in the sweetened water, in the little pot, in the piece of flannel. There was some in the stomach. The paste prepared for the rats had nothing poisonous, merely bicarbonate of soda. Explain that contrast. Arsenic is found where you say there was nothing but what was innocent; and on the other hand we find nothing but the innocuous where you pretended arsenic had been prodigally used?"

"If I could explain that," replied Madame Marie Lafarge, "I should be recognized as innocent."

It is quite clear on reading this case that there was overwhelming evidence against Marie Lafarge. If Charles Lafarge had been poisoned his wife was undoubtedly the person to go into the dock.

It was quite clear that Marie Lafarge had had possession of great quantities of arsenic; it was proved that this arsenic had not been employed in killing rats. It was alleged that it was buried; but when the stuff, that was buried, was dug up, it was found to be bicarbonate of soda. Witnesses swore they had seen Marie Lafarge putting a white powder in her husband's food. She said it was gum arabic. Charles Lafarge had exhibited the symptoms of arsenic poisoning—did he die from arsenic poisoning, and was that arsenic administered by his wife?

Dr Lespinasse, who had been brought by Denis and had been told about the arsenic, said he found some of the white powder, which it was alleged Marie Lafarge had used; he threw it on the fire and it smelt of garlic. He had no doubt whatever that Charles Lafarge had been poisoned.

But the autopsy had to prove that.

The evidence of the family went to prove the points that have been cited. They were clearly not in favour of the accused. The prosecution alleged that Marie Lafarge had persuaded her mother-in-law to write a letter to her son in Paris when the cakes were to be dispatched. This was obviously done, said the prosecution, with a view of throwing the blame on the mother if anything happened. Moreover, it was alleged, that Marie Lafarge showed very great anxiety after the cake had gone. She was said to have expressed a fear she might receive a black-edged envelope. Details of that damaging sort were many.

Denis—'Jean Denis Barbier'—was called as a witness, and as he has been mentioned with directness by some who have attempted to re-try Marie Lafarge, it may be worth while quoting some of his evidence.

"On the 8th of January," he said, "Madame Marie Lafarge, learning that I was going to Lubersac, sent for me. She took me on to the lawn and asked me to get her some arsenic and other things. I got the other things, but not the arsenic. The next day I bought a franc's worth of arsenic from M Lafosse. On the 11th, when I was going to Tulle on business, I received a letter from Madame Charles Lafarge through her maid. In it, she asked me to get for her some arsenic as well as some other things. Fearing Madame might be angry I said to my wife, 'I shall have to get this arsenic because this is the second time she has asked for it'. And I added, 'I'm very much afraid that this arsenic will help to kill M Lafarge'. I said that because Madame Charles had said before M Magnesaux that, if she wished, in twenty-four hours her husband would be dead. She had also said that she would wear weeds for a year as they do in Paris, if her husband died."

And Denis or Barbier was not shaken in his pertinent evidence. He had used the name of 'Denis', so that as Barbier he could sign bills and in that way aid his master to obtain money. But in reading his evidence in this trial he gives one the impression of speaking frankly and truly.

But the charge is that Charles Lafarge has died of arsenical poisoning, and that the arsenic was given him by his wife. That people saw her put white powder in his food; that she bought arsenic may be true; but was Charles Lafarge's death brought about by arsenic?

The Experts had to decide that.

Messieurs Tournadon, Bardou, Massenat and Lespinasse conducted an autopsy. It seems to have been an irregular affair, for bottles were not sealed, and some things were lost. However, this was their report:

1. That the egg and milk contained a large quantity of arsenical acid.

2. The sweetened water (eau sucrée) contained arsenical acid.

3. The beer, gum water and powdered sugar contained no venomous substance.

4. The liquids vomited contained no arsenical acid sensitive to the reactives.

5. The liquids in the stomach contained arsenical acid.

6. The death of Charles Joseph Pouch Lafarge was the result of arsenical acid poisoning.

This autopsy was considered to be valueless, and a new one was ordered. It was undertaken by Messieurs Dubois, father and son, and Dupuytren.

They declared they could find no traces of arsenic!

After all this time, all this evidence, the doctor said Charles Lafarge had not died of arsenical poisoning!

When this report of the analysts was being made the dense court was taut. There was no need for silence. And when the last words came, "*nous n'avons obtenu aucune tache arsenicale*", loud cheers stabbed the room. Marie Lafarge leaned forward and smiled; tears ran down M Paillet's face.

When the prosecution said there were still other resources, the bubbling excitement ceased. The tense calm was resumed. Wasn't it all over? . . .

M Lespinasse went back into the box. He said he knew nothing of the Marsh test; but he was still of the opinion Charles Lafarge had died of arsenical poisoning.

The Court ordered a fresh autopsy to be made. The name Orfila had already been invoked, so it was dramatically appropriate that he should be called in to undertake it. He was a distinguished man. His name carried weight. Professor, and author of a treatise on poisons, he was also a graceful man of the world. He made an autopsy with Messieurs Devergie and Chevallier. And when he went into the witness box with his report he said he would prove there was arsenic in the corpse of Lafarge.

It was a terrible opening for the defence.

M Orfila said they had found arsenic in the stomach, in the thorax, the liver, the heart, and the brain. He explained that there was naturally in man a certain amount of arsenic, but it was not to be found in the stomach, the liver, the kidneys, the heart nor the lungs. He suggested that the Marsh apparatus used by the previous autopsists was not up to date, and therefore had not given accurate results. He suggested for instance that at the previous post-mortem too strong a flame had been used and in consequence some of the arsenic had been volatilized. This case is interesting, as it is the first in which the Marsh Test was used.

Orfila's report turned white the hair of Marie Lafarge.

The prosecuting counsel went through the evidence:

Lafarge had been poisoned: Marie Lafarge had bought a great quantity of poison; a cake containing poison had been substituted for others, and sent to Paris by Marie Lafarge to her husband; Marie Lafarge has wished to get rid of her husband—the letter written on the day she arrived at le Glandier proved it. She detested her husband, and calmly set to work to poison him. There was the evidence of the purchases of arsenic: there was the evidence of Mademoiselle Brun, who had seen Marie Lafarge put powder in the food destined for her husband.

M Paillet for the defence quoted letters in which Marie Lafarge had spoken of herself as a happy member of the Lafarge family. He bravely denied that the prisoner had anything to do with the substitution of the poisoned cake for the *choux*, and the suggestion that she had given arsenic to her husband was preposterous and unthinkable. And he ended with one of those bursts of bombast, which at that time were thought eloquence, and may be welcomed to this day in easily impressed countries.

" Courage, however, courage, poor Marie ! I have hope that Providence who has so miraculously upheld you during this long trial will not henceforth abandon you. No. You will live for your family, which loves you so much; for your numerous friends; you will live for the judges themselves; you will live as a glorious testimony to human justice when it is confided to pure hands, to clear minds, to souls, feeling and compassionate."

When that kind of thing is insincere it rings like a cracked bell.

The question for the jury was: Marie Cappelle, widow of the late Pouch Lafarge, is she guilty of having, in December and January last, put to death her husband by means of substances capable of causing death, and which have in fact caused it?

It took that Tulle jury less than an hour to come to their verdict—by a majority: Guilty.

She was condemned to be exposed in the pillory and then to be executed.

She did not suffer the ignominy of the pillory nor was she executed. She was sent to prison, and in twelve years was released. But she had little use for liberty and in five months after her release she died.

The case had excited extraordinary interest. Marie Lafarge was young and well connected—the fables about her being beautiful are exaggerated. An intriguing note was struck by her letter to her husband. This was the first case in which distinguished men had argued over poisons and the Marsh test. And a young woman, attractive, even if not beautiful, will always have defenders, no matter what her trouble is.

Maître Lachaud, the young advocate, fell in love with her, so it is said. He regularly sent flowers to her grave. Others wrote poetry to and for her. This was the kind of thing:

> Ainsi, pauvre martyr, redressez votre tête
> Levez vos yeux au ciel, lui seul vous entendra.
> Vos larmes, vos douleurs, pour lui c'est la fête !
> Pardonnez-leur, Madame, et Dieu vous recevra.

Marie Lafarge had not much to forgive. Yet people insisted that she was innocent and many do so to this day. Two weighty Germans published a German volume on the subject. Marie Lafarge was clearly innocent in their view, and the real culprit was Denis. Denis did curious things : Denis said odd things : Denis disappeared !

This man Denis always crops up when people wish to find a substitute for Marie Lafarge. He happened to have used two names for the purpose of doing shady tricks for his master. He was also reported to have made use of some strong expression about Marie Lafarge. But a man who has been asked by his mistress to buy arsenic, and thinks his mistress is using the poison to kill her husband, is very likely to say something nasty about her.

Denis is no substitute for Marie Lafarge. She got the arsenic : she put white powder in Lafarge's food. There was arsenic in Lafarge's food. And with that hysterical letter Marie Lafarge showed her range. She was out of the normal. She may have been one of those women to whom marital relationship is distasteful. Candidly, in our view, she was hard, determined, merciless. She looks it. She had stolen from her friend and lied. It is very probable that Madame Garat's losses were due to Marie Cappelle.

That the marriage was not a love match we know. This is how Marie Cappelle described the affair.

"On Wednesday I saw a gentleman at Musard's ; he was pleased with me and I with him. On Thursday he called on my aunt and I liked him better. On Friday he formally asked for my hand. On Saturday I didn't say ' yes ' or ' no ' and on Sunday—to-day—the banns are being published ! "

Pretty quick—and pretty risky !

We cannot in going over this case see any reason for the extraordinary sympathy shown to Marie

Lafarge, except on the grounds that there are a great number of people who seem to have a lot of sympathy to spare for the wrong people.

Legalists will dispute the finding of the jury on the ground that it was not definitely proved that Lafarge died of arsenical poisoning.

Orfila found poison, it is true, but he did not find enough to justify the statement that Lafarge died of arsenic.

The reply was, big doses of arsenic did not necessarily leave traces.

All the symptoms of Charles Lafarge's death were those of arsenical poisoning and, in our view, Charles Lafarge died of poison administered by his wife.

IV

CHRISTIANA EDMUNDS

PASSION has played many sad pranks but it has rarely played one so oddly tragical as in the case of Christiana Edmunds.

Miss Edmunds lived with her widowed mother in Brighton. She had reached that dangerous age of forty-two, and was still disturbed by impulses or conquest, which are none the less real and poignant, and may be more bitter, when the woman is forty-two instead of twenty-two.

Miss Edmunds at this time made the acquaintance of a Dr Beard and his wife. It may be that at this time—the year was 1870—Miss Edmunds had not many opportunities of making the acquaintance of men whom she could encircle with the web of her dreams. Any presentable, desirable man, married or otherwise, might serve at that time. Christiana Edmunds was ready to translate commonplaces into subtle suggestions, the smile was something familiar and hinting, the handshake something tender and, after all, the medical profession has a " manner." Dr Beard may have been nothing more than doctor; Christiana Edmunds regarded him almost as *the* man.

It is not worth while attempting to inquire whether Dr Beard gave Miss Edmunds any grounds for imagining that he was a little more than Doctor and none the less a man. Letters subsequently passed between them that distinctly showed what she had thought of their relationship. They were certainly not the letters of patient to doctor, nor of the colour that would label them as mere friendly letters.

It is clearly plain that once Christiana Edmunds had got firmly fixed in her mind that Dr Beard was the man of her dreams, she must either solace herself with the dreary satisfaction of a secret and unrequited love or something must happen.

Love is capable of any urge. Christiana Edmunds was forty-two and of curious stock. She would be considered as " quite respectable " in those respectable Victorian days, and she and her mother visited Dr and Mrs Beard as friends.

On June the 13th, 1871, an inquest was held at " The Carpenter's Arms ", West Street, Brighton, on the body of Sidney Albert Barker, aged four years and a half.

At the time there seemed to be nothing to connect this inquest with Christiana Edmunds. Like many inquests it passed little noticed by the general public, though it had its tragic interest for those deeply concerned.

The case told at this inquest was peculiarly touching. The mother gave evidence first. She said she had noticed on the previous day that something was the matter with the deceased because he refused to come downstairs when they were ready to go a walk. The little nurse thought he was cross. But, said Mrs Barker, " I went back into the sitting-room and he clung to me and shivered a good deal. I took him on my lap, but Mrs Woodham (the landlady) took him away from me and said it was a fit. My eldest brother went for the doctor. Deceased shivered very much and his teeth were clenched, and he became very stiff and rigid. He got worse and worse. His face became black and he rolled his eyes about and seemed in great pain. The hot water and mustard that we put his feet in did not seem to do him any good. From the time he was taken ill to the time he died was not more than twenty minutes."

Charles David Miller, the uncle of the deceased, gave evidence. He said that about nine o'clock that morning he had eaten some chocolate creams himself and given three to the deceased. These sweets were pink and white in colour and one of the all pink ones, which the dead little boy had eaten, had a nasty taste. The witness also ate a pink one, and noticed its acid taste.

After eating the chocolate creams—say a quarter of an hour afterwards—the witness said he felt unwell. He trembled, his bones seemed to be loose, and a film spread before his eyes.

It was not the kind of thing he wished to make a fuss about, so he did not mention what he felt till the next morning, when he found he couldn't get up for breakfast. For half a minute he went rigid. He got better and then had another attack —and another, and became insensible. The doctor, a Mr Tuke, was sent for, and he said it was a fit; it was not the result of anything the witness had eaten.

About four o'clock Mr Miller, now feeling better, brought out his chocolate creams and handed some to his nephew and some to his brother. His nephew became ill; his brother disliked the nasty copper-penny taste of a sweet which burned the throat, and spat it out. Naturally, as the doctor had said the illness was not caused by food, the witness thought no ill of the chocolate creams.

The diagnosis of the doctor doesn't seem to have been a happy one.

The father of the dead boy confirmed rather than added to the evidence given by his wife and brother-in-law.

Mr Rugg, a surgeon who was called in to attend

to the boy, said he suspected poison at once. But he was too late. Before an emetic could be procured the little boy was dead.

The evidence, as one sees, was of a somewhat peculiar nature. Had these chocolates, bought in the ordinary way at a reputable shop in Brighton, caused the little boy's death? If so, it was a matter that had to be inquired into. So the inquest was adjourned.

In the meanwhile the police and the analysts worked on the case, and when the inquest was resumed noteworthy evidence was given by a Mrs Cole and . . . Miss Christiana Edmunds.

Mrs Cole kept a shop at 32 Church Street, and the story she told was that, two days after the inquest, she found some chocolate creams in a bag, which had on it the name of Maynard. She didn't know how the bag got in her shop and her explanation was that somebody must have left it. On the next day a boy called Henry Walker came into her shop and was given the creams.

And Henry Walker became ill.

Now appeared Christiana Edmunds. She had volunteered to give evidence; she was in no way considered a party to this case till she thrust herself into it as a witness. As her evidence is valuable we will quote it as it was given.

"I have bought chocolate creams at Mr Maynard's. I bought some in September last, which I fancied made me ill. I ate two and gave some to a friend, who was also ill. I did not notice any bad taste in them. I had violent internal pains and a burning in my throat, which came on about an hour afterwards. I took some brandy, which made me worse, and then some castor oil. On the 6th of March I bought some more chocolate creams, pink and white, at Mr Maynard's, on purpose to try them. I ate a portion of a white one, but the taste was so

bad I could not eat any more. It tasted like copper.
I was ill about ten minutes after. I felt a burning
sensation and tightness in my throat; saliva kept
coming into my mouth; I felt a trembling sensation
and looked livid. I took some brandy and water,
which made me feel worse, and then some castor oil.
About three or four in the afternoon I felt better, and
went and called on Mr Maynard and saw him in his
private room. Mrs Maynard was also present, and
I told them how ill I had been from the chocolates.
Mr Maynard said it could not be that, and that
metallic taste I complained of must have come from
something else I had been eating. They brought
several from the shop to try, and I tasted a very
small piece of some of them, but they were free from
the peculiar taste I had perceived in mine. I said
I should like to know what was in them, and Mr
Maynard said I was at liberty to have any analysed
out of the shop. I told him to try and find one like
that I had, for if he once tasted it he would believe
what I said. He said he was obliged to me for coming
and would write to his French agent. I gave one to
a lady at the same time I partook of one myself, and
it made her ill like myself, but she took a glass of
wine, which made her sick, and she soon after got
better. I took the remainder of the chocolates
that I had left to Mr Schweitzer, and told him how
I had felt, and I wanted to know how so small a
portion of chocolate cream could have made me so
strangely and suddenly ill. Mr Schweitzer treated
it very lightly. He thought I was nervous and
fanciful, but he altered his opinion after he had
tasted one himself, and he said he would make an
analysis and he gave me the result in writing. I gave
it to Mr Rugg but did not mention Mr Maynard's
name. Mrs Maynard ate several from the shop,
and tasted one of those I had left. Some of those
I had left were good, but others, I am convinced,

were bad. I did not communicate the analysis to Mr Maynard, as he seemed too sceptical. My object in going to him was to warn him."

Mr Maynard naturally was called, but his evidence was little more than that he could not understand how any poison could get into his chocolates. His children ate the chocolates regularly, and had never been ill.

Mr George Robert Ware of Marchmont Street, Russell Square, who made the chocolates, said he could not think how any poison could get into them. He had sometimes used poison to kill rats, but he did not see how that could get in the chocolate creams.

But the jury thought they saw better than he. There was undoubtedly poison in some chocolates, and Mr Ware had had poison for rats, so the verdict was, " We find that the child died from poisoning by strychnine, but we quite exonerate Mr Maynard from blame, and the other gentleman also, though we think he might be a little more careful in killing the rats ".

Mr Maynard promised to destroy all his stock of chocolate creams.

It reads like a ghastly accident, and might so have been recalled and related, but other events that followed seemed to have some sort of kinship with the death of the boy Barker, and Suspicion flapped her wings.

It is well to mention that three anonymous letters were received by Mr Barker, the father of the dead boy.

Sussex Square,
June 27, 1871.

" Sir,

Having seen the result of the investigation of the inquest of Thursday last, I feel great surprise to find that no blame is attached to anyone. I have felt great interest in the case and fully sympathize in your sad loss. Great dissatisfaction is felt at the result by most of the inhabitants, and we all feel it rests now with yourself to take proceedings against Mr Maynard. As a parent myself, I could not rest satisfied, nor would one in a hundred. I trust you will come forward for your own sake and in the public good. You shall have all the assistance possible. I feel sure the young lady will willingly come forward, as I know, from good authority, she was very dissatisfied with Mr Maynard's conduct; she of course supposed he would have taken the same step she did and have them analyzed. I can only say that Mr Maynard, after being duly warned that his chocolates were injurious, and had made three persons ill, ought to have them analyzed or destroy them. The public mind is not satisfied, and feel great blame is attached to him for selling to your family chocolates from the same stock he had been warned against. He spoke of investigating, and what was his investigation? Merely looking over and tasting a few chocolates with his shopwoman. Why, the young lady was not satisfied with that even; and as to writing to his French agent, it appears he never did. I hope no monetary considerations will prevent you taking proceedings. The Brighton inhabitants are all up in arms at the laxity of proceedings in the want of justice, and will assist you in every way, and, with the facts tried before unbiassed and unprejudiced men, I think Mr Maynard will not escape scot free. My feeling of disgust is felt by most of the respectable and influential inhabitants of this town.

I am, Sir,
An old Inhabitant and a Seeker for Justice."

P.S.—The Town Council cannot take up the case again; it rests with you, and you shall receive all the aid we can offer. The papers are taking this up both Brighton and London. See the London *Observer*.

The second letter was signed "C. G. B." and written the next day. The third was as follows:

BRIGHTON,
DEAR SIR, *July* 1, 1871.
Having seen your letter in the *Daily News* permit me to say that, as you seem doubtful whom you are to proceed against, it is generally thought that the seller of

the chocolates is the proper person and it is the firm conviction with all who know the case that this man, after being warned and making no investigation, is certainly answerable. Had he taken common precaution—had his sweets been properly examined—this sad event might never have occurred. Are persons' warnings to be disregarded because he chooses to think them nervously fanciful? Such negligence ought not to be tolerated. A letter from Mr Ware's solicitor makes the case worse, for he says if the sweetmeats were supplied by him, the poison must have got into them after leaving his premises. Now you have good grounds for pursuing your investigations, for who supplied these chocolates to the seller? As the *Brighton Times* observed to-day, the case cannot be dropped; that you are the person to take proceedings, and of course cannot rest satisfied—the public will not, I frankly confess. Had I lost my child in such a sad way, as a parent I should feel myself in duty bound to take proceedings against the seller of the sweets. Justice, I would have, and you have certainly not had it shown in your case. Excuse the liberty I take in advising you, but you may not see the papers, and know what is hoped for and expected from you.

I am, Sir, respectfully yours

A London Tradesman now a visitor at Brighton.

P.S.—I am sure that many London tradesmen, with myself, will second you in your efforts.

These three anonymous letters were subsequently found to be in Christiana Edmunds' handwriting.

The next chapter in this story was turned when Miss Christiana Edmunds was charged before the magistrates at Brighton with attempting to administer poison to Emily Beard with intent to commit murder.

It came out in the course of the trial that packets of cakes, preserved fruits and sweetmeats, had been received by various people in Brighton. These packets were usually accompanied by notes, saying they were for certain members of the family and came from an old friend. One of these notes bore the initials "G. M.". But the people who had eaten these cakes and sweetmeats from 'an old friend' had generally been taken ill and had to call in a doctor, which cast a doubt on the verity of the sender's friendship.

One day two boxes containing cakes, with a special packet of small cakes wrapped separately, arrived at Dr Beard's, addressed to Mrs Beard. There was a paper in the separate little parcel of cakes which read, "A few home-made cakes for the children, those done up are flavoured on purpose for *yourself* to enjoy. You will guess who this is from; I can't mystify you I fear. I hope this will arrive for you in time while the eatables are fresh ".

Mrs Beard, wife of Dr Beard of 64, Grand Parade, Brighton, said in her evidence, " On Thursday, the 10th of August, I received a parcel about half past seven, which I unpacked. . . . Inside the box I found the paper produced " (the note already quoted) " and also some cakes, preserved fruits and ginger bread-nuts. The note was wrapped round a plum cake, about the size of a tea-cup, which was different from the others. I cut the cake open on the following Saturday about midday, and then noticed something in it which looked to me like unbaked flour. I cut the piece out and said to my servant that it did not look nice, and gave it to her to take away. Two of my servants ate some of the cake and were taken ill the same afternoon, and Mr Blaker was called in to attend them. I and some other people in the house ate some of the other contents of the box and were not affected by so doing. . . . I gave up the box and paper to the police. I have known the prisoner five or six years. She was for some time a patient of Dr Beard's, and for some time I and my family have been on terms of intimacy with her. About a year ago a circumstance occurred in consequence of which the intimacy was discontinued.

The incident to which I allude occurred in our drawing-room in the evening. I was present, and so was Miss Edmunds and a Miss Richardson, an elderly lady who is deaf, and resides in the house. . . .

"Miss Edmunds, on the occasion in question, took from her pocket something which she called chocolates, and said she had brought them for the children. The children however were gone to bed, and she put one of the chocolates in my mouth. It had a very unpleasant, cold, metallic taste, and I spat it out directly. I experienced very unpleasant feelings after it, and saliva ran from my mouth all night. The next day I had an attack of diarrhoea and felt very unwell. I did not say anything to Miss Edmunds about it that night, nor at any other time. I mentioned what had occurred to Dr Beard within a day or two."

In cross examination Mrs Beard said "the occurrence was partly the cause of the intimacy being partially broken off".

Dr Beard also gave evidence, in the course of which he said the prisoner had written to him several times, and he had told her the letters must cease. What he said was, "This correspondence must not continue; it is not good for either of us."

The bench took up the cross-examination of Dr Beard, who said, "Between the 22nd of September and the 2nd of October last, I visited Mrs and Miss Edmunds at their residence and alluded to the illness of my wife after taking the chocolate given her by Miss Edmunds. I had my worst fears in my own mind, but I alluded to the matter as trivially as possible, in order to see what would come of it. I then, to prevent any recurrence of the kind, spoke of the great use which had lately been made of the spectroscope for the purpose of detecting the most minute particles of poison. From her answers I quite understood that she denied all intention of anything of the kind on her part " (meaning, of course, the intention to poison Mrs Beard), " and said that she herself had been ill from eating some chocolates. I saw Miss Edmunds at the commencement of this year at my house. She called on me and asked that she might be on the same friendly terms as formerly. I believe there had been a coldness between my wife and her, besides which I had been away from Brighton for three months. I refused her request, and told her I could not help fearing she had attempted to poison my wife. She was very indignant, and on the following morning she and her mother called to expostulate. I then laughed off the idea, simply because I could prove nothing, and did not wish to lay myself open to an action for libel. Besides, my wife was then fully on her guard ".

The first hearing before the magistrates was adjourned and before the second hearing the case had developed. The police had accumulated evidence to connect Miss Edmunds with the case of the boy, Barker. The reader will remember that on that occasion she thrust herself forward as a witness. The important chronological order is as follows:

(1) The poisoned chocolate given to Mrs Beard, which led to the coldness between Miss Edmunds and the Beards.

(2) The poisoning of the boy Barker.

(3) The cake sent to Mrs Beard, now traced to Miss Edmunds, and other parcels sent to various people in Brighton.

After the inquest on Sidney Albert Barker Miss Edmunds wrote the following letter to Dr Beard.

CARO MIO,
    I have been so miserable since my last letter to you. I can't go on without ever speaking to you. What made me write so ! I thought, perhaps, it would be better for both of us, but I have not strength of mind to bear it.
We met La Sposa the day after her return and were

glad to see her back again. La Madre thought she looked very thin and careworn; I hope she will feel the good now from her change. You must have missed her. I didn't enter on the poisoning case in the street, but I called and told her that I was obliged to appear at the inquest in a few days, and I hoped she would send you a paper and let you know, but she said No, she did not wish to unsettle you. However, dear, I mean you to know about this dreadful poisoning case, especially as I had to give evidence; and I know how interested you would be in it as you told me you would give anything to know what La Sposa swallowed. I sent you the analysis and have no means of knowing if it was sent you. Yes, through my analysis the police found me out and cited me to appear. You can fancy what I felt; such an array of gentlemen; and that clever Dr Letheby, looking so ugly and terrific, frightened me more than anyone; for, if I gave wrong symptoms, of course he would have known. You can fancy my feelings, standing before the public, looking very rosy and frightened as I was. When I saw the reporters' pens going and taking down all I uttered, Burn's lines rushed to my memory: "The chiel's amang them taking notes and faith he'll prent it."

I did the best I could, thankful when I had finished. It seemed so long and my evidence was useful. As the jury had nothing to say, my heart was thankful. When Mr Gell and Penfold attacked me—Mr G.: "Why didn't I show Maynard the analysis?"—it was so sudden, my ideas all left me, and I merely said, because I found Mr Maynard so sceptical and prejudiced, and I thought I had done sufficient. Oh! Why didn't I say as I meant. Because, I suppose Mr M. would take the same steps as I had done or else destroy his stock, and that, if those sold to Mr Miller were from the same stock, I had warned him against *these*—he was answerable.

If I had only said that, *for I had no friendly feeling towards Mr M*. That man's chocolates have been the cause of great suffering to me. The Inspector said he wished I had spoken as I felt and as I did to him when he came to me, earnestly and energetically. But La Madre told me I should be thought *flippant, so you see I was subdued.* It was unfortunate the woman Cole's case was dropped. The

Inspector told me Dr Letheby took one of the chocolates from the bag and said, "Good God! this is filled with strychnine". He felt the effects of it all day: it was rash of him. You see there were two poisons. Zinc was in La Sposa's case and mine. I was troubled to describe the taste. The reporters smiled when I said castor oil and brandy. The Coroner said, "Ah! Your usual remedy". I was stupid. He is so deaf. I was told to stand close to him. I took care to turn my back on the jury and on all I could. They were all very polite to me, even that fierce Mr Penfold. Dr Letheby's evidence was so interesting, and showed the different sweets in one glass tube, yet separated. His physique is large and grand, like his mind. Now, darling, rest assured through the whole affair I never mention *your name* or La Sposa's, and if I had been asked to mention a friend I should say Mrs Dix. She is very kind and fond of me, and would have come forward had they wanted her, to help me. No, the rack shouldn't have torn your name from me, and the only reason I said September was, that you might see I had concealed nothing. My dear boy, do esteem me now. I am sure you must. What trial it was to go through, that inquest! La Madre was angry I ever had the analysis; but you know *why* I had it—to clear myself in *my dear friend's eye*. She always says nothing was meant by you. No, darling; you wanted an excuse for my being so slighted. I never think of it; it was all a mistake. I called on La Sposa and told her how I got on. She said my evidence was very nice. She didn't ask me to come; but perhaps she mustn't. *Now there is no reason.* La Madre says if you were at home, she is sure you would ask me just the same as ever.

Come and see us, darling, you have time now. La Madre and I have been looking forward to your holiday to see you. She wants to know how you get on and like the North. Don't be biassed by any relatives: act as your kind heart tells you, and make a poor little thing happy, and fancy a long, long bacio from

DOROTHEA.

I haven't taken back your etchings yet, and I'll not call while you are not here, as I have just been and it will be better and right for you to come to us.

With that letter Christiana Edmunds unlocked her heart. The police were not dull, and at once began to gather together the threads of this remarkable case.

The issue before the magistrates was the charge of "attempting to administer poison to Mrs Beard", but as the case progressed and the police became possessed of more evidence the prisoner was definitely charged with the murder of the little boy Barker and with attempting to poison Mrs Beard, Mrs Boys and Mr Garrett, who had received poisoned cakes or sweetmeats.

The trial of Christiana Edmunds on these serious counts took place at the Old Bailey in January 1872, before Baron Martin.

Mr Serjeant Ballantine, with whom was Mr Straight, appeared as counsel for the prosecution; Mr Serjeant Parry, Mr Poland and Mr Worsley defended the prisoner.

The first witness was Mr Charles David Miller, who repeated the story he had told at the inquest; how he had bought the chocolate creams at Maynard's, how the little boy, after he had been given one began to cry, stiffened and died.

Dr Rugg, who attended the boy and made a postmortem examination, said he found the organs generally healthy, with the brain slightly congested, which would be the condition in a child dying of convulsions. The body was very rigid. It had been well nourished. There was nothing about it to indicate the cause of death. There was a quantity of indigested food which he preserved. Witness could form no opinion as to the cause of death. He never saw anyone die of strychnine.

The foregoing is evidence to make both the faculty and laymen lower their brows. What follows is more encouraging.

Dr Henry Letheby said he was a Professor of

chemistry and well acquainted with the symptoms produced by different descriptions of poisons. He had heard the account given in evidence of the boy's death and also his uncle's description of his symptoms. He had no doubt they were symptoms caused by the poison of strychnine. Some chocolate creams were afterwards handed to him by Inspector Gibbs, and he had since analysed them. He should say there was a quarter of a grain in them. A quarter of a grain had been known to kill an adult, and a 16th of a grain to kill a child between two and three years old. He had also examined the child Barker's stomach, which he had received from Inspector Gibbs on the 16th of June, and had analysed it. He found strychnine to the extent of a quarter of a grain in it.

Mr Isaac Garrett, the next witness, was a chemist in Queen's Row, Brighton. He said: "The prisoner has been in the habit of dealing at my shop for two years. She was a ready money customer, and I did not know her name. She came on the 28th of March and bought something. She afterwards asked me if I would supply her with a little strychnine to destroy cats. I objected strongly. She said she had a garden and the cats destroyed the seeds in it. She also said she was a married woman, and pressed me much to give it to her, adding that there were only her husband and herself; that they had no children, and the strychnine would not go out of their hands. I raised other objections, but ultimately I supplied her with 10 grains; I said I would not let her have it unless she brought a witness with her. She said the only person she knew in the neighbourhood was Mrs Stone, and she left the shop and fetched her. On their arrival I made an entry in my book, stating that the purchaser was Mrs Wood, and that the poison was purchased for the purpose of destroying cats. The prisoner signed in the name of Wood.

She remembered that I seemed very anxious about the matter, and said she was coming into Brighton again in a few days, and would call and tell me there had been no accident. She afterwards called and said she had burnt the paper, and there had been no mishap. On the 15th of April she called on me again and bought some more strychnine—10 grains—and I made an entry in my book of the transaction, she signing it as Mrs Wood, of Hillside, Kingston. It was witnessed by Mrs Stone. The prisoner said the strychnine I had sold her had no effect on the cats; they were as numerous as ever. I again told her the nature of strychnine, its great strength and danger, and again she overruled my scruples by referring to her husband. I supplied it. On the 11th of May she called again, and I sold her 10 grains of strychnine in the same name; the purpose, stated by her, being to kill a dog. The entry I made was signed by the prisoner, but not in the presence of any witness. She had said they were about to leave Kingston to go to Devonshire and that they had a dog which was old and diseased, that they could not take it with them, and that she wanted the strychnine to kill it. On the 8th of June I received a note produced by a little boy. It purported to come from Messrs Glaisyer and Kemp, of North Street, Brighton, chemists, and stated that they would be obliged if I could supply them with a little strychnine; that they were in immediate want of a quarter of an ounce, but a smaller quantity would do. They asked me to send it in a bottle sealed up, adding that the bearer of the note might be safely trusted with it. I did not act upon that letter, but sent a note to them by the boy in reply. He returned in about twenty minutes or half an hour with another note from them, stating that they would be quite satisfied with one drachm of strychnine until their own arrived, and would thank me to supply it; but if

I should feel in the least disinclined they would apply elsewhere. Half a crown was enclosed in the note. I then supplied one drachm of strychnine, put it into a bottle, sealed it up and labelled it 'Poison', and handed it to the boy with the change. I remember hearing of the inquest on the boy, Barker, and receiving on the 8th of July a letter purporting to come from the Borough Coroner (Mr D. Black). He asked for the loan of the book in which I registered the sale of poisonous drugs, adding that the request had no reference to anything I had sold in that way or to any irregularity in selling, but only to assist him in certain inquiries. I sealed up the book and handed it to the bearer. In about half an hour it was brought back by the same boy, and a few days afterwards I missed a leaf from it. It was the leaf preceding the entries of sale to 'Mrs Wood'. The last purchase of strychnine in my book was on the 11th of May."

Caroline Stone, a milliner, said her shop was three doors from that of Mr Garrett's. On or about the 20th of March the prisoner came into her shop and asked to see some Shetland "falls". When she first came in she said she had neuralgia in the face and was going to Mr Garrett's to get some stuff for it. She bought a fall, and after some conversation left the shop, but returned in about five minutes saying she wanted witness to do her the favour to go with her into Mr Garrett's shop and sign a book as she wanted some poison, she and her husband being naturalists. Witness hesitated a long time and at last went, after the prisoner had given her name and address as 'Mrs Wood of Kingston'. The prisoner afterwards called again, bought another veil, and asked her to go to Garrett's again and sign her name. She said she wanted more poison to stuff birds. She never used the word strychnine at all. Witness went into the shop and signed an entry again.

Mr Thomas Glaisyer, the senior partner in the firm of Glaisyer and Kemp, was shown the letters referred to by the witness Garrett. He said they were not in his handwriting nor in that of anybody connected with his establishment. He did not know the prisoner.

Mr Black, the coroner, swore that the letter asking Mr Garrett for his poison book was not written by him.

Adam May, a boy of eleven years of age, recognized the lady in the dock. "I have seen her before," he said, "at the top of King Street, Brighton. I think I first saw her in Portland Street. I remember her asking me if I would go an errand for her. I said I would. She asked me to go to Mr Maynard's shop and get her six pennyworth of large chocolate creams, and she gave me 6d. to buy them. I went and asked a young woman serving in the shop for six pennyworth of chocolate creams. She took them from a large case and put them in a paper bag. I went to the lady who sent me; she was then walking up and down near the bottom of Portland Street. I gave her the bag and she undid it, and then did it up again, saying they were not the right sort. I returned to the same shop and brought back a sixpenny box of small creams and gave them to her. She said they were the right sort and gave me a large piece of chocolate cream, which she took from a paper she had in her hand when I came back. I saw the same lady again about three months afterwards at the top of King Street. She asked me if I would go an errand for her. I asked if I could go and ask my mother. She said yes. I asked my mother, who said yes, and then the lady asked me to take a note to Mr Garrett, the chemist. I took it and brought back something like a book in a brown paper parcel. I found the lady in Duke Street—not where I had left her—and gave her the book. She gave me 4½d. I did not see her any more that day.

On another occasion, some time afterwards, I met her and she gave me some 'bull's-eyes'."

Anne Meadows, the shopwoman at Mr Maynard's who supplied the chocolates to the boy, corroborated his story from her side.

Kate Page, also an assistant in Mr Maynard's shop, told how she had given certain instructions to a man named Parker when she supplied a boy named Brooks with some chocolates.

Boys who came in innocently for chocolates were no longer regarded with purely commercial looks in Mr Maynard's establishment.

It appeared that this boy Brooks also bought chocolates for a lady and also, oddly enough, came back with them as being the 'wrong sort'—always the big French ones, that would hold a lot of cream.

And an assistant named Charles Schooley had also followed two boys, who had bought chocolates at the shop, and seen them hand the sweets to a lady—the prisoner.

Mr Maynard also gave evidence. He said he had sold chocolate creams in Brighton ever since they had been introduced and had no strychnine or poison of any kind in his establishment. After the inquest on the boy Barker he had sent the whole of his stock of chocolates to be analyzed and then had them destroyed.

Mrs Cole, the wife of a grocer in Church Street, said that in the preceding March the prisoner came to her husband's shop, and, after she had left, a bag containing chocolate creams was found. Witness's daughter and another young woman staying with them ate some of the creams and were very sick and ill. In June the prisoner again came to the shop and, after she had gone, witness found that a bag of chocolate creams and lemon bull's-eyes had been dropped into a zinc pail near the counter. Witness ate some of the bull's-eyes; her daughter broke a cream in her mouth and spat it out immediately. Witness gave the remainder of the creams to a little boy named Walker.

Mrs Walker took up the story. She was the mother of the little boy, and she ate some of the chocolate cream given her by her son, and felt a strange sensation in her head, as if she were likely to lose the use of her limbs. She went to get some water but could not hold it in her hands. She felt a bitter taste in her mouth and was ill for about an hour. She had felt nothing like it before or since.

William Henry Halliwell, aged thirteen, son of a stationer in North Road, Brighton, said he had seen the prisoner often at the shop. She came in March last. She bought something and, after she left the shop, he found a bag of chocolate creams with the name of Maynard on it. He went to look for her, but could not find her. Two or three days afterwards she came again, and he showed her the bag of creams and asked her if she had left it. She said she had not. A day or two afterwards she called again. Meanwhile he had eaten all the creams but one or two—there were about a dozen altogether. When he ate the last one he felt sick, his legs ached, there was a burning in his throat and a drawing-up of his limbs. He was obliged to go to bed and was ill ten days. He was quite well the day before he ate the creams. About a week or so after he recovered the prisoner called again, and after she had gone he found another bag of chocolate creams. He did not try them.

William Henry Halliwell was lucky.

Other witnesses were called, who testified to this promiscuous dropping of bags of chocolate creams, some of which had a bitter taste; and all were in some way or other connected with the prisoner.

The letters, purporting to have been written by Glaisyer and Kemp and Mr Black, the coroner, to

Mr Garrett, the chemist, were, in the opinion of an expert, in the handwriting of the prisoner.

Police-inspector Gibbs said he remembered having an interview on a Sunday in August last, at 16, Gloucester Place, Brighton, with the prisoner. She was lying on a couch just within the door, and she said, "Here I am again, Mr Gibbs, nearly poisoned. You have heard I have had a box sent me with some fruit in it. It came on Thursday evening by post. It is evidently no one well acquainted with me or the sender would have known my address and how to spell my name correctly." She said the box contained some strawberries, two apricots and a pair of new gloves. She said Mrs Edmunds, her mother, had the strawberries, which were all right, and she (prisoner) ate one apricot and found it so bitter that she had to spit it out. She asked if it were true other boxes had been received. She said she had heard Mrs Beard and Mrs Boys had received one, as had also Mr Curtis, editor of the *Gazette* in North Street. She said it was very strange, and felt certain witness would never find it out. Witness took her into custody on the 17th of August at her residence on the charge of attempting to poison Mrs Beard. She replied, "I poison Mrs Beard! Who can say so? I've been nearly poisoned myself".

That was the case against the prisoner. In one way it is remarkable: the evidence is architectural. Each stone raises up the edifice: there is no waste or wandering, not much overlapping, and little that is not immensely significant. The smallest action bore the importance of the pin or transom of a great structure.

If the court had not been in possession of the motive which had pushed this unhappy woman to her crime it might have found the case inexplicable, perhaps unravelable. How trace to a respectable lady of forty the death of an innocent little boy of four, who was a perfect stranger to her? Yet there was no gainsaying the evidence.

Mr Serjeant Parry had a difficult task. He could not deny that the prisoner had craftily got possession of a great quantity of a terrible poison. He, however, asked the jury to be sure in their own minds that the particular chocolate, which poisoned Sidney Albert Barker, was actually poisoned by the prisoner herself. He pleaded well on this, his one clear and well-chosen forensic ground. He said, "On the Monday morning when the witness Miller bought the creams, the shopwoman nearly emptied the compartment to serve him, and it was afterwards filled up. But, strange to say, the sweets that were subsequently purchased by Ernest Miller, his brother, which would have been taken from the top of the new heap and not from the bottom of the compartment where his brother's had been got, also contained strychnia. That fact alone proved almost to demonstration that the poison was not put there by the prisoner. . . ."

Mr Serjeant Parry was on a surer road to the jury's sympathy when he dealt with the antecedents of the prisoner. He said her father died at mid-age in a lunatic asylum, and had suffered from suicidal and homicidal mania; her brother died an epileptic idiot in Earlswood asylum; her sister suffered from constant hysteria. And the prisoner herself was so "idiotically vain" as to deny her real age; she said she was thirty-four; she was forty-three.

A dangerous argument to prove lunacy. But one forgives much in a counsel.

Mrs Edmunds said her daughter had suffered from paralysis and hysteria, and as a child walked in her sleep. Since she had known Dr Beard there had been a great change in her demeanour. While Mrs Edmunds gave her evidence the prisoner sobbed poignantly.

The doctors who were called laid emphasis on the inability of the prisoner to distinguish between right and wrong. One medical man said he regarded the prisoner's case as lying on the borderland between crime and insanity. He thought her intellect quite clear and free from any delusion, but that her moral sense was deficient. . . .

This is not the place to argue a case, but one obvious comment may be added: all deliberate murderers are morally deficient.

Mr Serjeant Ballantine said it had been contended that possibly the chocolate cream, causing the death of the unfortunate boy, did not originally come from the prisoner. If that had stood alone there might have been room for a doubt, to which the prisoner would be entitled: but he could not forget the artful manner in which the prisoner had obtained strychnia from the chemist, Mr Garrett, and the forgery to which she had had recourse in procuring it. . . . Folly always followed in the wake of crime, and even the crimes of very clever people. The primary motive of the prisoner was to absolve herself from blame in a family, with which she had been intimate, and a secondary one to fix on anybody else the culpability that would otherwise attach to herself. . . .

Baron Martin, in summing up to the jury said, if they believed she gave the boy May poisoned sweetmeats, intending that he should take them to Maynard's shop, and that they should be sold there; and if they also believed that one of these poisoned sweets was sold to a relative of the deceased boy Barker, and administered to him and that he died from its effects, the prisoner would be guilty of the murder of the child.

Referring to the prisoner's state of mind he said, if the jury in this case should think that the prisoner did not know right from wrong at the time she committed the crime with which she was charged, if she did commit it, they would acquit her; but if they so found, they would accompany their verdict with an intimation that they did so on the ground of insanity.

The jury, after an absence of one hour, returned a verdict of "Guilty"; they did not consider her insane.

Before sentence of death was passed the prisoner said it was owing to her intimacy with Dr Beard that she had been brought "into this dreadful business". Also she said she was pregnant.

A jury of matrons was at once empanelled from ladies who happened to be in court and they tried that issue, with the assistance of two doctors. The result was a verdict that the prisoner was not pregnant.

Sentence of death was passed, and it is noteworthy that the *Times'* reporter says that "when the jury returned to deliver their verdict, the prisoner walked to the front of the bar, her bearing at that supreme moment being singularly firm and betraying no visible emotion. It was also respectful and becoming. She heard the verdict without any apparent distress. Her countenance was slightly flushed and her eyes beamed with an unwonted expression. In the few words of complaint she addressed to the Judge she spoke with much modesty and propriety, and afterwards heard the sentence with fortitude."

The death penalty was not inflicted, Christiana Edmunds being treated as 'insane'.

The case is a peculiar one, not only for its strangeness, but for the light it sheds on the character of the neurotic woman. Christiana Edmunds, in the forties, meets a doctor with whom she falls in love. Apparently she desires to marry him and so attempts to poison his wife; that attempt having failed with opprobious results to herself, her one object is to rehabilitate herself in the eyes of the man whose esteem she values, and whose friendship meant so much to her. It was here that her moral deficiency asserted itself just as there is a time in many people's lives when their morality is put to the test. The vain, the morbid, the vengeful, the vicious, the weak fail. And society has to protect itself against such people.

There have been few crimes so wanton, pursued with such ruthlessness and determination. Christiana Edmunds was a remarkable criminal in that she had no spite or grievance against the majority of her victims : she didn't even know them. She wanted to be on familiar terms with the Beards, particularly with Dr Beard, and having done something to end that intimacy the only plan she could follow (it was an obvious idea) was one which involved suffering and danger to many people. She said to herself, " If only I can make the Beards believe that a number of people have been poisoned—and I among them—they will not hold me responsible for that poisoned chocolate, which I unfortunately gave to Mrs Beard." She had the heart of a 'woman scorned'; it beat for no one but herself, and she forthwith laid her schemes to spread poison about Brighton and took care to let the Beards know of the cases. Note her letter descriptive of the inquest on the boy Barker which she sent to Dr Beard : she thought that inquest would be conclusive and convincing. She hoped intimacy would be resumed. It wasn't. So she again attempted to poison Mrs Beard.

Christiana Edmunds was a determined murderess. She tried to kill, then killed to divert suspicion, and then attempted once more to kill the one person she obviously wished dead.

She was treated as insane. Certainly her ancestry was unhealthy; but nothing she did—outside the crime—was quoted that would convince a reasonable mind that she was not responsible for her actions, though many opinions were tendered.

V

MARIE DE MORELL

LIEUTENANT DE LA RONCIÈRE, who was attached to the Cavalry School at Saumur, had certainly not the best of reputations. He lived with his mistress, and there was a general tendency to cold-shoulder him. Melanic Lair realized this, and decided Paris and freedom would be pleasanter than Saumur and gossip.

It may have been when Emile de la Roncière's reputation was less pronouncedly 'fast' that General de Morell, who commanded the Cavalry School, thought the lieutenant might be invited to his house. General Baron de Morell's family consisted of Madame de Morell, his handsome and accomplished wife, Marie, his attractive daughter aged sixteen, a son Robert, aged twelve, and a pretty English governess, Miss Stone, aged twenty-four.

The Morells were well connected, Madame de Morell being a niece of Marshal Soult.

While the Morells had been living in Paris anonymous letters had been received by Madame de Morell. They scarcely seemed worth the writing: there was a reference to a mysterious society that boded the family no good; but the letters might have been concocted by Huck Finn and his friends. What the Morells thought of them we don't know.

The General and Madame de Morell entertained, and a Lieutenant Oclave d'Estouilly, whose pleasures were intellectual, artistic and religious, was a fairly frequent visitor. He presented Marie de Morell with a drawing and, oddly enough, shortly afterwards received an anonymous letter.

"I am neither man nor woman, neither angel nor demon, and for that reason inclined more to evil than good. I know you are happy, and I mean to disturb your happiness as well as that of the de Morell family. I have already destroyed the happiness of three women.

I have conversed with Mademoiselle de Morell on the sofa; I told her I was your intimate friend; Mademoiselle de Morell listened to me. I continued: M. d'Estouilly does not intend to remain at Saumur; he has been strongly urged to return to his family; his father has plans for him.

AN OFFICER."

On the face of it this was an odd letter for any officer to write. It starts off almost hysterically and comes to definite news, which happened to be true. M. d'Estouilly had been pressed by his father to return home and General de Morell had persuaded him to stay on at Saumur.

But what officer had written this letter?

M. d'Estouilly suddenly remembered he had seen de la Roncière sitting on the sofa with Miss de Morell. If M. d'Estouilly had had enough imagination to realize the romantic as well as the moral side of life he might not have taken this letter so seriously.

When next he met Mademoiselle de Morell at a dance he asked her if she knew that his plans had been changed. Mademoiselle had the air of one slightly embarrassed. "Yes. . . . She had heard. . . . But, really, what can it matter to me?"

M. d'Estouilly then pressed her to tell him who had given her the information. She said nothing.

Just then la Roncière passed them.

"Is that the man?" asked d'Estouilly.

"Yes," replied Marie de Morell.

Three days later d'Estouilly received another anonymous letter.

"I wrote a letter to Marie to-day in which I told her a good many humiliating things. This letter is signed d'Estouilly. It will reach her, I am sure, because I bribed a servant with five francs."

It scarcely seems to have been worth the cost of a stamp.

M. d'Estouilly began to feel the awkwardness of the situation. He went frequently to dances at the Morell's and now took pains to avoid dancing with Marie de Morell.

So he received this letter:

"You have changed your behaviour, it seems to me, without giving me any warning. How can I help you? Several things made me imagine you have told all to Madame de Morell. I congratulate you: it was the best way to annoy Marie. In the first place, her mother has given her a fine talking to. If you show indifference she may think she is not going to see you again.

I have got some of her handwriting through a friend. I have tried to copy it and send you the fruit of my labours. Take this pretended letter from Marie to her mother, whose fury will then rise to its height. Your heroine will be shut up and you and I, my friend, will laugh in our sleeves.

You may be assured I shall make life pretty miserable for her. I have had placed in her room, in her books, little papers where she is described as ugly, stupid and disagreeable—which is true, so far as I am concerned. I had one of these papers put in her prayer-book: that was devilishly smart.

Adieu. I sharpen my pen to say some pretty things about the poor desolate.

R."

And with this strange epistle there was the one which copied Marie de Morell's handwriting.

"How wicked you are not to pay any attention to me. If you knew the trouble that causes me! You didn't ask me to dance on Saturday and I did so want to! I see you are as hard as a rock and I, who am so tender. . . . You hurt me. I pray the good God to change you, but he is as deaf as you. I love you—you are so attractive.

MARIE DE MORELL."

The matter of these letters is interesting. At the time they may have presented the indications of a fantastic idiocy or something stupidly sinister, but to-day we can read them with understanding.

M. d'Estouilly naturally was ill at ease. He was the recipient of strange letters and did not know what to do.

His friend, Lieutenant Ambert, called on him and d'Estouilly showed the letters.

And together they agreed that the writing was the writing of de la Roncière—but disguised.

So the next night when Lieutenant d'Estouilly happened to be at the Morell's he showed the last letter he had received to the Baroness, also the one signed 'Marie de Morell'.

And Madame de Morell said, "Yes . . . That is my daughter's handwriting, but she writes a more leaning hand."

And apparently nothing was done!

All this time, too, Marie de Morell had said to the friends she met, that when she saw Lieutenant de la Roncière for the first time he said, "You have a charming mother: it is a pity you are not like her."

And the General so far had said nothing about this.

But anonymous letters were a feature of the Morell household. They turned up at all times and in all sorts of places.

Marie de Morell showed one she had found:

"Madame de Morell is charming, Robert is very nice. Mademoiselle de Morell is very wicked."

Miss Allen found one which flattered her. A few days later she found another which gave her no cause for rejoicing. But almost always Marie de Morell was quoted with belittlement.

Marie de Morell told this story to her mother:

"I was near the window about an hour ago, playing on the piano, when I heard someone applauding in the street. I went to the window and there was a man going through the most extraordinary gestures. I watched him go. He went straight to the river, threw off his cloak and dived in. I was going to cry out when I saw some men go out in a boat and rescue him. . . . Oh! It was awful . . ."

But a few days before Madame de Morell had been singing and playing by the window and there were 'bravos' shouted from the street. Madame de Morell went to see who presumed, and thought she saw someone dressed in an officer's uniform—so she said.

It may be as well to mention here that nobody in the town of Saumur had heard of the man who threw himself into the River Loire and was rescued, as Marie de Morell had so touchingly described.

The General himself received an anonymous letter. They are not all worth quoting, for we can see the strain. This began:

"General, it has been my wish to spread trouble and discord in your household," and ended appropriately with "le mot de Cambronne".

Madame de Morell received the following:

"I tremble with the desire to let you know the name of him who adores you. It is the first sweet feeling that has filled my heart, and such homage should be agreeable to you. I hope that all I have written to your daughter has not upset you. At any rate you must know that all I have said is true, and, before sending them, I took care to get to know if you loved her and it was only when I learnt the contrary that I began to torment her. I had a great idea. I can't carry it out here, but one day it will be fatal to her. I have written more than thirty anonymous letters to people who know her in Paris: to Mademoiselle de B, who is at Neuchatel-en-Bry to Madame du M., who is at Ancy-le-Franc. You see I know everybody.

I shall be round your house to-day, and if I see you going out permit me to believe that you accept the homage of respectful love from your obedient servant

E. DE LA R."

One would say there was not much anonymity about "E. de la R". He might as well have written the name in full.

Madame de Morell went out.

The General looked from the window and saw de la Roncière on the bridge.

During the trial la Roncière's answer to this was:

"There is nothing extraordinary in that. After exercises we took a walk and the only walk was the bridge."

And when Marie de Morell went to play the piano, almost at the same time that her mother walked in the streets of Saumur, she found this letter:

"MADEMOISELLE,
As I don't know if your mother lets you see the letters she receives, I hasten to tell you that I have sworn a hatred for you that time will not weaken. If I could hack you, kill you, I would. Later, my hate will have results, which will take all happiness and all peace from your life. I have not won over merely one person in your house, but three: I know all that goes on. You have found a letter in the curtains: you will find this in the piano. Your father knows something of all this, but he knows nothing of my letter of yesterday. No, all this is no joke: death would be a relief for you, for your life will always be miserable and troubled.

R."

How did these letters get into the house. The General suspected his valet, Samuel, of being the accomplice who placed the letters. He discharged him.

M. d'Estouilly received another letter:

"You have in no way followed my advice: on the contrary you have treated it with contempt. That cries for vengeance. It is begun, but it can only be assuaged by death. This young girl worships you. I saw her last night hidden behind the window at eleven o'clock hoping to get a glimpse of you. Instead of replying to this love of a girl of sixteen with the coldness of your years, which would have made her suffer, you insist on going three times a week to be bored at the Morell's; your frequent walks on the bridge—all that can make someone in love feel she is loved in return. I have too much confidence in your good since to think that has anything to do with it, but you think that a big fortune can make one overlook ugliness and stupidity. You are as naughty as I to pit your cold and calculating mind against that kind of admiration. But don't cherish too many illusions. In a short time that young girl will be but a degraded creature, an object of pity for everyone. If you would have her then, she will be thrown in your arms, her parents too happy to get rid of her. She will be pure and innocent; it is the only thing I can't take from her; but in the eyes of everybody she will be guilty. All this, my dear friend, will happen in the month of January, and you will be the cause of it, for I should like to tell you this: I love her to distraction—that is to say, her money and in my own fashion. I should like to have won her; her air of disdain has prevented me from speaking. Also, I will have vengeance on her for her love for you. I have had put in her room by the person whom I have bought the most outrageous letter. Since you were so foolish as to tell her mother everything she is worried and watched at every turn. The flames of Hell devour her!
                                                              R."

That letter is worth analysis. It lays bare the writer. Its wild romantic touch of revenge that only

death can assuage; its application of the adjective
'naughty' to a man, its echoes of Don Juan and its
stupid mention of the person in the house who has
been bribed to place the letters—all these things
present no difficulties when one has the key.

But M d'Estouilly had not the key. He held an
anonymous letter in his hand, and wondered at the
shamelessness of the person who would write it.

So d'Estouilly handed the letter to General de
Morell.

The General called Captain Jacquemin to him, informed him that he was receiving a number of
anonymous letters and that he suspected the author
to be de la Roncière.

Captain Jacquemin suggested the General should
forbid la Roncière to his house. And, at a special
function one evening, when Lieutenant de la Roncière
presented himself with the other officers at the Morell's,
the General asked Captain Jacquemin to bring la
Roncière to him in another room.

"Monsieur," said the General to de la Roncière,
"I have special reason for asking you not to come
to my house. Will you retire?"

Lieutenant de la Roncière bowed and withdrew.

The General said, "Ah! He goes without pro-
testing: he doesn't say a word. He is guilty!"

Innocence behaves oddly at times, but it is practically certain that a guilty man would have made
some protest: generally he protests too much. As
a matter of fact de la Roncière went the next morning to ask Captain Jacquemin why he had been asked
to leave the Morell's house. Jacquemin told him
it was because he was suspected of writing anonymous
letters. "Writing anonymous letters ... Absurd!
Preposterous!" La Roncière protested against the
charges and swore he had never done anything of
the kind.

Then came this incident:

Miss Allen, who slept in a room adjoining that of Marie de Morell, was awakened by the sound of groans. She got up, but found the communicating door barred, which was unusual. However, she managed to force it open, so that it could not have been locked securely. The window was open; the silver moon flooded the room, and stretched on the floor was Marie de Morell, who was groaning. She had a cord tied round her; a handkerchief was round her neck; there was blood on her breast and on her nightdress. . . .

After a while Marie de Morell recovered sufficiently to be able to say that she had been awakened by hearing the window broken; a man dashed in the room. She jumped out of bed and got behind a chair. The man first fastened the door and then turned on her.

"His glance froze me with terror. The lower part of his face was hidden by a cravat of black silk; his look was terrifying. He wore a red undress military cap with silver braid I think I recognized . . . M. de la Roncière. I trembled. 'I have come to be avenged,' he said."

He had seized her, pulled off her nightdress and her camisole, tried to choke her with the handkerchief and then tied her with the rope for some romantic or desperate reason. He walked on her and then hit her on the arms and the chest. He bit her in the right wrist and jabbed some sharp instrument between her thighs, but this last incident was not thought of at the time. It was remembered some weeks later. The miscreant actually took a letter from his pocket, threw it on the commode and then went away.

And neither Miss Allen nor Marie de Morell, the wounded, abused and outraged girl, had so far made the slightest noise, that would waken anybody else in the house.

When Marie was in bed Miss Allen said she would rouse Madame de Morell, but Marie wouldn't hear of it, and so with the beams from the silver moon caressing them Miss Allen and Marie slept together with their dread secret till the morning.

In the morning Madame de Morell was told what had happened. The General was told that La Roncière had almost killed his daughter. And he told his wife and daughter and Miss Allen not to breathe a word of the event to anybody!

Marie de Morell got up as usual apparently and found this letter:

"You alone know the real motive of the crime that I am about to commit, for it certainly is a crime to soil what is purest in the world. I have loved you, worshipped you. You have treated me with scorn. I prefer hate and I am going to give you the right to hate me. One day I asked you to go out and you shut yourself up in your room. The love which consumes me will serve you for vengeance. I suffer the torments of Hell. The wretch has had the imprudence to tell everything to M de Morell. I have written to him that wherever I should meet him I would brand him with the seal of infamy. Adieu. I leave you only to destroy you. I add that everybody in Paris will learn of the shame of Saumur. I leave without having the satisfaction of your grief. I will be silent. May you suffer one half of what I have suffered for you."

That same day the General also received a letter which was dated "Wednesday—four o'clock in the morning", and came by post.

"You laughed at my letters, eh! This catastrophe will teach you that I am more redoubtable than you thought. I must gather all my hate to write to you. Unhappy father! I entered your daughter's room: I got in without the aid of anybody by the window. The noise I made in breaking the window woke her; she threw herself at the foot of the bed; I threw myself on her. I nearly strangled her with a handkerchief. Pain made her fall in a faint and covered with blood. I was thirsty for her blood and for her honour. I had everything. After having taken from her her honour, after having made her an object of shame, I went away without being seen by anybody. What a night! Do you see me soiling a young girl, cold as death? In the adjoining room a woman hurled herself at the door, which I had locked, and cursed me. I knew Madame de Morell had gone to Palenne, and your daughter had taken a walk with her brother and Miss Allen. With the aid of a false key I got into the room and made all my arrangements. My first care was to prevent help by shutting the door. Physical suffering took from her all power of crying out. Now that all has been done, now that your daughter will have a pledge of her misery, I can tell you that it is Samuel, who has distributed the letters at five francs each, money which I don't wish to reclaim. I promised him 1,000 francs if he would introduce me into her room in a less dangerous way than by the window and he refused. In three days I shall have left Saumur. In Paris you will see your daughter's shame. Here nobody knows of it. I fear the affection and respect of the Saumurite pigs and of my comrades who behave infamously towards me."

And that letter was supposed to have been written by a person who had daringly broken into the house of General de Morell, assaulted his daughter and got away without disturbing any other member of the household. But why drag in Samuel?

And what did the General do after having heard the story from his daughter and after having read that letter? Nothing.

Didn't he believe the story his daughter had told him and which was repeated in the anonymous letter? Let us record the fact that on September 24th, he did nothing. He might have shirked a public scandal, but what was to hinder him having an interview with La Roncière?

Other things were to happen before General de Morell moved in the matter.

Mr and Madame de Morell having received letters, the epistolary edifice was appropriately crowned when Marie de Morell received one.

"I am the happiest of men. Fortune has smiled on me in a most unlooked-for way. You see what it means in this world to love the good and to pursue it. You are the most miserable of creatures and the man who has had the imprudence to stand up for you is half dead. All that for me. A frenzied joy has got me. But that is another thought which I enjoy. It is this: you are now completely dependent on me. An atrocious tie unites us and soon you will be obliged to seek me to give you and another a name. Nothing can save you from this last humiliation. So you see where I have been carried by a frantic love. I never hated you; you generally inspired me with interest; but your mother's contempt has made me capable of anything. Let her come and beg mercy at my feet and then I will consent perhaps to give you back your honour in marrying you. I am the only person who can save you from an eternal disgrace. And even in my consent there will still be vengeance because I know you love another.
Believe me."

We have almost quoted enough of these strange letters; but they are extraordinary effusions and are worthy of care in the reading.

M d'Estouilly had not been overlooked, and a letter to him led to a climax.

"You are a wretch and a coward. After all the letters I have written anybody else would have asked me for an explanation; instead of which you merely denounce me to the General. I shall deny all, for what I have done I have done to annoy you—and I've done it. Ambert is all right but you are a coward; you are afraid of your skin. After having dishonoured your epaulette you thought you could throw it away and your cowardice would be forgotten. If you have any courage, then after this letter, you will call me out. But, wretch that you are, you daren't. Receive the assurance of my contempt. And one day I will brand you on the face with the seal of infamy and then we shall see what will happen.

EMILE DE LA RON . . ."

Why stop at Emile de la Ron.? Either in full or not at all.

La Roncière is supposed to have written this letter on the top of all the other letters and to have signed it 'Emile de la Ron'. One has to admit that if he did it he was mad.

D'Estouilly at once answered the above letter with a challenge. La Roncière, when seen by Ambert, d'Estouilly's second, said he couldn't understand the question of anonymous letters—knew, in fact, nothing about them. He said the same to d'Estouilly when they met. D'Estouilly, believing the letters to have come from de la Roncière, shrugged his shoulders at the explanation and refused to accept it.

So they fought. D'Estouilly was wounded.

One hour after the duel had been fought Ambert met de la Roncière. According to what was cited afterwards this is how de la Roncière had spent that morning.

At one o'clock he had written a letter to Madame de Morell.

At two o'clock he had burst into Marie de Morell's bedroom and done all the vile things that had been reported by the girl of sixteen.

At four o'clock he had written a letter to General de Morell in which he had set out all the details of the assault on the General's daughter, a feat in a lieutenant that makes one gasp.

At some other hour he had written to Marie de Morell.

He had had sundry interviews with his brother officers and then fought a duel.

An hour after the duel he was chatting gaily with comrades as if there was not a cloud in his sky.

Following the duel d'Estouilly and Ambert put their heads together. They believed de la Roncière was the author of the anonymous letters, and they came to the conclusion that something must be done.

The duel was talked of. Gossip got hold of the letters.

Partly by threats and partly by persuasion de la Roncière was persuaded that the best way to settle the trouble was for him to write a letter confessing he was the anonymous author.

And the extraordinary thing that de la Roncière wrote a letter confessing he was the author of the anonymous letters.

So far—assuming he was not the author—he had only seen one of these letters and that was shown him by d'Estouilly when they fought the duel. That letter de la Roncière had not even digested, for as he stumbled over the phrases d'Estouilly called him a hypocrite, and that stops concentrated reading.

Lieutenant de la Roncière was not an ideal man. He had led a gay and foolish life. He had, as we have seen, openly paraded his mistress in this town of Saumur. He had certainly been extravagant, and his career was probably littered with debts. His father was a stern parent of the old French School. Emile de la Roncière was afraid of his father, who was a lieutenant-general, with a distinguished career, and had already expressed disapproval of many of the doings of his son, Emile.

It may have been that de la Roncière said to himself: "I look like getting into another unholy mess. . . . Council of Honour, eh? . . . What will be said there? Everything. . . . What will my father say? He will think I am no good. . . . What are these anonymous letters? . . . Stupidities, I suppose . . . Oh! Well, if admitting I wrote those will keep people quiet, why not? . . ."

Emile de la Roncière's reasoning may have run on those lines. This is what he signed. The original had been drawn up by Ambert and d'Estouilly, and de la Roncière altered certain phrases.

" . . . Considering the material proofs against me, which would overwhelm me in a court of justice, I consider— I owe a duty to my family, whose honour might be smirched —my poor father at the close of so brilliant a career would not survive this affront : my condemnation would make his last days too bitter ; so, Monsieur, in the name of all possible considerations, I rely on your generosity and hope that this unhappy affair will be buried in oblivion.

I disavow all the expressions in the letters you have received, and in confessing myself the author offer my apologies. Accept them, Sir, and be generous and discreet.

It costs me much to make this confession. I have been pushed to it by no personal consideration because my career is lost. It is my family, whom I cannot disturb, that has decided me. Spare them—that is all I ask and I rely on you.

E. DE LA RONCIÈRE."

Saumur, Sep. 25, 1834.

When de la Roncière handed this confession to Lieutenant Berail, who acted as go-between, he reiterated his innocence and that he made the confession for the sake of his father.

But the letter wasn't strong enough for d'Estouilly. He had received letters and he knew of those that had been sent to the Morells. So he wrote to La Roncière, told him that three experts recognized his writing and that he had saved himself five years' penal servitude.

M d'Estouilly was stretching truth. Three experts had not recognized the anonymous letters to be in La Roncière's handwriting, but the hint was enough to wring a full confession from de la Roncière, who was probably sick and weary of the whole business by now.

And Ambert added a note.

"Your affair is becoming public; there is talk of a Council of Honour. . . . Leave the school. I think the General will give you leave. Lose no time, for you have many enemies.

AMBERT."

P.S.—You can rely on my discretion. I owe that to your father and your old friendship.

These honourable people, who trample on honour in their eagerness to protect it, overstepped the limit. There was no more talk of a Council of Honour than there was a judgment by the experts on the handwriting of the anonymous letters. But de la Roncière had to be persuaded. And if the end justified the means in the eyes of these honourable men then Lieutenants Ambert and d'Estouilly must have rejoiced, for de la Roncière wrote this :

" MONSIEUR,
I thought you would have been satisfied with my letter of this morning. You overwhelm me in my distress and ask me to retract certain letters which you mention. I will do it ; and may this step on my part give my family peace. I declare, therefore, that I am the author of the anonymous letters which have been received by General, Madame and Mademoiselle de Morell.

I also declare that I have sent to Mademoiselle de Morell a letter signed ' d'Estouilly ' and to you one signed ' Marie de Morell '.

I have just asked for leave and shall quit the school to-night. That, I imagine, will satisfy you. Instead of trying to damage my unhappy family I hope you will see this affair is spoken of as little as possible.

E. DE LA RONCIÈRE."

It is uneasy to get past that confession. The feeling that an honest man owns to roguery is disagreeable. In the box Lieutenant Berail repeated without equivocation that when de la Roncière handed him the letter he protested his innocence and said he merely made the confession to get rid of d'Estouilly's importunities. It is intelligible if one considers that de la Roncière had a record to hide, particularly from his father, and that the consequence of this confession meant no more than the resignation from a regiment where he was regarded with disfavour by his commanding officer. Also, that he knew nothing of what was in the anonymous letters.

But another troubling item is the fact that when de la Roncière asked for leave General de Morell granted it at once. And General de Morell had heard his daughter's terrible story of the attack by the light of the moon and had read these abominable letters purporting to come from the same Lieutenant de la Roncière.

But the General had done one bold thing: he had discharged his valet Samuel, who had been in the service of the Morells for sixteen years.

This fact came to de la Roncière at Paris. Mademoiselle Annette Roualt told him that Samuel had been dismissed, and was leaving by a certain diligence. La Roncière met the diligence and said to Samuel, " I haven't much money, but if you can tell me who is the author of the anonymous letters, I will give you twelve hundred francs."

And Samuel said, " I should like to know that. I thought perhaps you could help me."

La Roncière was not content to leave the matter as it stood. He went to a friend, a M de Chelaincourt, told him the whole story, and asked him to do the best to discover the author of the anonymous letters. This friend interviewed Samuel, but got nothing out of him. Samuel in all probability had never actually seen any of the anonymous letters.

And the very day de la Roncière left Saumur Madame de Morell had received another letter signed 'E. de la R.'.

It is preposterous to pretend that kind of thing is anonymous. This is how the letter began:

"You probably think that my vengeance is slaked. No, madame, a love like mine, a love that is despised has need of a deal of blood, of tears, of torture before it can get satisfaction. . . ."

An officer who could write that stuff wouldn't be fit to command a platoon.

What did Madame de Morell think of this? We don't know. What did she do? Nothing.

Marie de Morell, in spite of that awful scene in the moonlit room, seemed to enjoy life as usual. Five days later she was at a ball, and nobody guessed from her behaviour what had happened that night the window of her bedroom was broken and she lay groaning on the floor with a cord and handkerchief round her, caressed by silvery beams till Miss Allen found her.

And a fortnight later—it is now October 12th—Madame de Morell received another letter. Part of it is worth quoting:

" . . . I would agree to marry your daughter. My unfortunate position would now prevent me from opposing your wishes. Of course, that was my original plan. I meant to compromise her with M d'Estouilly, thinking he would boast and show her letter. . . .

For the rest, I should have thought that there are things that a coquettish mother and a mean father can't do even to save their daughter from disgrace. But it would be the limit of horror if your daughter should consent and you should refuse (and it must be with a very handsome dot, remember). . . .

E. R."

This letter was posted at Saumur. But de la Roncière and Samuel were not in Saumur.

On the 21st of October Marie de Morell fell down in a faint. Her mother ran to her and found this paper in her hand:

> "While you thought yourself safe the greatest disasters are preparing for you. Those you love most in the world, your mother, your father, M d'Estouilly, in a few months will die. You have refused me. I shall have vengeance on him.
>
> E. R."

Marie de Morell had an attack of nerves.

But who gave her the letter? . . .

And the next day Madame de Morell received another letter:

> "I have done nothing less than killed your daughter. I intended to give her an awful disease from which she would have died in great agony. I gave her blows from a knife in certain parts. She raised my courage by these words, 'If my poor mother could hear me', thinking that if she had told you all that had happened you would not have failed to think that I had done as I wished with her. . . .
>
> Now, vengeance! Vengeance! Blood! Blood! Your august M Gisquet won't be able to protect you. I am going to fill your house with letters. To Paris—death!"

At last, at long last, General de Morell acted. He wrote a short note headed "Crime", in which he loosed his feelings and achieved a tone that might link him in relationship with the actual writer of the anonymous letters. He handed all the anonymous letters he had to the Public Prosecutor, and on October 28th de la Roncière was arrested.

And while de la Roncière was in prison the anonymous letters still descended on the town where lived the persecuted Marie de Morell! Someone, signing himself (or herself) 'Victorine Moyert' wrote that M de la Roncière did not know his address and had therefore asked him (the said 'Moyert') to forward a letter.

But clearly the one thing de la Roncière would know would be the address of the officers at the Cavalry School at Saumur.

The letter to d'Estouilly was even stranger than the forgetting of an address: it was signed "E. de la Ronsière".

Spelt with an 's' you notice. La Roncière had presumably forgotten how to spell his own name!!

The last of these letters dropped suddenly in a carriage as Marie de Morell was driving with her mother. Marie suddenly said, "They are breaking my arm," and drew her right arm back into the carriage. As she did so a ball of paper fell on her knees. It was an anonymous letter!

" . . . The less malicious say that if you had been a good mother, in place of covering your daughter with contempt, you would have made sacrifices to marry her to her seducer, whom it pleases you to call her assassin. Nobody is duped by that. The malicious all say that your seducer is not the son of a lieutenant-general, but merely your valet. And they are the greater number. If the outrage actually occurred and if Madame de Morell has any heart, before three months have passed she will marry her daughter to put an end to the awful calumnies which are spread about this poor young girl. That's what they say in modern Babylon."

It was the same handwriting as the other letters. And M de la Roncière was in prison!

Now, at any rate, the matter would soon be settled.

The judge examined de la Roncière and informed him he was accused of having attempted to assault Mademoiselle de Morell.

"What!" And he nearly knocked the chair over as he sprang up. "But. . . . But what does that mean?"

"You've admitted it."

"Admitted it?"

"Yes. You have confessed to being the author of the anonymous letters, and the attempted outrage is detailed in hose letters."

"I never wrote a single one of those letters. I have been taken in an infamous trap." And he thereupon explained matters to the judge exactly as he had explained them to M de Chelaincourt.

The trial took place in Paris. It was a sensational case. The papers had already showered imagination and other details to a feverish world. No wonder the court was packed, and society ladies fell on their knees or squatted anywhere rather than be turned out. A thousand years in emotion's sight are but as yesterday.

The counsel for the *partie civile*—the family of de Morell—were Odilon Barrot and Berryer, two of the most distinguished and able men at the French bar. They were capable of justifying infamy and carrying injustice to triumph.

M Chaix d'Est-Ange defended La Roncière.

When the plaintiffs entered the court they suggested a Red Book. With Baron de Morell were Messieurs de Mornay, Madame de Mornay (a daughter of Marshal Soult), M and Madame de Montesquion, the Duke and Duchess de Vincence, M de St Aignan, M de Lameth. Victor Hugo followed the case from beginning to end. There were also the Duchess de Maillè, the Countess de Jobal, the Countess de la Riboissière.

By this time the atmosphere of the court was one of general hostility to La Roncière. He was a wild soldier, who, after living a mistral sort of life, had attempted to violate a pure girl of sixteen years of age. Some of them no doubt believed all the stories that were invented and told about La Roncière and they therefore regarded a man, with a reputation of such Cimmerian pitch, as a miscreant and ergo guilty before he stood in the dock.

The charge was that La Roncière had attempted to violate Marie de Morell and had wounded her. Samuel Gilieron, the valet, and Julie Genier the maid were charged with being his accomplices.

The confession that La Roncière had signed told heavily against him. It prejudiced the case. Why confess to writing anonymous letters if you haven't written them?

And his career, painted according to fancy, was held out as fitting that of a man who would climb into a young girl's bedroom by the light of the moon.

La Roncière was taken through his patchwork past and probably went through it as well as the average officer would have done. He denied now he was the author of the letters and said he would never have pretended he had written them if he had known what they contained.

His brother officers were called as witnesses, and their evidence generally was not in La Roncière's favour. Ambert was confident La Roncière had written the letters—he recognized the writing. M and Madame de Morell repeated what Marie had told them, and the court seemed greatly impressed.

The dramatic nature of Marie de Morell's evidence could not be gainsaid. It might have been arranged by M Lemaître, for medical men gave it as their opinion that, considering the state of her health, her evidence should be heard at midnight, for then she would be at her best.

And in that crowded court, tense with the day's drama, with everybody, at the request of the considerate judge, maintaining a sympathetic silence, entered Marie de Morell, leaning on a lady's arm, and followed with solemn step by her parents. At midnight . . .

One can see every eye in that court turned on her. Her own eyes were of a magnificent blue. She was tall, well made, and wore a straw hat with a white veil. She walked in steadily and calmly and sat in the court as comfortably as she had sat in her own room writing letters.

The value of her evidence was the effect it had on the jury. She answered the president's carefully chosen questions with ease and readiness. She went through the details of that moonlit scene in the bedroom without hesitation and without faltering. Marie de Morell's account of the bedroom scene as she gave it in court is worth reproduction for it allows us to see exactly what the charge against La Roncière was, and what it was worth.

"I was asleep. . . . A voice woke me. Someone broke a window. In turning round I heard a man jump into my room. He was wearing a bonnet de police (an undress military cap). I saw at once it was M de la Roncière. He took off my camisole. He placed a handkerchief round my neck and a cord round my body. He said he had come for vengeance. He struck me on the arms and the legs. He bit me . . . he walked on me. . . . He struck me on the mouth. . . . During this time he said he wanted to be revenged. . . . .

"My cries smothered, my groans were at last heard, Miss Allen knocked at the door and opened it by force. M de la Roncière went away the same way he came. I heard him say as he went, 'That's enough for me'. I then opened my eyes and saw he had gone. I heard someone say 'Hold fast'."

The President very naturally asked her why she hadn't cried out. She said fear prevented her.

When she was asked the question: "Are you certain that the person who entered your room was de la Roncière?" She answered without a moment's pause "I am certain."

She was reminded of the seriousness of the charge.

"It was he," she repeated.

She said the moonlight was so clear she could distinguish colours. And when she was reminded that she had said that her assailant wore a red cap, whereas the undress caps of de la Roncière's regiment were blue, she said she might have been mistaken.

Naturally there was much anxiety amongst M de Morell's family at the storm of anonymous letters. Some came by post, but others seemed to spring out of pianos, chairs, walls . . .

This was a question the President put to Marie de Morell which she did not answer:

"Samuel Gilieron has said that, going into the drawing-room, where he looked to see if there were any anonymous letters, and coming out with the certainty that there were none, he heard you say a little time afterwards that you had just found one. Also, you said you had found it pinned to the wall, and Samuel asserts that it was impossible to put a pin in that wall?"

To that pertinent question Marie de Morell had no answer.

She insisted and re-insisted that Lieutenant de la Roncière was the man who had broken into her room and assaulted her.

And then the President raised his hand for silence; necks were craned and eyes stared as Marie de Morell with buoyant step walked out of the court, smiling at friends, having been spared all cross-examination!

The defence called Miss Elisa Roualt, where de la Roncière lodged, who swore she locked the door and put the key in her pocket (as she did whenever she worked at night) on the evening when the alleged assault took place.

The glazier who mended the broken window of Marie de Morell's room swore that the pane was broken at the bottom and that one couldn't reach the latch from the hole except by thrusting through an arm, and that would have necessitated a bigger hole.

Miss Allen and M de Morell swore the hole was at the top of the pane.

The handwriting experts brought a fresh note.

Two of them declared that all the letters came from the same hand, and that hand was certainly not de la Roncière's, also that the note signed ' Marie de Morell ' had been written by a woman.

The two other experts said that of all the letters attributed by the Baron de Morell and M d'Estouilly to de la Roncière not one was wholly or partly written by him ; that the letter signed ' Marie de Morell ' and addressed to M d'Estouilly, as well as the letter signed ' Victorie Moyert', also addressed to d'Estouilly, had been written by Marie de Morell !

They concluded that all the fourteen letters had been written by the same hand, *and that hand was Marie de Morell's !*

The mob in the court lost all restraint when the defence actually dared, not merely to plead not guilty, but to accuse Marie de Morell of being the writer of the anonymous letters and the inventor of the story of the outrage by moonlight.

The jury were of those who did not feel that this beautiful girl in her teens could have lied so hideously and so calmly. So if she had not invented this story—which to them was an incredible hypothesis—then the roué, de la Roncière, must be guilty. Counsel for the prosecution had merely to dot the i's and cross the t's of the prejudices of the jury.

Odilon Barot talked of La Roncière's record as if

the untruths that had been circulated were truths.
He said La Roncière wished to have vengeance on
the de Morells and on d'Estouilly. And he hung on
to the confession of the prisoner. He said these
letters could only have been written by a vicious
cynic and . . . there was the roué, self-confessed;
here was the sweet innocent . . .

This speech lasted for four hours and a half and
cheers rewarded the eloquent advocate at the end.

M Chaix d'Est-Ange, before making his speech
for the defence, introduced a witness who swore that
the paper on which the anonymous letters had been
written was identical with that used by Marie de
Morell.

M Chaix d'Est-Ange had something to do to cut
through the prejudice of that heavily saturated
court.

He showed that the tales which had been circulated about de la Roncière and used by the prosecution were not true. He was not the scamp he was
alleged to be. He had had a mistress and he had had
debts—so had other officers. And there were anonymous letters received by the Morells in Paris, before
Madame de Morell and her daughter arrived at
Saumur.

M Chaix d'Est-Ange suggested that no reasonable
motive could be assigned to de la Roncière for writing
the letters. If he wanted to make a rich marriage
he behaved like a fool. He didn't make love to
Madame de Morell. And how could he get the letters
into the house? The prosecution say that two of
the servants were his accomplices, but all deny it,
and common sense says they wouldn't have betrayed
their master and mistress for what La Roncière
could give them. Besides, there was not a scrap of
evidence to support this statement.

What about the letter received when La Roncière
was in prison? How did he get that delivered?

Counsel asked the jury to compare the letters with Marie de Morell's writing. There were tricks that La Roncière had, which were not in the anonymous letters. And when General de Morell was asked for specimens of his daughter's handwriting he replied he had not got any! He said that twice. But at last he brought just those specimens he wanted to bring. And as a contrast La Roncière's rooms, as well as his past, were ransacked so that nothing was hid.

M Chaix grappled with the confession. As men under torture confessed when they were not guilty, so La Roncière, who may have been a moral coward, confessed to writing anonymous letters (knowing nothing of their contents) to save himself from things that he dreaded.

And how did La Roncière get into Mademoiselle de Morell's bedroom? It needed a thirty-five feet ladder and three men to manage it. And the moon was at her best!

But suppose La Roncière had managed to get into Marie de Morell's room? A shriek from her and he was lost. And she didn't give that cry.

M Berryer followed. He had the silvery voice and apt gesture. Someone has lied: it is either La Roncière with the abominable record, or that pure virgin, Marie de Morell. . . . That was the kind of stuff the jury wanted.

The President summed up fairly on the whole, but even he was impressed by the terrible alternative: If La Roncière is innocent then this beautiful young girl of virgin purity and Biblical upbringing has invented this story. . . .

And that is apparently how the minds of the jury worked.

They found La Roncière guilty—with extenuating circumstances! What were these extenuating circumstances? The fact that he had practically said his accuser ought to be in his place?

Samuel Gilieron and Julie Genier were found not guilty and discharged.

La Roncière was sentenced to ten years' imprisonment.

But that was not the end of the matter. Even in France people began to realize that there had been a poor case against La Roncière. It stood, for all intents and consideration, on the uncross-examined word of a girl of sixteen, who was in such a condition that she had to be listened to at midnight and let out on a doctor's certificate.

Lord Abinger wrote disagreeing with the verdict: He said that in an English trial de la Roncière's confession would not have been admitted as evidence, and, speaking judiciously, he said he was not persuaded of the defendant's guilt. And those who had been interested in the case began to be moved—and to move.

The Presiding Judge tried to get the sentence revised. Berryer at length admitted that "the verdict, till now a subject of regret, is beginning to become one of remorse".

And Time's irony decreed that when Odilon Barrot was Minister of Justice, de la Roncière, already released from prison, was rehabilitated after a full inquiry, and made a Commandant in the National Guard. He afterwards held high Colonial appointments and received the Legion of Honour.

The case is particularly interesting because it brings us face to face with the young woman's possibilities. The argument, "She is young, therefore she did not do that terrible thing," is silly. The annals of crime show the tremendous possibilities of human nature, and the young girl is probably capable of astounding us the most.

In our view Marie de Morell was a hysterical subject. Her mother attempted to bring her up on old stern repressed lines. Her literature was the Bible. But if a mother imagines a daughter will never hear or read about things not in the Bible up to the age of sixteen she has very little imagination, and her Paradise is the fool's. Miss Allen, the English governess, had been chosen with care. She was the daughter of an English chaplain; but daughters of English chaplains read novels. The romantic note in that age, which was still weltering in Byronesque heroes, must often have been struck by governesses and pupil. A picture, a cavalier, a look from a pair of dark eyes, would have been enough to set tingling the nerves of Marie de Morell. Her complexes were sex.

It is obvious that La Roncière had not written the anonymous letters when Madame de Morell and her daughter were living in Paris and had not yet met de la Roncière.

Madame de Morell was very beautiful, very accomplished and very young-looking. Marie, seeing the attention her mother attracted, had her complexes disturbed. Note how often in the letters she attacks herself. The tone, too, is that of wild romance. A Corsair gesture runs through them all. Marie de Morell was the young girl sighing for the Sheik.

It was unfortunate that de la Roncière crossed her path. If she had heard a hint of his purple past that would be enough to set her lurid desires agalloping.

If one sees Marie de Morell as the author of the anonymous letters all is as clear as sunlight. And there is no doubt of that, in our opinion. There was no letter which she could not have placed or posted. The moment one assumes de la Roncière to have been the author difficulties crop up like verdure after tropical rains. Why did he write them? He had no sex complex, which could be assuaged by the writing of hysterical letters. He was French to the marrow. And if an officer wished to avoid more trouble—as de la Roncière did—the last thing he would have done would have been to attack the family of his commanding officer. Why the letters to d'Estouilly? And how did the letters get in the carriage? How did letters get pinned on walls or hidden in the piano? Marie de Morell could do all that. La Roncière could not possibly have done it. An accomplice might have helped in the house, but one ceases to think of such a thing when de la Roncière is trying to clear himself from the charge of writing these letters, and still they fall on the General's family.

Take the alleged assault. If we assume it was a manifestation of Marie de Morell's hysteria, running its Sheikish gamut, we can understand. She breaks the window—at the wrong end and not enough—she takes off her nightdress and her camisole, ties a cord round body and a handkerchief round her neck. Then she thumps herself with something and bites her thumb.

All is ready. The door that communicates with Miss Allen's room is in some queer way made to be a hindrance, but not a stubborn one. The delicate-minded governess has to be able to open it. So Marie de Morell lies down and groans in the pale moonlight.

The tale of the terrible Corsair is told and the two ladies sleep together. Not a word to mother!

It is fantasy from beginning to end.

Marie de Morell was behaving as usual the next day. It had cost her no more to plan and relate this scene than to write an anonymous letter.

And it was not till five weeks afterwards that she thought of telling her mother that the villain who assaulted her had done terribly indelicate things to her.

It seems to us that de la Roncière's counsel should not have let this young neurasthenic off so easily.

She should have been cross-examined. A girl who doesn't cry out when her nightdress is taken off, when her camisole is dragged off, when a rope is being put round her doesn't want to cry out.

And we are suspicious of M and Madame de Morell. Madame de Morell had said that the letter received by d'Estouilly was written by her daughter. Surely she had suspected her daughter before? She must have recognized the writing of the anonymous letters was her daughter's as the expert did. The silence of General and Madame de Morell is explicable on no other ground but that they suspected, to say the least, that the letters were written by Marie and that she was capable of weaving strange stories.

Marie de Morell's behaviour at the trial was extraordinary. After giving her evidence she smiled as if she were going into the desert with her Sheik. She hadn't the moral courage to confess then, and she must have had a heart of sawdust to know she was deliberately sending an innocent officer to prison for ten years!

The young girl's possibility for crime is not sufficiently realized. In our view Marie de Morell and Madame Lafarge were very similar: it was merely circumstance that dictated their different crimes.

Marie de Morell married, as that type of woman was bound to do.

Lieutenant Ambert rose to be a general and wrote books about religion. M d'Estouilly became a monk. The religious strain in these two officers might have predisposed them to regard the libertine de la Roncière as capable of anything—and therefore guilty.

VI

HELÈNE JAGADO

Scene : *The Assize Court of D'Ille-et-Vilaine*
            Date : December 6th, 1851.

The President (M Boucly, first president of the Court of Appeal at Rennes) : At what age did you go out to service ?

Helène Jagado : I was seven years old when I went to M Riallant, the curé at Bubry, where I lived with my aunts. I was twenty-five when I left there. I was eleven years at Séglien, with M le Curé.

The Judge : Wasn't there a young girl there ? Didn't she find some flax grains in her soup one day and refuse to take any more bread from you ?

Helène Jagado : No, sir. I left because someone else came who wanted my place.

The Judge : Did you not go at once to the presbytery at Guern, and didn't a number of people die there ?

Helène Jagado : The rector's bed caught on fire and caused such an emotion that a lot of people died.

The Judge : The seven persons who died were the father, the mother, a child, a woman who ate at the house, the curé himself, Françoise Duffray and finally your own sister ?

Helène Jagado : It is true ; they all died vomiting. My sister didn't vomit much.

The Judge : Didn't you get your sister's place with the curé of Bubry ?

Helène Jagado : Yes, sir.

The Judge: Was there at that time any epidemic in the commune? Were you not the cook? Didn't you nurse the sick?

Helène Jagado: Yes. I always nursed the sick—that has been my misfortune. That's the cause of my trouble to-day.

The Judge: M Le Drogo, the curé, was a strong and vigorous man, and he died in thirty-two hours?

Helène Jagado: Yes, sir.

The Judge: Didn't his little niece die in an astonishing way? You went out of that empty house and you took your sister's place with the curé of Bubry and three people die?

Helène Jagado: Yes. My aunt, the niece of the rector and a young girl.

The Judge: Didn't your aunt notice something after a cup of tea you gave her?

Helène Jagado: No. My aunt only drank milk.

The Judge: You left the presbytery at Bubry?

Helène Jagado: Yes. Because the bishop didn't want the curés to have servants under forty years of age, and I was too young.

The Judge: Where did you go?

Helène Jagado: To Locminé. I went to learn sewing. I was always ill.

The Judge: In the Leboucher family two people died?

Helène Jagado: Only the mother died—not the daughter.

The Judge: Didn't you say to the daughter, "I fear your mother will die. I carry death with me"?

Helène Jagado: I said I was very sorry to see her mother suffer.

The Judge: When you left the Leboucher family, didn't they find on the top of your bed certain papers—kinds of plasters?

Helène Jagado: They never found anything like that.

Helene Jagado

The Judge: Didn't you stay with a widow a few days? Wasn't she slightly ill and you nursed her, and after you had given her some soup she got terribly worse and died in agony?

Helène Jagado: No. I don't remember that.

The Judge: About May, 1835, you went to the family Toussaint? Didn't some deaths occur there?

Helène Jagado: Yes. Monsieur died, then a demoiselle Eveno. She caught something going to Auray—she was hot and cold.

The Judge: She died in five days, didn't she? And didn't Mademoiselle Julie Toussaint also die in agony?

Helène Jagado: I don't remember.

The Judge: And Madame Toussaint died after you had gone?

Helène Jagado: Yes, sir.

The Judge: Didn't a woman called Helene Rolland receive from Madame Toussaint a cup of chocolate that had been prepared by you, and didn't she refuse to drink it? Three people who did drink were ill, weren't they?

Helène Jagado: No, sir.

The Judge: Weren't you ill at this time when you went to Marie Perel? And didn't they find you had a lot of keys and also that you had packets of powder, one brownish, the other white?

Helène Jagado: Impossible.

The Judge: Nasty rumours were afloat about you at this time: you were actually insulted in the streets of Locminé. Didn't they suggest you had a fatal influence and call you the " white-livered woman "?

Helène Jagado: Never. When I left Locminé I went to the convent at Auray.

The Judge: Why did you leave the convent?

Helène Jagado: I don't know. The Superintendent said I was too old to learn to read and write.

The Judge: As a matter of fact, didn't they find

the linen in the cupboards cut in pieces ? And wasn't that the reason why you were expelled ?

Helène Jagado: The sisters never reproached me with anything.

The Judge: Then you went to Anne Lecorbec, and one day you boasted about your ability to make a soup ?

Helène Jagado: Yes. I said how it ought to be made.

The Judge: And you made some of that soup and served it, and Anne Lecorbec died in agony, showing that bluish colour again ?

Helène Jagado: I had nothing to do with it.

The Judge: Didn't you say about this time, "Death follows me everywhere" ?

Helène Jagado: I don't remember.

The Judge: Then you went to Madame Lefur at Plumeret. She soon fell dangerously ill ?

Helène Jagado: Yes. She vomited a little.

The Judge: And you left her without giving notice ?

Helène Jagado: No.

The Judge: And didn't you make a great show of religion and at the same time have a lot to do with the soldiers ?

Helène Jagado: Nobody can say that of me.

The Judge: Weren't you thrown out from a Madame Etain ? Did her son-in-law throw your things outside and everything you had prepared ?

Helène Jagado: Never.

The Judge: Wasn't the reason of this that some ecclesiastics having dined with Madame Etain, said you were a dangerous woman ? You went to Jouanneau at Pontivy and didn't a child die after vomiting ?

Helène Jagado: He had been beaten at college: he was a naughty boy. When he was dead Madame told me to go.

The Judge: In 1831, in the month of June, you

went to a M Kéraly at Hennebon? Somebody spoke to Mademoiselle Kéraly of your fatal influence, and when you went to join her father in the country he fell ill and returned home to die?

Hélène Jagado: Yes.

The Judge: Didn't the chambermaid die too and weren't you put outside?

Hélène Jagado: Nobody made any complaint.

The Judge: You went to a M Vernon and didn't Madame Vernon die after vomiting?

Hélène Jagado: If her doctor were alive he would say it was her own fault for eating while she was convalescent.

The Judge: You went to a Madame Dupuis. Because one of the children had had small-pox they were going into the country—you didn't like that?

Hélène Jagado: No. It was too far to go for provisions.

The Judge: That child was sent to its grandmother. But the little girl who had some soup and a cake that you had made vomited, didn't she? The next day the child was better. When they arrived in the country it died. Wasn't everybody in the house ill and vomiting?

Hélène Jagado: I don't remember. Nobody spoke to me about it. (Followed some questions concerning thefts.)

The Judge: When you were about to leave a Madame Carrère didn't she take some medicine you had prepared, and wasn't she so ill that she could scarcely satisfy her thirst?

Hélène Jagado: Madame Carrère was no worse that day than any other day.

The Judge: Madame Ozanne's son was ill?

Hélène Jagado: Yes. Madame thought it was worms. The doctor thought he died of croup.

The Judge: Before you went to M Ozanne you were with a M Robot. When you went there a child was convalescent, but was worse again after eating some soup?

Helène Jagado: I don't remember.

The Judge: Up till then the child hadn't vomited. But after taking the soup you had prepared he vomited and died in terrible convulsions. After his death M and Madame Robot went into the country with their mother, Madame Brière. Soon, Madame Robot and Madame Brière were ill: they vomited and continued to vomit as long as you were in the house. Madame Robot stopped the vomiting as soon as she got a nurse to prepare her food. When people asked after her, didn't you say she had the same disease as her child?

Helène Jagado: I never said that.

The Judge: You complained of Madame Brière?

Helène Jagado: I said she used to grumble.

The Judge: On leaving M Ozanne you went to the Bout-au-Monde; there you were found with an umbrella belonging to the servant of Hippolyte Roussel?

Helène Jagado: Yes.

The Judge: Naturally something was said to you about that, and didn't Madame Roussel threaten to send you away?

Helène Jagado: Never. I liked Madame Roussel.

The Judge: Wasn't Madame Roussel accustomed to take a little bowl of soup by herself?

Helène Jagado: Yes.

The Judge: And after she scolded you for stealing the umbrella she vomited after taking her soup?

Helène Jagado: She would have vomited whether she had taken the soup or not.

The Judge: She got worse and could scarcely walk?

Helène Jagado: She could scarcely walk before.

The Judge: Didn't you suspect another servant in the house, Perrotte Macé, of having reported you for dirtiness?

Helène Jagado: I liked her very much. I did what I could to help her. I am too fond of people.

The Judge: Didn't you make overtures of marriage to an ostler named André?

Helène Jagado: He was ill and I gave him some broth. The other servants joked about it and said he was my sweetheart.

The Judge: Didn't you say you would be a good match for him?

Helène Jagado: It was only in fun.

The Judge: Didn't you suspect that André preferred Perrotte?

Helène Jagado: No.

The Judge: Perrotte had been five years in that house. She was trusted. Weren't you jealous of her? Didn't she fall ill after a meal you prepared? She vomited and then when she got a little better you suggested you should make her a soup which you knew so well how to make?

Helène Jagado: She herself made the soup which caused her to vomit.

The Judge: You were very anxious to look after her. She found you gave her things that burnt her. She disliked you intensely. And when the doctor saw nothing serious in her condition you said she was mortally ill?

Helène Jagado: I said that the doctors didn't understand her case.

The Judge: Perrotte died. There was a post-mortem and it was found that she had died of arsenical poisoning. Who could have put arsenic in her food if not you?

Helène Jagado: I never put anything in her food. I am innocent. I don't know any poisons. God will be merciful enough to keep me ignorant of them!

The Judge: You left the hotel with that coffin behind you. You went to M Bidard. Wasn't there a strong healthy girl with him—Rose Tessier? She was trusted by M Bidard and you had to account for your spendings to her. Didn't you say you didn't like her?

Helène Jagado: Yes. I said I was sorry I had come because she didn't like other servants in the house.

The Judge: She was quite well on Sunday. She went out in the morning and was taken ill after a meal that you and she had together. You got her a cup of tea. She vomited and afterwards got a little better. But she died on the 3rd of November. You are the only person who attended to her.

Helène Jagado: I have nothing to reproach myself with.

The Judge: At the autopsy they found in this unfortunate creature more arsenic than was found in Perrotte. After the death of Rose Tessier a Françoise Huriaux came to M Bidard. You got her under your hand: you told the master she stole the bread she ate. And after she had eaten some soup made by you she vomited.

Helène Jagado: I saw her vomit twice.

The Judge: And when she wouldn't touch soup again, you said, "Do you think I want to poison you?"

Helène Jagado: It did make me angry to see the soup wasted.

The Judge: That girl broke out in swellings. She was ill all the time she was at M Bidard's and only got better when she left. Rosalie Sarrazin came. M Bidard then said he wanted to see your accounts, and matters henceforward would go on as in the time of Rose Tessier.

Helène Jagado: I told her to put things down in the book, and she told me I wasn't there to give her orders. M Bidard afterwards said I could find another place.

The Judge: Weren't you ill after this quarrel?

Helène Jagado: Yes. They got M Pitois to attend to me.

The Judge: Didn't you refuse to let Rosalie look after you and then complain that she did nothing for you ?

Helène Jagado: I told M Bidard she never looked after me, and didn't want to see me. I wasn't angry with her.

The Judge: On the 10th of June, after supper, Rosalie began to vomit. She had eaten some peas which you had prepared although against orders. You asked M Bidard why he didn't eat them. Rosalie ate them and was ill. She was getting better when she had some soup prepared by you, and she began to vomit again.

Helène Jagado: I didn't make it.

The Judge: On Sunday the 22nd she was ill again after you gave her a purgative.

Helène Jagado: I told her she took too many medicines and only gave her what was ordered.

The Judge: It was the second glass you gave her that caused the vomiting. When M Bidard gave her one nothing like that happened. And she took some syrup with aerated water. Her mother gave her two glasses and she liked them. You gave her the third and she found it detestable. She said, " That isn't the same thing."

Helène Jagado: I tasted the bottle : it was all right.

The Judge: Didn't you tell M Bidard that you tasted everything she took ?

Helène Jagado: I never said that.

The Judge: In the evening of the 28th of June didn't you fetch a prescription in which there was acetate of morphia ?

Helène Jagado: I don't remember. I went with the doctor.

The Judge: And you sat up with her part of the

night, when you gave her some spoonsful of that prescription? Didn't she vomit every time she took it?

Hélène Jagado: She didn't vomit that night.

The Judge: The next day she was very ill. The doctors, suspecting poison, gave her a big dose of magnesia. On the Sunday night you didn't leave her?

Hélène Jagado: I was there with a nurse.

The Judge: After having received a drink from you she vomited for the last time?

Hélène Jagado: It wasn't much, and they kept it.

The Judge: Yes, and in it and in the prescription and in the viscera of Rosalie Sarrazin they found arsenic?

Hélène Jagado: I never gave anything to Rosalie, nor to the others. What I gave I gave to relieve them.

After the death of Rosalie Sarrazin the doctors were disquieted. Two servants dead in the same house and both poisoned. . . . So Drs Pinault and Baudoin went to the Procureur Général and informed him of the matter.

So Law strode to the house of M Bidard and said, "A servant has died here and poison is suspected."

"I am innocent," said Helen Jagado.

"Innocent of what?" asked the judge. "You haven't been accused of anything."

At first the law looked into the deaths of Françoise Huriaux and Rose Tessier. The doctors who had been called in to see Rose Tessier concluded she had either ruptured the diaphragm or had been poisoned. As they did not wish to think of poisoning, they suggested the cause of death was the rupturing of the diaphragm.

But when Françoise Huriaux, a lusty girl of

nineteen, also died in the same house with similar symptoms, these two doctors threw over their theory of a ruptured diaphragm.

Hélène Jagado was arrested, and then there rose the dread secrets of her life. Along the path she had travelled voices came from the tomb; the living began to talk. And before the trial a terrible catalogue was laid at Hélène Jagado's prison door.

She was an orphan at seven years of age. The training of children is either cruel or stupid even with the best; orphans take the chances of wild beasts.

Hélène Jagado at seven may be thought to have had a chance, since she was taken into a curé's house where her two aunts were servants. One never knows how older people may warp and twist and spoil the young. . . .

After staying seventeen years in the same village she went with one of her aunts to Séglien to another curé. It was here that were first remarked this terrible creature's propensity for evil.

Above all things we are interested in human nature: we desire to know it in its depths and heights, and we should like to understand how these tempestuous creatures come to their villainies. We may get a glimpse of the psychology of Hélène Jagado before the tale is ended.

At Séglien a little shepherdess found some grains of flax in a soup made by Hélène Jagado, and afterwards refused to touch anything Jagado had prepared—not even buttered bread!

Now read the catalogue.

Hélène Jagado at Guern. Seven people died. The doctors suspected and nodded and suggested. . . .

Hélène Jagado at Bubry. Three people died. Presumably the doctors behaved as those at Guern.

Hélène Jagado at Locminé. Two people died. There probably would have been a third only the child hated Jagado, and refused to take anything from her.

Jagado changed her place. Another death. Another place: four deaths.

Helène Jagado in a convent. Put out for wanton destruction.

Took a place. Mistress died.

At Plumeret. A death.

At Auray. A death.

At Pontivy. A child died. There was an autopsy and the doctors suggested the child had died through drinking vinegar.

At Hennebon. A death.

At Lorient. A death and some narrow escapes.

The catalogue between 1833 and 1841 was twenty-three deaths, five sick, several thefts.

The new series began about 1848 so far as the Law was concerned.

At Rennes. A death and some narrow escapes.

Still at Rennes. A child died and the doctors suggested "croup"! There followed the deaths of Perrotte Macé, Rose Tessier and Rosalie Sarrazin.

Helène Jagado was charged with having committed eleven thefts, with having caused three deaths by poisoning, and with having attempted to poison three other people.

The Statute of Limitations wiped from the charge sheet twenty-three poisonings, five attempts and a good many thefts.

Helène Jagado must have been a curious creature as she stood in the dock. She was forty-eight years of age, uneducated, shrewd with the instinct of self-preservation, betraying surely in her face some of those strange and fearful complexes. Her coarse features and hypocritical mannerisms—she had been brought up in the curé's house—gave her a repugnant air, which was perhaps slightly relieved by her Breton accent. She took snuff and was dirty.

M Julien Guimart, the vicar of Séglien, where Hélène passed so many of her moulding years, said there was arsenic in the house. It was apparently used to kill rats and the servants had free access to it. In all probability Helène Jagado took a quantity of this arsenic and had therefore no need to go to chemists to procure it. And this *power* was too much for a creature who readily nursed grievances and easily manufactured wrongs. This is what one witness said of her : " Helène's conversation ran on deaths. She was full of jeremiads, complained of her lot, and would sit for a long time silent and thoughtful. When she went out she said, ' I am going out. I have no happiness.' "

At the convent they didn't consider she had sufficient intelligence to learn to read.

Her thievings were condoned. Perhaps it was a pity. If she had been handed over to justice the arsenic might have been found, and the course of Helène Jagado's life altered. The course of others too. She was not prosecuted because it was desired not to spoil her chances of getting another place. Sometimes a good, sometimes a foolish decision.

Jagado swore she had never had any arsenic and didn't know what arsenic was. Like the hardened criminal she faced her judges well, even if her way was that of the shifty peasant. Now and again the sweat stood out on her face.

In the course of the trial one gathered traits of this terrible woman.

Poor Perrotte Macé said to Jagado, " How dirty you are, you wretched Breton ! "

When M Roussel caught her stealing wine and threatened to tell his brother she " threw at him a look that had something infernal in it."

The crime had to be brought home. As is the custom in French trials all evidence is permissible that tends to show the character of the prisoner, hence there were many witnesses to tell of incidents that had nothing to do with the charges that were before the court.

The evidence of M Bidard, professor at the Faculty of Law at Rennes, was pertinent to the case.

He said Helène came to him with excellent testimonials. And at first she gave proof of a good deal of intelligence. Also he considered her good-hearted for, according to what she said, she worked for two poor creatures and her mother. But Rose Tessier, her companion, soon began to feel the rigours of her nature.

Rose suffered from a pain in the back, as the result of a fall. Although it was not at all serious, Helène insisted on prognosticating terrible consequences. One night she got up and cried out in a sepulchral voice, 'Rose! Rose!' Poor Rose was so frightened she hid under the counterpane. Rose complained to him (Prof. Bidard) about it, and he spoke to the servants. Helène pretended it was one of the manservants and added, "I heard someone knock at my door. I thought it was the end of poor Rose!"

On Sunday the 3rd of November, Rose, after having dinner with Helène, was very sick. Helène looked after her like a mother. She made tea for her and spent the night with her. Rose, although ill, got up the next day. Helène gave her some more tea and Rose was terribly sick, with awful vomiting. She was only better when he had himself given her some tea. M Pinault, who was called in, diagnosed nerves. But there was more vomiting on the 5th, and it was then Helen said, "The doctors don't understand what the matter is. Rose will die."

At that time it seemed a preposterous thing to say, for Rose had no fever and a good pulse.

Tuesday night was calm; but on Wednesday there were intense vomitings with awful pains in the stomach. From this time on to the end Rose was in agony. She burned: she was consumed by a burning fire. She died on Friday evening at five o'clock. During the whole of her illness she had two nurses, the witness (Prof. Bidard) and Helène Jagado.

Rose's mother came. She was broken-hearted. Rose was her support. Helène's sorrow seemed to equal hers. She had tears in her eyes and her expression of regrets was extraordinary. When they had returned from the cemetery the witness noticed a kind of joy in Helène's grief and thought for a moment she was a hypocrite. But for days afterwards Helène kept speaking of "Poor Rose! Oh! How I loved that girl!"

When M Bidard wished to fill Rose's place Helène objected. She said she would do anything not to have another chambermaid. But Françoise Huriaux was engaged. She was weak-willed and weak-minded. Helène dominated her and made her life miserable. Françoise was afraid of Helène and did all Helène wished. But Françoise had swellings and as they got so bad she had to be sent away.

When Rosalie was engaged the witness said to her, "You have got a difficult companion. Don't be mastered by her. I don't want you to be treated like she treated Françoise."

At first Helène and Rosalie were like sisters. But that didn't last. The witness wanted an account from Helène, and Helène was furious with Rosalie, who said she preferred to take orders from her master and not from Helène.

At this time Helène was sick. (One wonders if this were an ordinary illness, or was it provoked?

Did Hélène in her spite attempt to poison herself but refuse to continue? The sickness gave Hélène an opportunity to complain to M Bidard about Rose, who (so said Hélène) had not waited on her at all. Quarrels followed. These were so frequent that witness told Hélène she had better find another place. Hélène retorted, " It's because of that girl I have to go ! "

On the 10th of June Hélène was sent to Saint-Jean. He was given at his dinner in the evening some peas, which he never touched. Hélène served them, and when she saw he hadn't touched them she said, " Why haven't you eaten those peas? They are very good." She took them in the kitchen; Rosalie ate some of them and was ill at once and vomited. Hélène said she wasn't hungry and didn't eat. . . .

When he heard of this the next morning he asked for the peas, but they had disappeared. But Rosalie's vomiting continued, so the witness told her to go and see her doctor. Hélène went with her. Dr Baudoin gave her an emetic and Rosalie was better.

On the 15th Rosalie was quite well. In the meanwhile Hélène had learnt that a new cook had been after her place. Rosalie had been ordered some herb broth and Hélène made it. Rosalie ate it and was at once ill with terrible vomitings. That same day Hélène went to the witness and said, " You are going to send me away on account of that young girl ? " " Very well, " said M Bidard, " promise to get on well with Rosalie and you can stay." And Rosalie got better.

On the 21st M Bidard went into the country, taking Rosalie with him. They came back on the 22nd and the witness, himself, went to the chemist to get some Epsom Salts, which had been ordered by the doctor for Rosalie. The witness divided the salts into three portions and put them into three portions of milk prepared by Helène. The witness gave Rosalie the first. But Helène gave the last. The invalid vomited it. The night was bad. Helène shook her head and said, " She'll die. She'll die."

On the 23rd Dr Baudoin prescribed leeches and a poultice and Helène railed against the doctors again. " You will see, Monsieur, it's to-morrow her day, and they are going to try leeches."

M Bidard, feeling somewhat anxious, sent for his own doctor, M Pinault, who came the next day. M Baudoin ordered syrup and seltzer water and Rosalie drank two glasses. But when she had a third given her by Helène she cried out, " I don't know what Helène has put in that glass, but it's burning like a red-hot iron."

M Bidard at that questioned Helène. He said that only twice in his life had he caught her eye. He caught it then; it was turned on Rosalie and was like that of a wild beast's—a tiger cat's. He actually thought at that moment of tying her up and handing her over to justice. But he hesitated. He couldn't do that from mere suspicion. Either she was a poisoner or a woman of remarkable devotion.

The witness had an anxious night, but was glad the next morning he had done nothing, for Helène came to him with the good news that Rosalie was better. And on the 27th she appeared to be cured.

The witness went into the country. But he heard the next morning that Rosalie had been taken ill again and at once hastened back to Rennes.

On the 28th the vomitings continued. The medicine ordered by M Baudoin didn't seem to do Rosalie any good, so the witness got up and made a strong infusion of garlic, thinking perhaps Rosalie had worms. The vomiting ceased, but returned six hours later.

The witness went to Dr Pinault, whom he met in the street with his confrère, M Guijot. He said to them, " There is no doubt about it ; it is either worms or poison that is causing Rosalie's vomitings." " I thought as much after the death of the other one, " replied M Pinault.

The doctors returned to the house with the witness ; strong doses of magnesia were administered ; the vomiting ceased. But it was too late.

The witness had given orders that all the ejections of the invalid should be kept, but Helen had always seen they were not kept. She was careful to clean all vessels. But M Bidard put the last under lock and key and Helène looked anxious . . .

Rosalie was tended by her mother and a nurse. Helène tried to get these women sent away. She said they only drank. And the witness couldn't keep her from sitting with the mother.

Rosalie was a prey to the most atrocious agony. The last night was awful. The poor girl struggled terribly. She jumped from one side to the other. Sometimes she got straight up, then she would double herself up—it was heart-rending to watch her. And Helène all the time watched her victim. She hadn't, however, the courage to see her die. At five o'clock she went to the market, leaving the mother alone with her daughter. It happened that when the half-dead mother went out to get help that Rosalie died with only the witness present.

When Helène returned and learned Rosalie was dead she wished to clean the vessels, but she was not allowed.

And M Bidard added that apart from this criminal charge he had considered Helène a faithful servant. But she had proved to be nothing of the kind. She had stolen all sorts of things, including a diamond belonging to his daughter.

When M Bidard was subsequently asked what he

thought of Helen's intelligence he said he had never had a servant as intelligent as she.

One of those small incidents that show the terrifying wickedness of Helène Jagado: Françoise Huriaux was drying a dress in her room. Helène went to the room above, bored a hole in the floor and then poured vitriol through it so that it fell on the dress and burnt it!

The result of the autopsies on the three bodies enabled the doctors to state that Rosalie Sarrazin, Perrotte Macé and Rose Tessier had all died from arsenical poisoning.

It is clear that a woman like Helène Jagado could not appear in court without exciting an interest far beyond the usual. The case led some of the witnesses to discuss matters that seemed almost outside the province of the court. One doctor discussed human anomalies and divided our intelligence "into two orders of substances: one ethereal, unponderable, which could not be cut with a knife; the other, the brain, indispensable for any kind of human manifestation." The witness, who proclaimed the possibilities of human behaviour, was asked if hypocrisy could become a sort of mono-mania, as it was suggested that the prisoner was a prodigy of hypocrisy. The witness did not believe in this mono-mania. . . . "What I have gathered," he said, "is a strong proof of intelligence; with a complete absence of morality, which serves as a counterpoise in life. Beings so formed go straight to their goal without bothering with obstacles. It is with the same indifference that they will break a piece of wood, destroy an animal or a human being. They are susceptible neither to remorse nor to repentance, they have only regrets, and especially that they haven't got rid of those people who have found them out!"

For those who would understand all the manifestations of human nature that saying is valuable, for it is true.

The Procureur Général had a plain task. The evidence against Helène Jagado was devastating.

Had we been in court we might have wondered what sort of a defence would be set up. This woman was almost incapable of defence. The years of her life were marked with gravestones. She had slain ruthlessly, agonizingly.

The defence admitted the crimes: they were undeniable.

"It is a phenomenon we have before us—a mystery if you prefer it: one of those impenetrable mysteries which we can see and touch but can't explain. It is a phenomenon as exceptional in the moral order as are idiots in the order of intelligence and monsters in nature. . . .

"If we can establish that these crimes had no real admissible motives, we must see in Helen a mono-maniac. She is an anomaly, morally perturbed —irresponsible."

And so forth.

It was the best line to take. Human nature in the decent is revolted by the actions of an Helène Jagado. The species is besmirched. We want to call her abnormal—a monster even. And yet she could work well; she could deceive people by pursuing a line of conduct that was normal and common. Only in this secret chamber of hers could she pull down the blinds and do her terrible deeds. . . .

The witness who talked of those people who went to their ends regardlessly and ruthlessly had put his finger on the nature of Helène Jagado. But there is another point to be considered, and all people as well as criminologists may fruitfully consider the story of Helène Jagado because of the light it sheds on the wretched creature who has once successfully committed a terrible crime like murder. The motive for it grows less and less. There is, to the average healthy person, an entire absence of motive. Helène Jagado would poison a person who contradicted her in an argument. She would dwell for a moment on the rebuff and at once think of revenge. She must now and again—and perhaps very often now and again—have poisoned from sheer wantonness.

What a figure she is!

She was of humble stock. At an early age she is set to work and probably made a sort of drudge. What wishes and desires she had we don't know. That she was inclined to be vicious we learned from a witness, and that may have been a disturbing element in her life.

In all probability she stole the packet of arsenic when she was with the curé at Seglien and where she had already shown she was developing a disposition towards the villainous. Once possessed of this arsenic she could not resist using it. In all probability it was because she used it with no adequate motive that she was left to carry on her nefarious traffic so long.

Once she had poisoned one or two people she used the arsenic with the ease with which other people would use an axe to chop wood.

She was an object of hate. The people howled at her in the street. Her hypocrisy was only a criminal's cloak. She was annoyed, she was jealous, she was found fault with—she poisoned!

And to her victims she behaved as if she really enjoyed nursing them! She would tend with zeal and sympathy—and continue her poisoning!

Helène Jagado was surely one of the most extraordinary women who leer in the criminal's catalogue.

She was found guilty. Her appeal was rejected.

That she was an unmoral creature is shown by what happened when she was facing death. With her hand on the latch of eternity she said she had been started on her abominable career and aided in her first crimes by a woman, whose name she gave.

And when this was inquired into it was found that this poor woman whom Helène had named was a paralytic, whose life had been exemplary and who had been regarded as a saint!

VII

MADELEINE SMITH

PASSION is unpredictable. No one can tell where it will lead.

Pierre Emile l'Angelier was described as a 'respectable' person in 1854. He was a clerk in the firm of Huggins & Co., merchants, of Glasgow. At that time he was acquainted with a youth, Robert Baird, seventeen years of age, whose family knew some people living in India Street, Glasgow, called Smith.

Madeleine Hamilton Smith was the eldest daughter. Her father was an architect of good social standing in the city, and when Emile l'Angelier saw Madeleine Smith she had just left boarding school and was about nineteen.

We don't know very much about L'Angelier, but we have glimpses of him working hard and pursuing women like a Frenchman. To quote from the speech of the Dean of the Faculty, "He was an unknown adventurer; utterly unknown at that time, so far as we can see. For how he procured his introduction into the employment of Huggins & Co. does not appear; and even the persons, who knew him there, knew nothing of his history or antecedents. . . . We find he is a native of Jersey; and we have discovered that at a very early period of his life, in the year 1843, he was in Scotland; he was known for three years at that time to one of the witnesses as being in Edinburgh, and the impression which he made as a very young man, which he then was, was certainly, to say the least of it, not of a very favourable kind. He goes to the Continent; he is there during the French Revolution, and he returns to this country, and is found in Edinburgh again in the year 1851. And in what condition is he then? In great poverty, in deep dejection, living upon the bounty of a tavern keeper, associating and sleeping in the same bed with the waiter of that establishment. He goes from Edinburgh to Dundee, and we trace his history there; at length we find him in Glasgow in 1853. In considering the character and conduct of the individual, whose history it is impossible to dissociate from this inquiry, we are bound to form as just an estimate as we can of what his qualities were, of what his character was, of what were the principles and motives that were likely to influence his conduct. We find him, according to the confession of all those who observed him then most narrowly, vain, conceited, pretentious, with a great opinion of his own personal attractions and a very silly expectation of admiration from the other sex. That he was to a certain extent successful in attracting such admiration may be a fact; but, at all events, his own prevailing idea seems to have been that he was calculated to be very successful in paying attentions to ladies, and that he was looking to push his fortune by that means. And accordingly once and again we find him engaged in attempts to get married to women of some station at least in society; we have heard of one disappointment which he met with in England, and another we heard a good deal of connected with a lady in the county of Fife; and the manner in which he bore his disappointment on those two occasions is perhaps the best indication and light we have as to the true character of the man. He was depressed and melancholy beyond description; he threatened—whether he intended or not—to commit suicide in consequence of his disappointment. . . ."

The Dean of the Faculty, in making those remarks, was desirous of removing sympathy from Emile L'Angelier. They seem to go a little too far when the man's hard life is pointed out as if in scorn. There is credit in rising from the half-bed of the tavern keeper. Even Robert Bruce had his moments of disappointment, and many a Scotsman could point with pride to a humble cot. " Honour and shame from no condition rise." But the rest of the picture gives us something of the mercurial woman chaser. There is no need for us to slander the dead: Emile L'Angelier was attracted by women. He was attracted by this girl, who had left boarding school and, whether his motives were social advancement or mere sexual urge, he was determined to know Madeleine Smith.

He got to know her.

One is inclined to think of their first meetings. The girl, brought up in a well-to-do, but probably strict, Glasgow home, meets a Frenchman. . . . To her at that moment a good deal of the romance of her silent hours is flowering. . . . He is experienced. He sees the glow in her eyes, the enchantment of her parted lips, and talks with just that ease and fire and desire to captivate, that the Frenchman can summon up for these pursuing occasions. Others too, of course.

The acquaintance ripens. She must have been thrilled by these early meetings. They were all clandestine, for she dared not tell her father. Then she had qualms. Perhaps she feared discovery and thought the best way was to end the business. But it is easier to dive into the stream of love than to get out of it.

Letters passed. Almost all are Madeleine Smith's, for his were no doubt destroyed. They are a revelation of what passion can do. Not to read these letters is not to understand Madeleine Smith.

MY DEAR EMILE,
I do not feel as if I were writing to you for the first time. Though our intercourse has been very short, yet we have become as familiar friends. May we long continue so. And ere long may you be a friend of Papa's is my most earnest desire. We feel it rather dull here after the excitement of a town's life. But then we have much more time to devote to study and improvement. I often wish you were near us, we could take such charming walks. One enjoys walking with a pleasant companion, and where could we find one equal to yourself?

I am trying to break myself of all my *very* bad habits, it is you I have to thank for this, which I do sincerely from my heart. Your flower is fading.

> "I never cast a flower away,
> The gift of one who cared for me
> A little flower, a faded flower.
> But it was done reluctantly."

I wish I understood Botany for your sake, as I might send you some specimens of moss. But alas! I know nothing of that study. We shall be in Town next week. We are going to the Ball on the 20th of this month, so we will be several times in Glasgow before that. Papa and Mama are not going to town next Sunday. So of course you do *not* come to Row. We shall not expect you. Bessie desires me to remember her to you. Write on Wednesday or Thursday. I must now say adieu.
With kind love, believe me,
Yours very sincerely,
MADELEINE.

(Dated 3rd April, 1855).

MY DEAR EMILE,
Many thanks for your kind epistle. We are to be in town to-morrow (Wednesday). Bessie said I was not to let you know. But I must tell you why! Well, some friend was kind enough to tell papa that you were in the habit of walking with us. Papa was very angry with

me for walking with a gentleman unknown to him. I told him he had been introduced and I saw no harm in it. Bessie joins with Papa and blames me for the whole affair. She does not know I am writing you, so don't mention it. We are to call at our old quarters in the Square on Wednesday about quarter past 12 o'c. So if you could be in Mr McCall's lodgings—see us come out of Mrs Ramsay's—come after us—say you are astonished to see us in Town without letting you know—and we shall see how Bessie acts. She says she is not going to write you. We are to be in Town all night. We are to be with Mrs Anderson. Rest assured I shall not mention to anyone that you have written me. I know from experience that the world is not lenient in its observations. But I don't care for the world's remarks so long as my own heart tells me I am doing nothing wrong. Only if the day is fine expect us to-morrow. Not a word of this letter. Adieu till we meet. Believe me, yours most sincerely.

MADELEINE.

MY DEAR EMILE,
I now perform the promise I made in parting to write you soon. We are to be in Glasgow to-morrow (Thursday). But as my time shall not be at my own disposal I cannot fix any time to see you. Chance may throw you in my way.

I think you will agree with me in what I intend proposing, viz. : That for the present the correspondence had better *stop*. I know your good feeling will not take this unkind, it is meant quite the reverse. By continuing to correspond harm may arise. In *dis*continuing it nothing can be said. It would have afforded me great pleasure to have placed your name on. . . .

That letter was not read further in the court.

L'Angelier was not to be cast aside with ease. He replied :

"In the first place I did not deserve to be treated as you have done. How you astonish me by writing such a note without condescending to explain the reasons why your father refuses to consent. He must have reasons, and I am not allowed to clear myself of accusations.

I should have written you before, but I preferred waiting until I got over surprise your last letter caused me, and also to be able to write to you in a calm and collected manner, free from any animosity whatever.

Never, dear Madeleine, could I have believed you were capable of such conduct. I thought and believed you unfit for such a step. I believed you true to your *honour*. I will put questions to you, which answer to yourself. What would you think if even one of your servants had played with anyone's affections as you have done, or what would you say to hear that any lady friends had done what you have—or what am I to think of you now. What is your opinion of your own self after those solemn vows you uttered and wrote to me. Show my letters to anyone, Madeleine, I don't care who, and if any find that I misled you I will free you from all blame. I warned you repeatedly not to be rash in your engagement and vows to me, but you persisted in that false and deceitful flirtation, playing with affections which you knew to be pure and undivided, and knowing at the same time that at a word from your father you would break all your engagement.

You have deceived your father as you have deceived me. You never told him how solemnly you bound yourself to me, or if you had, for the honour of his daughter he could not have asked to break off an engagement as ours. Madeleine, you have truly acted wrong. May this be a lesson to you never to trifle with any again. I wish you every happiness. I shall be truly happy to hear that you are happy with another. You desire and now you are at liberty to recognize or cut me just as you wish—but I give you my word of honour I shall act always as a gentleman towards you. We may meet yet, as my intentions of going to Lima are now at an end. I would have gone for your sake. Yes, I would have sacrificed all to have you with me, and to leave Glasgow and your friends you detested so very much. Think what your father would say if I lent him your letters for a perusal. Do you think he would sanction your breaking your promises. No, Madeleine, I leave your conscience to speak for itself.

I flatter myself he can only accuse me of a want of fortune. But he must remember he too had to begin the world with dark clouds round him.

I cannot put it into my mind that you are yet at the bottom of all this."

A letter to him from her seems to have ignored this estrangement. It may have been wrongly numbered. The next one suggests the complete break.

DEAREST MISS PERRY,
                    Many kind thanks for all your kindness to me. Emile will tell you I have bid him adieu. My papa would not give his consent so I am in duty bound to obey him, comfort dear Emile. It is a heavy blow to us both. I had hoped some day to have been happy with him, but alas it was not intended. We were doomed to be disappointed. You have been a kind friend to him. Oh! Continue so. I hope and trust he may prosper in the step he is about to take. I am glad now that he is leaving this country, for it would have caused me great pain to have to meet him. Think my conduct not unkind. I have a father to please and a kind father too. Farewell, dear Miss Perry, and with much love,
                    Believe me,
                        Yours most sincerely,
                            MIMI.

Most of these letters were undated, but the first was written on the 3rd of April, 1855. It showed the bud of friendship. The one we have just quoted suggests that in the bud was a canker. But the next, bearing the post-mark September 4th, 1855, has a dramatic turn that can scarcely have been expected after the epistle to Miss Perry.

MY DEAREST EMILE,
                    How I long to see you. It looks an age since I bid you adieu. Will you be able to come down the Sunday after next? You will be in Town by 14th. I do not intend to say anything till I have seen you. I shall be

guided by you entirely, and who could be a better guide to me than my intended husband. I hope you have given up all idea of going to Lima. I will never be allowed to go to Lima with you—so I shall fancy you want to get quit of your Mimi. You can get plenty of appointments in Europe—any place in Europe. For my sake do not go. . . . I am quite tired of company. What would I not give for to be with you alone. Oh! Would we not be happy. Ah! Happy as the day was long. Give dear Miss P. my love and a kiss when you write. I love her so. What a friend she would be to us. I feel very nervous to-day. My hand shakes so. I have not felt well since I got your last letter, and I try to appear cheerful before my family, and it is not easy to appear in good spirits when there is a pain at the heart. It will break my heart if you go away. You know not how I love you, Emile. I live for you alone. I adore you. I never could love another as I do you. Oh! dearest Emile, would I might clasp you now to my heart. Adieu for to-day—if I have time I shall write another note—before I post this. If not— I shall have a letter at the Garden for you. So adieu, dearest love, and a fond embrace.
  Believe me your ever devoted and fond
  MIMI.

The next day she wrote again and sent "a kiss", the first she has given him by letter.

After the temporary set-back, when she attempted to break off the understanding or engagement, she has returned with heated heart to the connection. The following letter was written on December 3rd:

My own darling husband,
  I am afraid I may be too late to write you this evening, so as all are out I shall do it now my sweet one. I did not expect the pleasure of seeing you last evening, of being *fondeled* by you, dear, dear Emile. Our cook was ill and went to bed at 10—that was the reason I could see you—but I trust ere long to have a long long interview with you sweet one of my soul, my love, my all, my own best beloved. I hope you slept well last evening and find

yourself better to-day. .... Never fear me. I love you
well, my own sweet darling Emile. Do go to Edr. and
visit the Lanes—also, my sweet love, go to the ball given
to the officers. I think you should consult Dr McFarlan
—that is, go and see him; get him to sound you—tell
you what is wrong with you. Ask him to prescribe for
you—and, if you have any love for your Mimi, follow
his advice and oh! Sweet love, do not try and Dr. yourself—but oh, sweet love, follow the M.D. advice be good
for once and I am sure you will be well. .... This is a
horrid scroll as I have been stopped twice with that bore,
visitors. My own sweet beloved, I can say nothing as to
our marriage as it is not certain when they may go from
home, or when I may go to Edr. it is uncertain. My
beloved, will we require to be married (if it is in Edr.) in
Edr. or will it do here? You know I know nothing of
these things. I fear the banns in Glasgow there are so
many people know me. If I had any other name but
Madeleine it might pass—but it is not a very common one.
But we must manage in some way to be united ere we
leave Town. .... I shall never forget the first visit I
payed with my own beloved husband, my own sweet dear
Emile—you sweet dear darling. If ever I again show
temper (which I hope to God I won't) don't mind it—it
is not with you I am cross. Sweet love, I adore you with
my heart and soul. I must have a letter from you soon.
I am engaged up till Friday night. Sweet pet, will that be
too soon for you to write. .... When may be may we meet
again—soon soon I hope and trust. Sweet darling, you
are kind to me, very kind and loving. I ought never in
any way to vex or annoy you. .... Much much love,
kisses, tender long embraces, kisses, love. I am thy own,
thy ever fond, thy own dear loving wife, thy

MIMI L'ANGELIER.

That's the clarion note of love. These people
were writing and meeting clandestinely. One can
almost see her with eager eyes, waiting for the next
encounter. There is the hint of the physical in the
fondeled, the kisses, the embraces. After all, love
is physical.

Through the winter this secret engagement was carried on, with no diminution in her fervour. It would have been interesting to read his letters, but they were destroyed.

This tell-tale epistle was written about the 7th of May, 1856, at 5 o'clock in the morning:

MY OWN, MY BELOVED HUSBAND,
     I trust to God you got home safe and were not much the worse of being out. Thank you my love for coming so far to see your Mimi. It is truly a pleasure to see you, my Emile. Beloved if we did wrong last night it was in the excitement of our love. Yes beloved I did truly love you with my soul. I was happy, it was a pleasure to be with you. Oh! if we could have remained never more to be parted. But we must hope the time shall come. I must have been very stupid to you last night. But everything goes out of my head when I see you my darling, my love. I often think I must be very very stupid in your eyes. You must be disappointed with me. I wonder you like me in the least. But I trust and pray the day may come when you shall like me better. Beloved, we shall wait till you are quite ready. I shall see and speak to Jack on Sunday. I shall consider about telling Mama. But I don't see any hope from her—I know her mind. You, of course, cannot judge of my parents. You know them not. . . . Darling Emile, did I seem cold to you last night? Darling, I love you. Yes, my own Emile I love you with my heart and soul. Am I not your wife? Yes I am. And you may rest assured after what has passed I cannot be the wife of any other but dear dear Emile. No, now it would be a sin. . . . I dread next winter. Only fancy beloved us both in the same town and unable to write or see each other; it breaks my heart to think of it. Why, beloved, are we so unfortunate? I thank you very much for your dear long letter. You were kind to me love. I am sorry for your cold. You were not well last night; I saw you were not yourself. Beloved pet take care of it. When may we meet (Oh! that blot!) again? A long time—is it not sad? I weep to think of it; to be separated thus; if you were far away it would not be so bad—but

to think you near me. . . . Emile, beloved, I have sometimes thought would you not like to go to Lima after we are married? Would that not do? Any place with you pet. I did not bleed in the least last night—but I had a good deal of pain during the night. Tell me pet, were you angry at me for allowing you to do what you did, was it very bad for me? We should, I suppose, have waited till we were married. I shall always remember last night. Will we not often talk of our evening meetings after we are married. Why do you say in your letter—'If we are *not* married?' I would not regret knowing you. Beloved, have you a doubt but that we shall be married some day. I shall write dear Mary soon. What would she say if she knew we were so intimate—lose all her good opinion of us both—would she not? My kind love to your sisters when you write. Tell me the names of your sisters. They shall be my sisters some day. I shall love if they are like their dear brother, my dear husband. I know you can have little confidence in me. But dear, I shall not flirt. I do not think it is right of me. I should only be pleasant to gentlemen. Free with none my pet in conversation but yourself. . . . Adieu again my dear husband. God bless you and make you well. And may you yet be very very happy with your Mimi as your little wife. Kindest fond love embrace and kisses from thy own true and ever devoted Mimi thy faithful

WIFE.

The following was found in L.'Angelier's lodgings, and the court decided it could not be read as it was not signed, and there was no evidence of it—or a copy—having been sent by post. As it was clearly written by L'Angelier we will quote it as it helps us to see his view-point.

MY DEAREST AND BELOVED WIFE, MIMI,
         I got home quite safe after leaving you, but I think it did my cold no good. I was fearfully excited the whole night. I was truly happy with you my pet; too much so, for I am now too sad. I wish from the bottom of my heart we had not been parted. Though we have

sinned, ask earnestly God's forgiveness and blessings that all the obstacles in our way may be removed from us. I was disappointed, my love, at the little you had to say but I can understand why. You are not stupid, Mimi, and if you disappoint me in information, and I have cause to reproach you of it, you will have no one to blame but yourself. Sometimes I think you take no notice of my wishes and desires but say yes for mere matter of form. Mimi, unless Huggins helps me I cannot see how I shall be able to marry you for years. What misery to have such a future in one's mind. Do speak to your brother, open your heart to him, and try and win his friendship. Tell him if he loves you to take your part. And besides, my dear, if once you can trust how pleasant it would be for you and me to meet. I could come over to Helensburgh when you would be riding or driving or of a Sunday. Mimi dearest, you must take a bold step to be my wife. I entreat you pet, by the love you have for me Mimi, do speak to your mother —tell her it is the last time you ever shall speak of me to her. You are right, Mimi, you cannot be the wife of anyone else than me. I shall ever blame myself for what has taken place. I never never can be happy until you are my own, my dear fond wife. Oh! Mimi, be bold for once, do not fear them—tell them you are my wife before God. Do not let them leave you without being married, for I cannot answer what would happen. My conscience reproaches me of a sin that marriage can only efface. . . . We must not be separated all next winter, for I know Mimi, you will be as giddy as last. You will be going to public balls and that I cannot endure. On my honour, dearest, sooner than see you or hear of you running about as you did last, I would leave Glasgow myself. Though I have truly forgiven you. I do not forget the misery I endured for your sake. . . .

The date of the foregoing was probably June. The date of the next was about June 14th.

MY OWN, MY DARLING HUSBAND,
   To-morrow night by this time I shall be in possession of your dear letter. I shall kiss it and press it to my bosom. Hearing from you is my greatest pleasure:

it is next to seeing you my sweet love. My fond Emile—
Are you well, darling of my soul? . . . I am longing to
see you my sweet pet—to kiss and pet you. Oh! for the
day when I could do so at any time. I fear we shall spoil
each other when we are married, we shall be so loving and
kind. We shall be so happy happy—in our own little
room—no one to annoy us—to disturb us. All to ourselves we shall so enjoy that life. . . .

I'm thy Wife, thy own true
MIMI.

The first P.S. ended: "A kiss dear love from thy devoted and loving, much attached wife, thine own, Mimi."

The second P.S. ended: "I am thine until death do separate us, thy Mimi."

The next bore the postmark of Helensburg, June 27, 1856:

Friday night.

Beloved, dearly beloved husband, sweet Emile. How
I long to call you mine, never more to leave you. What
must occur ere that takes place God only knows. I often
fear some cloud may yet fall on our path and mar our happiness for a long time. I shall never cause you unhappiness
again. No, I was unkind, cruel, unloving—but it shall
never be repeated. No, I am now a wife, a wife in every
sense of the word, and it is my duty to conduct myself as
such. Yes, I shall behave now more to your mind. . . .
Your income would be quite enough for me—don't for
a moment fancy I want you to better your income for me—
no dearest, I am quite content with the sum you named.
When I first loved you I knew you were poor. I felt then
I would be content with your lot however humble it might
be. Yes. Your home in whatever place, or whatever
kind, would suit me. If you only saw me now—I am all
alone in my little bedroom—you would never mention
your home as being humble. I have a small room on the
ground floor, very small—so don't fancy I could not put
up in small rooms, and with humble fare. . . . Oh how
I love that name of Mimi. You shall always call me by

that name—and dearest Emile if ever we should have a daughter I should like you to allow me to call her Mimi for her father's sake. You like that name and I love it. . . .

Helensburg postmark.
July 15, 1856.

My sweet beloved and dearest Emile,
    I shall begin and answer your dear long letter. In the first place, how are you? Better I trust. You know I did feel disappointed at our marriage not taking place in Sp! . . . Emile, dear husband, how can you express such words—that you mar my amusements and that you are a bore to me. Fie, fie, dear Emile. You must not say so again—you must not even think so, it is so very unkind of you. Why I would be very unhappy if you were not near me. . . . Our intimacy has not been *criminal* as I am your wife before God—so it has been no sin—our loving each other. No, darling fond Emile I am your wife. . . .

Date, *July*, 1856.

Beloved and darling husband dear Emile,
    I have just received your letter. A thousand thanks for it. It is kind and I shall love you more for writing me such a letter. Dearest I do love you for telling me all you think of me. Emile I am sorry you are ill. I trust to God you are better. . . . Yes Emile, you ought in those sad moments to consider you have a wife. I am as much your wife as if we had been married a year. You cannot—will not leave—me, your wife. Oh! For pity's sake do not go. I will do all you ask—only remain in this country. I shall keep all my promises. I shall not be thoughtless and indifferent to you. On my soul I love you and adore you with the love of a wife. I will do anything —I will do all you mention in your letter—to please you— only do not leave me or forsake. I entreat of you, my husband, my fondly loved Emile, only stay and be my guide, my husband dear. You are my all—my only dear love. Have confidence in me sweet pet. Trust me. Heaven is my witness I shall never prove untrue to you—I shall—

I am your wife. No other one shall I ever marry. . . .
I adore you with my heart and soul. Emile, I swear to you
I shall do all you wish and ask me. I love you more than
life. I am thine. Thine own Mimi L'Angelier. Emile,
you shall *have all* your letters the first time we meet. It
may cost me a sigh and a pang, but you shall have them
all. . . . Minnoch left this morning—say nothing to
him in passing. It will only give him cause to say you did
not behave in a gentlemanly manner. Do not do it. He
said nothing to me out of place—but I was not a moment
with him by myself. I did not wish to be alone with
him. . . . Love, my pet, my husband, my fond and
ever dearly beloved Emile. Good-night. May God grant
you better health. Be happy. Adieu, sweet one. I am
thy wife, thy own fond pet—

MADELEINE SMITH,
alias MIMI L'ANGELIER.

Date about *August* 14, 1856.

BELOVED AND EVER DEAR EMILE,
All by myself. So I shall write to you dear
husband. Your visit of last night is over. I longed for it.
How fast it passed—it looked but a few minutes ere you
left me. You did, love, look cross at first, but thank Heaven
you looked yourself ere you left—your old smile. Dear
fond Emile I love you more and more. Emile, I know you
will not go away from me. I am your wife. You cannot
leave me for ever. Could you Emile? I spoke in jest of
your going last night. For I do not think you will go very
far away from me Emile, your wife. Would you leave
me to the end of my days in misery? For I can never
be the wife of another, after our intimacy. But, sweet love,
I do not regret that—never did and never shall. Emile,
you were not pleased because I would not let you *love* me
last night. Your last visit you said, " You would not do
it again till we were married. . . ." No one heard you
last night. Next night—it shall be a different window—
that one is much too small.

Probably the next letter in sequence, but the
post-mark was obliterated. This is interesting because

it lets us see what she read and it mentions Mr Minnoch:

MY OWN DEAR EMILE,
         Now must I thank you for your kind dear letter. Accept a fond embrace and dear kisses and assurances that I love you as much as ever and have never regretted what has occurred. I forgive you freely from my heart for that picture; never do the same thing again. . . . I told you what I liked in the August *Blackwood*. I shall read the Sept. one on Monday. I think you should not mind getting a Ring but you shall have the size. I don't know which finger it ought to be I am sure. I have never noticed these things. I did tell you at one time that I did not like William Minnoch, but he was so pleasant that he quite raised himself in my estimation. I wrote to his sisters to see if they would come and visit us next week, also him, but they cannot. . . . You ask me what I have been reading. Well then I shall tell you. The lives of 'Leonardo de Vinci' and 'M. Angelo' and 'Andrea del Sarto'—all first-class painters. I am fond of reading the lives of painters. The life of Andrea del Sarto quite makes me feel melancholy. His life was a life of unhappiness—he was a prey to sorrow—he never knew what it was to be happy. . . ."

From a letter dated about October 8th, 1856:

" . . . I know you will, I feel sure you will quarrel with me this winter. I know it well, sweet love—but only know dearest, that I have no desire ever to be parted from you, so Emile, my own sweet Emile, if we should ever part it will be on your side, not mine. I sometimes fancy you are disappointed with me. I am not what you once thought I was. I am too much of a child to please you. I am too fond of amusement to suit your fancy. I am too indifferent, and I do not mind what the world says, not in the least— I never did. I promise to marry you knowing I would never have my father's consent. I would be obliged to marry you in a clandestine way; I knew you were poor. All these I do not mind. I knew the world would condemn me for it, but I did not mind. I trust you have days of happiness before us—but God knows we have days of misery too. Emile, my own, my ever dear husband, I have suffered much on your account from my family. They have laughed at my love for you—they taunted me regarding you. I was watched all last winter. I was not allowed out by myself for fear I should meet you—but if I can I shall cheat them this winter."

And so these letters go on. Her passion and rapture are not abated. Towards the end of January, 1857, she wrote :

Sunday night, ½ past 11 o'c.

EMILE, MY OWN BELIVED,
 You have just left me. Oh, sweet darling, at this moment my heart and soul burns with love for thee ; my husband, my own sweet one. Emile, what would I not give at this moment to be your fond wife ? We would be happy. Emile, I adore you. I love you with my heart and soul. I do vex and annoy you, but oh ! sweet love, I do fondly truly love you with my soul to be your wife, your own sweet wife. . . ."

And the next letter was this. Suggested date, early February, 1857.

I felt truly astonished to have my last letter returned to me. But it will be the last you shall have an opportunity of returning to me. When you are not pleased with the letters I send you, then our correspondence shall be at an end, and as there is coolness on both sides our engagement had better be broken. This may astonish you, but you have more than once returned me my letters, and my mind was made up that I should not stand the same thing again. And you also annoyed me much on Saturday by your conduct in coming so near me. Altogether I think owing to coolness and indifference (nothing else) that we had better for the future consider ourselves as strangers. I trust to your honour as a gentleman that you will not reveal any thing that may have passed between us. I shall feel obliged by your bringing me my letters and likeness on Thursday evening at 7—be at the Area Gate and C. H. will take the parcel from you. I trust you may yet be happy and get one more worthy of you than I. On Thursday at 7 o'c.

I am, etc.,

M.

You may be astonished at this sudden change—but for some time back you must have noticed a coolness in my notes. My love for you has ceased and that is why I was cool. I did once love you truly, fondly, but for some time back I have lost much of that love. There is no other reason for my conduct, and I think it but fair to let you know this. I might have gone on and become your wife, but I could not have loved you as I ought. My conduct you will condemn, but I did at one time love you with heart and soul. It has cost me much to tell you this—sleepless nights, but it is necessary you should know. If you remain in Glasgow or go away, I hope you may succeed in all your endeavours. I know you will never injure the character of one you so fondly love. No, Emile I know you have honour and are a Gentleman. What has passed you will not mention. I know when I ask you that you will comply. Adieu."

"Astonished at this sudden change! . . ." One would certainly guess that. Not more than a fortnight before she was his "own dear, sweet little pet wife", and now "I am, etc. M."

Astonished! He was more than astonished.

It is worth while trying to understand what has really happened.

Madeleine Smith, the daughter of a well-to-do Glasgow architect, was clearly a romantic creature very much in love with love. The romantic note is struck now and then in her phrases "You know them not." "Ere this. . . ." Her eyes are gazing for romance. But she had much more in her than a thirst for romance.

And this man, L'Angelier, was a woman chaser. It is ours merely to set down what we believe to be true. Mr E. V. Mackay, a Dublin merchant, said he had seen quite enough of L'Angelier to enable him to form an opinion of his character and disposition: "I formed anything but a good opinion of him. I considered him a vain, lying fellow. He was very boastful of his personal appearance and parties admiring him, ladies particularly. ... He said ladies admired him very often. I remember one occasion particularly, when he came in when I was reading the papers in the Rainbow. He told me he had met a lady in Princes Street with another lady, and she had remarked to her companion what pretty little feet he had. I had said he was a rather pretty little person, and he had gone out and concocted the story of the lady's remark. I never believed anything he said afterwards."

Someone else thought him "rather a forward man and full of pretension." And someone else, "well-behaved, well-principled, religious."

Industrious, ambitious, probably agreeable in conversation, vain, religious and somewhat carnal —that may sum him up.

And it was this man L'Angelier, who thrust himself, with true Gallic audacity in love matters, on to Madeleine Smith, when she was in a mood to regard a man as a prince in disguise.

The letters have told us what happened. But the 'how' is interesting. Letters were addressed to a Miss Perry, a friend of L'Angelier. The lovers met—and met at the Smiths' house! Her daring was amazing and is an indication of her character. She actually let this man L'Angelier into the house —probably into her room, certainly into the laundry and the drawing-room—when her parents had no idea that she was having anything at all to do with him. She was helped by one of the servants, "C.H."

—Christina Haggart. But she didn't need help. This is from her letter of the 21st November.

> "If Mama and Papa were from home I would take you in very well at the front door, just the same way as I did in India Street, and I won't let a chance pass . . ."

So we get the story of the letters and visits. The Smiths were not always in Glasgow, but L'Angelier was willing to travel any distance to see his Mimi.

That he should regard the capture of the daughter of a rich Glasgow architect with pride was natural. The opposition of the parents was something to be got over. His small salary was also more than a reproach. He would probably have been glad of a runaway match with the hope of the parents recognizing the inevitable, for he certainly fixed a date for the wedding.

And then this jilting blow came. What had happened?

Madeleine Smith had become engaged to a Mr William Minnoch—the name appears in sundry letters—on January 28th, 1857. Mr Minnoch had been paying his addresses to her for some time. Mr Smith probably favoured the match. Mr Minnoch was a well-to-do merchant, older than Madeleine Smith, but suggesting romance with all domestic comforts, whereas poor Emile L'Angelier promised a hectic business in a cold room.

No man likes to be jilted. L'Angelier was really in love with Miss Smith; he and she had held each other in the abandon of love and now she writes, "My love for you has ceased."

Love doesn't run down quite like a musical-box.

In any case L'Angelier won't take this lying down. What he wrote we don't know because his letters were destroyed, but the appeals on her part came from the heart, even if it was a heart that recked of nothing but self.

Emile,
I have just had your note. Emile for the love you once had for me do nothing till I see you—for God's sake do not bring your once loved Mimi to an open shame. Emile, I have deceived you. I have deceived my mother ... I deceived you by telling you she still knew of our engagement. She did not. ... Emile write to no one, to Papa or any other. Oh! do not till I see you on Wednesday night—be at the Hamiltons at 12, and I shall open my shutter and then you come to the Area Gate, I shall see you. It would break my mother's heart. Oh, Emile be not harsh to me. I am the most guilty, miserable wretch on the face of the earth. Emile, do not drive me to death. When I ceased to love you, believe me, it was not to love another. I am free from all engagement at present. Emile, for God's sake do not send my letters to Papa. It will be an open rupture. I will leave the house. I will die. Emile do nothing till I see you. ...

And so on. He had evidently threatened to show her letters to her Papa. She goes on with that writhing pleading. She grovels. Then she reverts to the "Dearest, Sweet Emile" again. It was "Bring my letters, darling." "Let me have my letters, sweet Emile."

It was early in February she wrote the cold letter to L'Angelier telling him she no longer loved him. On the 28th of January she had accepted Mr William Minnoch as her future husband. Her plan was clear; she meant by pleading, by cajolery, by any means to get her letters from L'Angelier and stop his mouth.

She tried making love again.

But he had heard she was engaged to Mr Minnoch and was jealous. "And is it true?" he asked her, "that you are, directly or indirectly, engaged to Mr Minnoch or to anyone else but me?" He wrote that on March 5th, so she was playing a dangerous game.

On March 12th Madeleine is with Minnoch at Bridge of Allan and they walk together and talk, together and agree to get married on June 18th.

Mr Minnoch, returning to Glasgow, receives this letter from his betrothed from Bridge of Allan:

> My dearest William,
> It is but fair, after your kindness to me that I should write you a note. The day I part from friends I always feel sad, but to part from one I love, as I do you, makes me feel truly sad and dull. . . . My aim through life shall be to please and study you. . . . Accept my warmest, kindest love, and ever believe me to be yours with affection.
>
> MADELEINE.

On the 19th she dined with her father and mother at Mr Minnoch's and went with him to the opera. She got home about 11 o'clock. And she had fixed a meeting with L'Angelier at midnight to whom she was writing about that time as "Dearest and Beloved . . . Sweet one of my heart, my only dear love . . . Ever yours with love and fond kisses . . ."

Some dates are useful.

On January 28th Madeleine Smith became engaged to William Minnoch.

Early in February she decided to break off with L'Angelier.

And also early in February—between the 6th and the 12th—she sent a boy, who acted as page in the family, to buy a bottle of prussic acid.

A firm of druggists had this entry on February 21st.

"Miss Smith, 7 Blythswood Square, 6d. worth of arsenic for garden and country house. M. H. Smith."

L'Angelier was the jealous man. Minnoch was the happy man. Madeleine Smith was the tortured soul, for she wanted to marry Minnoch and had called L'Angelier her husband. No wonder the letters between Madeleine Smith and L'Angelier are scorching.

He had already spoken of the whole matter to a Mr Kennedy, the cashier at Huggins & Co. He told him that he had been asked to return her letters and said he would never allow her to marry another man as long as he lived. "She will be the death of me," he said.

In February he was ill and vomited. He told his landlady he had been taken ill on the road home. She fixed the date of the second illness about February 22nd and the first one about a week before. He got leave from business and went to Edinburgh. When he returned to Glasgow on the 17th of March he was naturally eager to get a letter. There was none.

So on Thursday the 19th he went to Bridge of Allan. And when he had gone the letter came. It was forwarded to him and he was back in Glasgow on Sunday, much to the surprise of his landlady. "The letter brought me home," he said in answer to her question. He had walked fifteen miles then. He was looking well. And, after all, a fifteen mile walk was a fair test of his health. He went out that night at nine o'clock and suggested he might be late.

What had taken him out?

We have not all the evidence, but the missed interview, probably due to the missed letter, is explained by this letter which was posted in Glasgow on the 21st of March and delivered the same afternoon.

"Why my beloved did you not come to me. Oh, beloved are you ill? Come to me, sweet one. I waited and waited for you, but you came not. I shall wait again to-morrow night same hour and arrangement. Do come sweet love, my own dear love of a sweetheart. Come beloved and clasp me to your heart. Come and we shall be happy. A kiss fond love. Adieu with tender embraces ever believe me to be your own

Ever dear fond,
MIMI.

And she has already asked Miss Buchanan to be her bridesmaid when she marries William Minnoch in June.

L'Angelier went to that interview. He never told what happened. Mrs Ann Jenkins's story lets us see the end of Emile L'Angelier.

"He took tea and toast that Sunday night," she said. "I cannot say what he had on when he went out on Sunday nor when he came in next morning. The gas was out in the lobby, and when I went into the bedroom he was half undressed. He said he had been very bad but he did not say what it was; nor did he say he had been vomiting on the way home. After he came back he vomited a great quantity of stuff. The chamber pot was quite full, but he did not vomit much after I emptied it. He purged twice, once before I went for the doctor and once after. I gave him hot water, he vomited much, and got better. That was before the chamber-pot was emptied, which was done after the doctor came and by his orders. Before he came I told L'Angelier I would keep what he had vomited and let the doctor see it . . . Dr Steven assured me that L'Angelier would get over it the same as before. I think on the morning of his death he complained of his throat, but I cannot say. . . . His right hand was clenched when he died."

He was between twenty-eight and thirty years of age. Madeleine Smith was then twenty-one.

L'Angelier's friends were communicated with; they took possession of those letters. The last one beginning, "Why my beloved did you not come to me . . ." was found in his pocket. Messrs. Huggins & Co., L'Angelier's employers, requested Drs Thomson and Steven to make a post-mortem examination of the body. The stomach being tied at both extremities was removed for chemical analysis. Dr Penny, Professor of Chemistry in the Andersonian University, Glasgow, analyzed the stomach and the liquid that had been contained in it. He made a detailed report and came to these conclusions :

> " Having carefully considered the results of this investigation I am clearly of opinion that they are conclusive in showing :
>
> First. That the matters subjected to examination and analysis contained arsenic ; and
>
> Secondly. That the quantity of arsenic found was considerably more than sufficient to destroy life.
>
> All this is true on my soul and conscience.
>
> <div style="text-align:right">(<i>Signed</i>) FREDERICK PENNY,
> Professor of Chemistry.

The body was exhumed and portions were sent to Dr Penny for analysis. His conclusions were :

1. That the body of the deceased Pierre Emile L'Angelier contained arsenic.
2. That the arsenic must have been taken by or administered to him while living.

Dr Robert Christison confirmed the report with an additional analysis.

There were about 82 grains of arsenic in the stomach.

What of Madeleine Smith during this time ?

On Thursday the 26th she bolted. Mr Minnoch called to see her, found she was not in the house; went to search for her in the company of her brother and found her on board a steamer going to Rowaleyn.

They drove back together. Yet he was ignorant of her acquaintanceship with L'Angelier. He knew nothing of these terrible letters. She promised to explain it all later. And she, casually, on a subsequent occasion, alluded to the report that L'Angelier had been poisoned with arsenic and remarked that she had been in the habit of buying arsenic, as she had learned at Clapton School that it was good for the complexion.

That day she was arrested.

We get a vision of her before the arrest in the evidence given at the trial by M Auguste Jauvert de Mean, Chancellor to the French Consul in Glasgow. He knew L'Angelier and the Smiths. He also knew of the understanding between L'Angelier and Madeleine, so, on the evening of L'Angelier's death, he called on Mr Smith and told him of the letters from his daughter that had been in the dead man's possession. He continued, " Having heard some rumours meanwhile, one day I am not sure which, I saw Miss Smith in presence of her mother. I apprised her of the death of L'Angelier. She asked me if it was of my own will that I came to tell her; and I told her it was not so, but that I came at the special request of her father. I asked her if she had seen L'Angelier on Sunday night; she told me she did not see him. I asked her to put me in a position to contradict the statements which were being made as to her relations with L'Angelier. I asked her if she had seen L'Angelier on Sunday night, and she told me she had not. I said to Miss Smith that the best advice that a friend could give to her in the circumstances was to tell the truth about it. . . . Miss Smith then got up from her chair and told me, ' I swear to you, M Mean, that I have not seen L'Angelier, not on that Sunday only, but not for three weeks ', —or ' for six weeks ', I am not sure which."

In these glimpses that we have of Madeleine

Smith after the death of the 'darling, adored, husband' we discern not the suspicion of a tear.

On Tuesday the 30th of June, 1857, began the trial of Madeleine Hamilton Smith for having (1) on two separate occasions in February, 1857, administered arsenic, or other poison, to Pierre Emile L'Angelier, with intent to murder him; and (2) on an occasion in March, 1857, by means of poison, did murder Pierre Emile L'Angelier.

The Judges were Lord Justice-Clerk (Hope) and Lords Ivory and Handyside.

Those who appeared on behalf of the crown were, the Lord Advocate, the Solicitor-General, Mr Donald Mackenzie, Advocate-Depute. Crown Agent, Mr J. C. Brodie, W.S. For the defence there were the Dean of Faculty, Mr George Young and Mr Alexr. Moncrieff, advocates.

It was a "sensational" case. The newspapers had not then captured the big caption habit, but the people were the same. They packed the courthouse and crowded the approaches. There was a tense silence just before the chief figure entered. "She appeared about half past ten o'clock," says a contemporary record, "accompanied by two policemen and a female attendant, and took her seat with the most perfect self-possession. She is probably about twenty years of age, ladylike in appearance, of middle height and fair complexion, and wore a brown silk dress and straw bonnet trimmed with white ribbon. Her features wore an expression indicative of extraordinary nerve; and it was only by those nearest to the dock that any difference could be seen in the manner of the prisoner from that of the surrounding spectators. Throughout the entire proceedings the prisoner manifested the same composure, paying nevertheless the closest attention to every item of the evidence."

Another description said, "In the midst of all

this excitement, passing through the eager crowd from and to prison, seated at the bar with hundreds of eyes fixed steadily upon her, Madeleine Smith is the only unmoved, cool personage to be seen. From the first moment to the last she has preserved that undaunted, defiant attitude of perfect repose, which has struck every spectator with astonishment. She passed from the cab to the Court-room—or, rather, to the cell beneath the dock—with the air of a belle entering a ball-room. She ascends the narrow staircase leading into the dock with a cool jaunty air, an unveiled countenance, the same perpetual smile—or smirk, rather, for it lacks all the elements of a genuine smile—the same healthy glow of colour and the same confident ease. . . . Miss Smith never ceases surveying all that goes on around her, returning every stare with compound interest, glancing every second minute at the down-turned eyes in the side galleries, and even turning right round upon the reporters immediately behind her to see how they get along with the note-taking, which is carrying her name and deeds into every British home. . . . The Dean of Faculty, her leading counsel, bids her good morning, or says a word to her when the proceedings close for the day, and she smiles so cheerily that you listen to hear her laugh. Whoever speaks, counsel or witness, must be sensible of the fixed, penetrating glance of her large black eye . . ."

Emile L'Angelier had died of poison. Had that poison been given to him by Madeleine Smith?

The prosecution found their difficulty in proving that Madeleine Smith and the deceased had met immediately preceding his attacks. The indictment charged the prisoner with having administered arsenic to L'Angelier in February as well as in March. It will be remembered that Mrs Jenkins swore to his illness in February.

In L'Angelier's diary, which was not admitted as evidence and therefore was not a matter for the consideration of the jury, there occur these items for February:

Thurs. 19.—Saw Mimi a few minutes. Was very ill during the night.
Fri. 20.—Passed two pleasant hours with M. in the drawing-room.
Sat. 21.—Don't feel well. Went to T. F. Kennedy's.
Sun. 22.—Saw Mimi in drawing-room. Promised me French Bible. Taken very ill.

Landladies can't remember whether lodgers are out for a couple of hours or more on certain nights, when they are asked weeks and months afterwards. Besides, L'Angelier's visits to Madeleine were kept as secret as possible.

Miss Buchanan swore she had gone to a druggist's shop with Miss Smith on March 6th, when the latter had bought some arsenic.

Mr Murdock, a druggist, swore he had sold arsenic to Miss Smith on February 21st.

Mr Haliburton, assistant to Mr Currie, chemist, said he had sold Miss Smith arsenic on March 6th. She said it was for rats. Christina Haggart said there were no rats at the house in Blythswood Square.

Did that arsenic go to the rats or to Emile L'Angelier?

The witnesses could get no nearer the core than has been suggested.

Madeleine Smith's declaration was as follows:

"My name is Madeleine Smith. I am a native of Glasgow, twenty-one years of age; and I reside with my father, James Smith, architect, at No. 7, Blythswood Square, Glasgow. For about the last two years I have been acquainted with P. Emile L'Angelier, who was in the employment of W. B. Huggins & Co.

in Bothwell Street and who lodged at 11, Franklin
Place. He recently paid his addresses to me, and
I have met with him on a variety of occasions.
I learned about his death on the afternoon of Monday,
the 23rd March current, from Mamma, to whom it
had been mentioned by a lady named Miss Perry,
a friend of M L'Angelier. I had not seen M L'Angelier
for about three weeks before his death, and the last
time I saw him was on a night about half past ten
o'clock. On that occasion he tapped at my bedroom
window, which is on the ground floor, and fronts Main
Street. I talked to him from the window, which is
stanchioned outside, and I did not go out to him,
nor did he come in to me. This occasion, which as
already said, was about three weeks before his death,
was the last time I saw him. He was in the habit
of writing notes to me, and I was in the habit of
replying to him by notes. The last note I wrote to
him was on the Friday before his death, viz. Friday,
the 20th March current. In consequence of that
note I expected him to visit me on Saturday night,
the 21st current, at my bedroom window, in the
same way as formerly mentioned, but he did not
come and sent no notice. There was no tapping
at my windows on said Saturday night, or on the
following night, being Sunday. . . . I remember
giving him some cocoa from my window one night
some time ago, but I cannot specify the time particularly. He took the cup in his hand, and barely
tasted the contents; and I gave him no bread to
it. I was taking some cocoa myself at the time, and
had prepared it myself. . . . As I had attributed
his sickness to want of food, I proposed, as stated
in the note, to give him a loaf of bread, but I said
that merely in a joke and, in point of fact, I never
gave him any bread. I have bought arsenic on
several occasions. . . . I used it as a cosmetic,
and applied it to my face, neck and arms, diluted

with water . . . I never administered or caused to be administered to M L'Angelier arsenic or anything injurious. And this I declare to be truth.

"(Signed) MADELEINE SMITH."

Counsel did their best. It is agreed that both the prosecution and the defence were at their heights. The Dean of Faculty could let himself go with more fervour than the prosecuting Lord Advocate and he made the utmost of his brief.

This is from the Lord Advocate's address:

"There was an appointment for Thursday the 19th. On Wednesday, the 18th, she bought her third packet of arsenic. She went back to Currie's shop on the 18th, told him that the first rats had been killed, that they had found a great many large ones lying in the house; and, as she had got arsenic before, appeared to be a respectable person, and told her story without hesitation, on the 18th March she got her third packet of arsenic. That letter was enclosed by Thuau to L'Angelier on the same day with the rest. He enclosed it in a letter of his own, in which he says that the letter came at half past twelve, and that he 'hastens to put it into the post if there is time.' L'Angelier got that letter after nine o'clock at Stirling on Sunday morning. He started with a man called Ross in perfect health to walk to Glasgow. He arrived at his lodgings at eight o'clock, and his landlady said he was immensely improved in health. He said a letter had brought him back and his landlady never doubted he was going to visit the lady. He is seen sauntering along in the direction of Blythswood Square about twenty minutes past nine. It is too early. He knows the way of the house and that they have prayers on Sunday night. He must beguile the time a little, and so he goes past Blythswood Square, down to the other side, and makes a call on his acquaintance

McAlester, in Terrace Street, but he does not find him at home. The maid-servant recognized him, and says he was there about half past nine. Here my clue fails me; we lose sight of him for the period of two or three hours, and my learned friends on the other side are equally unsuccessful in their endeavours to trace him; but there is no attempt to show that any mortal man saw him anywhere else than the only place he was going to. He went out with the determination of seeing her; and believing that he had an appointment at that place. You cannot doubt that, after coming from the Bridge of Allan, post haste, to see her, walking first from Bridge of Allan to Stirling, then travelling from Stirling to Coatbridge, walking from Coatbridge to Glasgow, and then walking from his lodgings in the direction of Blythswood Square—you cannot believe that he would give up his purpose within a hundred yards of the house. The thing is incredible, impossible. . . . When and how do we see him next? He is found at his own door, without strength to open the latch, at two o'clock in the morning, doubled up with agony, speechless with exhaustion and pain, parched with thirst, and burning with fever; vomiting commences instantly, and the former symptoms, with great aggravations, go on from two till about eleven o'clock when the man dies of arsenic."

The Dean of Faculty laid emphasis on the fact that L'Angelier's landlady has said he was ill eight or ten days before the 22nd of February. "You have it proved very distinctly, I think—to an absolute certainty almost—that on the 19th February the prisoner was not in possession of arsenic. . . ." He contended there was no evidence that L'Angelier and the prisoner had met on Sunday evening and that there was much more to be said for suicide than for the prisoner's guilt.

(It may as well be mentioned that L'Angelier was not known to have purchased arsenic.)

The Dean of Faculty read one of Madeleine Smith's passionately pleading letters, while she was engaged to Minnoch and was afraid L'Angelier would go to her father, and then he said, " Is that the state of mind of a murderess, or can anyone affect that frame of mind ? Will you for one minute listen to the suggestion that the letter covers a piece of deceit ? No : the finest actress that ever lived could not have written that letter unless she had felt it. And is that the condition in which a woman goes about to compass the death of him whom she has loved ? . . . A motive to commit a crime must be something a great deal more than the mere fact that the result of that crime might be advantageous to the person committing it. You must see the motive in action and you must see it influencing the conduct before you can deal with it as a motive."

But we know very well that the " mere fact that the result of a crime might be advantageous to the person committing it " has been ample motive for many crimes. And in many instances even the bare advantage has been kept naked.

The Dean of Faculty continued : " On the 28th of January Mr Minnoch proposes, and, if I understand the theory of my learned friend's case aright, from that day the whole character of this girl's mind and feelings was changed, and she set herself to prepare for the perpetration of what my learned friend has called one of the most foul, cool, deliberate murders that ever was committed. Gentlemen, I will not say that such a thing is absolutely impossible, but I shall venture to say it is well nigh incredible. He will be a bold man who will seek to set limits to the depths of human depravity ; but this at least all past experience teaches us, that perfection, even in depravity, is not rapidly attained, and that it is not by such short and easy stages as the prosecutor has been able to trace in the career of Madeleine Smith, that a gentle loving girl passed at once into the savage grandeur of a Medea or the appalling wickedness of a Borgia. No, gentlemen, such a thing is not possible. There is and must be a certain progress in guilt, and it is quite out of all human experience, judging from the tone of the letters which I have last read to you, that there should be a sudden transition from affection to the savage desire of removing by any means the obstruction to her wishes and purposes, that the persecutor imputes to the prisoner."

That may have had its effect on the jury. They had to decide whether a bonny Scotch lassie, belonging to one of the most respectable of families in Glasgow had or had not poisoned a licentious Frenchman. Did she say as she handed him a cup of cocoa, "Drink this", as she had done before? And was there arsenic in it? Or did they not meet?

The jury found, by a majority, she was not guilty of the first charge in the indictment—that was administering arsenic to L'Angelier in February. And their verdict on the murder charge was "*Not proven*".

Enthusiastic cheering echoed the verdict.

A line of comment on the case from the *Examiner* may be quoted: " . . . But strange and unnatural to say, to Madeleine Smith alone his horrible death seems to have been no shock, no grief, and she demeaned herself on her trial as if L'Angelier had never had a place in her affections. If it had been a trial for poisoning a dog the indifference could not have been greater. . . . After what had passed between her and the deceased L'Angelier, her composure, in our view, wears the aspect of heartless callousness."

She wrote to a friend, " I did not feel in the least put about when the jury were out considering whether they should send me home or keep me. I think I must have had several hundred letters, all from Gentlemen, some offering me consolation, and some their hearts and homes. . . ."

She was subsequently married, but not to Mr Minnoch.

Madeleine Smith was lucky.

VIII

MARIE MICHEL

Phase One

MADAME Mottet was an austere lady—eighty years of age when we have to notice her —who had disapproved of the conduct of her brother. She would not tolerate his irregular *liaison* and determined that no money of hers should go to him when she died.

One Louis Cauvin, the son of a watchmaker of Marseilles, had crept into her heart when he was a child, and so when Madame Mottet decided to disinherit her blood relation she also decided to make Louis Cauvin her heir.

She lived in a villa at La Blancarde, one of the suburbs of Marseilles, with Marie Michel, a little maid aged fifteen, one of those pitiful drudges whose minds are not sufficiently disclosed to a world that seems incurious about them.

Cauvin lived in a villa not far from Madame Mottet, and he made a point of calling on her every day.

Those who know the mentality of the small bourgeoisie in France will understand how the good fortune of Louis Cauvin would be a theme for the gossiping tongues in the neighbourhood. Money occupies an almost sacred place amongst the French peasantry and middle-class.

The gossiping tongues were probably loosed afresh or with added vigour concerning Louis Cauvin, when it was known that a reconciliation had been affected between Madame Mottet and her brother in Marseilles, who had now espoused the lady he had been living with.

Madame Mottet's sense of morality being appeased, the obvious question arose: what would she do with her money? We can imagine the neighbours asking what Louis Cauvin thought about it all. . . . Would Madame Mottet alter her will? Rumour said Madame Mottet had so decided, which clearly could not be to Louis Cauvin's advantage, since it meant the reinstating of the reconciled brother as an inheritor.

But the gossips had much more in which to dip their tongues.

Madame Mottet did not alter her will. At eighty one ought perhaps to hurry, but eighty won't be hurried. It is eighteen with so much time that hurries. Madame Mottet accepted an invitation to stay with her brother in Toulon after Christmas.

But in December, 1891, she was found dead.

It was Cauvin who informed the police.

He said he had been wakened the preceding night—nearly about one o'clock in the morning—by Marie Michel, Madame Mottet's servant, who told him she had heard her mistress groaning and crying, "I'm choking . . . I'm being choked," and that she was so afraid she had run straight out of the house to call him.

Cauvin was apparently a fearsome soul, for he armed himself with a stick, a revolver, and a candle, went with the maid, and found Madame Mottet lying in bed, the clothes thrown back and one arm slightly raised in the air. He touched this arm, and, finding it cold, concluded the old lady was dead. So, after locking the door of the house, he returned home, leaving Madame Mottet in her dead loneliness.

About five o'clock in the morning (four hours

after the other visit) he went again to the Villa Mottet, this time accompanied by his wife, his mother-in-law, his servant and Marie Michel. Marie Michel was sent to a gardener named Coulomb, who lived near, to get him to prepare the corpse.

Apparently Cauvin, his wife and mother-in-law viewed the body and talked over what should be done. The doctor was called. When he arrived Cauvin told him that Madame Mottet had died from suffocation; but the man of medicine, after noticing scratches on the dead woman's face, suggested she had been murdered. Cauvin suggested that was unlikely, as there had been no robbery; and that perhaps the scratches had been made by the old lady herself struggling against a natural suffocation.

The doctor disagreed. He examined Madame Mottet's fingers to show there were no traces of blood there—as there should have been if she had scratched herself—and the body had not then been washed. No, no, he couldn't agree that Madame Mottet had died of suffocation, and he refused to give a death certificate.

The police were notified of this by Cauvin. A proper autopsy was made, and it was the view of the doctor that Madame Mottet had been strangled.

Who was the murderer?

The police looked for the beneficiary and found—Cauvin.

The gossips of the neighbourhood accused Cauvin at once. Had he not considered himself Madame Mottet's heir, and was he not furious that a reconciliation had been effected between Madame and her brother? . . . Who else could be the murderer?

Neighbours get to know things. It was common knowledge that Madame Mottet had given Cauvin money when he married and had even read her will to his wife.

Cauvin's father-in-law had had losses, and Cauvin

and his wife were not so well off as they had anticipated. Madame Mottet had lent them two thousand five hundred francs, and Cauvin's wife plied her needle to earn extra money.

Cauvin had not repaid the loan, so no wonder the neighbours said he had a great interest in the death of his benefactress.

The police arrested Cauvin and Marie Michel.

Marie Michel at first corroborated Cauvin's story, but when the usual inquiries, questionings, re-questionings, cross-questionings had taken place the little drudge said she had a story to tell: She would confess!

This was her confession. On the evening of December 16th, Cauvin came to the villa and took her—Marie Michel—out in the garden. She said she thought he was going to make love to her, but soon discovered her error. Cauvin told her it was time Madame Mottet died. She must help him, and he would give her three thousand francs and guarantee to keep her as a servant as long as she lived.

She was afraid, but she accepted. Cauvin said Madame Mottet must die that night.

So they waited together in the dark in Marie's bedroom while the clock ticked the doom of the old lady, who slept peacefully in her bed.

Then at midnight they crept out. Cauvin went first with a candle in his hand, Marie Michel just behind. Cauvin opened Madame Mottet's door and in a stride had his hands round the old lady's throat. But in spite of her eighty years Madame Mottet put up a desperate fight. She actually threw Cauvin off the bed. Cauvin told Marie Michel to push back a piece of furniture and then Marie Michel held the struggling woman, who was making great gestures with her arms as she struggled for breath. . . . And when it was all over Cauvin washed his hands,

wiped them on the sheet and went home to the
"Villa Dahomey".

Cauvin protested that this story was a string
of lies.

But Marie Michel persisted it was true. Cauvin
turned on her fiercely.

"You wretch! You lie!" he exclaimed.

Marie Michel replied calmly.

"No. I am speaking the truth."

"Look at the people who hear you and dare to
lie again."

Marie Michel looked as she had looked before—
the epitome of the scullery.

"I am speaking the truth," she repeated.

Although the people in the Court were generally
antagonistic to Cauvin, and atmosphere has far too
great an influence with a French jury, there was
no denying the genuine anger and indignation in
Cauvin's tone and attitude. He was either innocent
or a wonderful actor.

This was Provence, where people are emotional.
And they had already made up their minds that
Cauvin was guilty.

There were one or two disturbing features. One
of Cauvin's shirts bore traces of blood. But he said
he did not wear that shirt that night.

Some bed linen, which also bore blood-stains, had
disappeared before the gardener, Coulomb, got into
the death chamber, and the only people who had
preceded him, so the prosecution said, were the
members of the Cauvin family. Why had it disappeared? . . .

This is a snatch of the dialogue between the
President of the Court and Louis Cauvin.

The President: Didn't you say to Marie
Michel—"When she dies, I shall get her money"?

Cauvin: Never. My word is as good as Marie
Michel's.

The President: Your conduct is incomprehensible. As soon as you saw your benefactress was dead you left.

Cauvin: I stayed a few minutes in the room, deeply moved, then I left.

The President: Your duty was to call the neighbours and try to reanimate the poor woman and not to leave her alone for five hours. What did you do when you went home?

Cauvin: I told the family of the deceased, then I prepared messages for her brother. I lay down on a couch, and at five o'clock I returned to the Villa Mottet.

The President: Why did you take 50,000 francs in stocks?

Cauvin: I merely carried out the orders of the deceased, so as to avoid paying succession duty.

Doctor Flavard, one of the witnesses, said, "The murderer left his signature on Madame Mottet's body; the scratches were done by someone with long nails, pointed and hard—like those of Cauvin the day he was arrested."

The President asked: "Could Marie Michel have committed the crime alone?"

"I don't think so," replied the doctor. "To produce the effects I have detailed it needed a large and powerful hand. Marie Michel has a short hand and is not strong enough."

The suggestion that Madame Mottet might have scratched herself was met by the amputation of her hand and its preservation in spirit—one of the ghastly exhibits of the trial.

The case excited extraordinary interest and was remarkable for most uncommon scenes. The court was cleared on one occasion on account of the tumult, and all the women driven out; but the President had not bargained with the jury. They had to go home and they probably felt a finer appreciation of the affair than the judge. They calmly struck! They refused to carry on unless their wives were admitted and they won!

The story as outlined neither gains nor loses much by the addition of more details. One sees at once the case against Cauvin, and so there is perhaps not much surprise at the verdict.

Louis Cauvin was found guilty, with extenuating circumstances (these " extenuating circumstances " !) and Marie Michel innocent. Cauvin was condemned to penal servitude for life. He appealed, lost and began to serve his sentence.

When one imagines that the feeling of the neighbourhood would naturally be against Cauvin, that he would be regarded with suspicion by the countryside, which would harbour the usual envy of one who was to benefit by an old lady's whim and will, it is not really surprising considering the evidence, that the verdict was one of guilty.

But the case was not done with. Four years later Marie Michel confessed she had falsely accused Cauvin, that he was innocent and that she was the murderess!

Phase Two

Louis Cauvin, the convict, had been in the hospital at Avignon, or he might have been in New Caledonia. He was brought from prison to stand once more in the court beside Marie Michel.

The history of this drab creature was essentially drab. She was a foundling, early sent out to work for various peasants and farmers in the neighbourhood. She was seduced when she was twelve years of age by a shepherd, but was not, so far as one gathers, a mere wanton. She was regarded almost as a model servant by the Sisters of the Hospital, in spite of her moral lapse, and so they recommended her with confidence as a trustworthy maid for the somewhat *difficile* lady, Madame Mottet.

After Cauvin was condemned Marie Michel, after a short period of service with a private family, returned to the Sisters of the Hospital at Toulon, and on the 2nd of March, 1896, she stole out, went to the *Procureur de la Republique* at Marseilles and made her confession.

It was this confession which had to be inquired into, and at this trial Louis Cauvin appeared as a witness dressed in his own clothes.

Marie Michel was clothed in blue, with a black straw hat. Tears were her portion. She was a figure of pathos.

The President: You are an illegitimate child?

Marie Michel: Yes.

The President: You have never known either your father or mother?

Marie Michel: No.

The President: You were satisfied with your mistress? (He referred to Madame Mottet.)

Marie Michel: Yes, sir.

The President: And yet you say you killed her —alone?

Marie Michel: Yes, sir.

The President: How do you explain that?

Marie wept intermittently.

"Were you assisted by anyone?" asked the President when Marie had sobbed a little.

Marie Michel: No, sir.

The President: Did you assist anybody?

Marie Michel: No, sir. (More sobbing.)

Marie was then reminded of what she had said at Cauvin's trial and at his appeal. She had sworn he was guilty at the appeal, and this evidence she had given after she herself had been declared innocent.

The President: Now when you accused Cauvin of having strangled his victim, did you speak the truth?

Marie Michel: Oh! No, Monsieur. (After sobs) It was because I saw that the *juge d'instruction* believed what I said that I persisted in accusing Cauvin.

That is interesting. Did it flatter her to be believed? To feel that her words had power—she, a little drudge? Did she suddenly realize she was riding a little whirlwind of her own blowing? M Cauvin, who lived in the Villa Dahomey, who was the heir to her late mistress, was disbelieved and she—the scullion—was believed. She was actually wielding power. . . .

She added afterwards, " I accused Cauvin like an idiot: I lied."

The President: All the objurgations of the president of the assizes at Montpellier were to get the truth out of you; and all the time you persisted in accusing Cauvin. Why?

Marie Michel: Because then, I hadn't the courage to confess myself guilty alone.

The President: In 1893 after the trial you were placed with a Dr Gospitalier, at Toulon, by M Simond, Madame Mottet's brother. After a scene there you left him, and in your room after you had gone there was found an open book, which the doctor had given you—a volume of poetry, by Piron. On one of the pages you had written: " My life is lost for ever. You will never see me again; I am going to expiate my fault." You were caught and taken back; but you wouldn't explain that. Two years more elapsed before you decided to speak?

Marie Michel: Yes, sir.

The President: Now while you were being tried with Cauvin one could understand you accusing him; but at the second trial, you couldn't be retaken.

Marie Michel: I didn't know that.

The President: Why accuse Cauvin?

Marie Michel: It was to hide the crime for which my conscience reproached me.

The President: And your conscience didn't reproach you with accusing an innocent man?

Sobs were her only answer.

The President: Cauvin was very kind to you?

Marie Michel: Madame Cauvin was.

The President: You had nothing to complain of about him?

Marie Michel: Nothing at all.

She told how she had gone to confess her crime to the procureur of the Republic.

The President: It was while you were in Toulon that you were touched by the sermon of a preacher? And then you decided to denounce yourself?

Marie Michel: Yes, sir.

The President: Are you quite sure you heard this sermon?

Marie Michel: Oh, yes.

The President: What was the subject?

Marie Michel: I don't remember.

The President: Did you go to confession?

Marie Michel: Yes.

The President: Without wishing to betray the secret of the confessional perhaps I can ask you if the priest suggested you should speak?

Marie Michel: Oh! No. I said to him, " My father, I accuse myself of having got an innocent man condemned and of having myself murdered my mistress in her room."

The President: What advice did your father confessor give you?

Marie Michel: To go to the archpriest of Toulon and ask his advice. He told me to confess my crime to the procureur of the Republic.

The President: And did anyone dictate the letter you wrote him?

Marie Michel: No, sir.

The President: And that to Madame Cauvin—did you compose that by yourself?

Marie Michel: By myself.

This was the letter to the procureur de la Republique:

> "It is with great repentance that I give myself into the hands of justice to render honour to Cauvin and all his family. He is innocent of this crime: I alone am guilty. It was after resentment for reproaches from my mistress and in anger that I decided to get rid of her."

To Madame Cauvin she wrote:

> "I am giving myself into the hands of justice to repair your honour and render your husband his liberty, because, as you know, he is innocent. The good God will, I hope, allow these things to be settled. . . ."

After the reading of these letters Marie Michel was invited to tell the jury how she committed the crime.

"On the 16th of December I had broken a dish and Madame Mottet grumbled at me. 'Little rascal!' she said. 'You are always breaking something.' 'Give me the money,' I replied, 'and I'll replace it.' 'What!' she said. 'Instead of asking pardon you assume the hoity-toity!' I replied, that rather than ask pardon I'd go and drown myself. In the evening she told me to be careful and not break anything else, or she would stop it out of my wages. I replied, 'You are rich enough. When you die they won't put your money in your box.'

"After this I had a long quarrel with Madame Mottet, and if I had had some poison at that moment I should have put it in her soup. I determined to be revenged when my mistress went to bed. About eight o'clock Madame Mottet went to her room.

Instead of closing her door, as I usually did, I left it ajar. I sat down and waited."

"How were you dressed?" asked the judge.

"In my night-dress: I had my petticoat over it."

"In December, sitting there you waited?"

"Yes, sir."

"Now tell us how you killed her."

"I opened the door and flung myself on her. I put both my knees on her chest and my two thumbs in her mouth. I waited for death to come . . ."

"Did she recognize you?"

"Oh! Yes."

"We shall see if it was possible in the darkness of the room for her to recognize you. What did she say?"

"'You little ungrateful creature! After all I've done for you, you want to take my life'."

"Put your two thumbs in your mouth," said the President, "and repeat those words."

She couldn't. Her sobbing was heart-rending.

Again the president tried to persuade her. But she made no response.

"Go on," he said. "Show the jury how you did it. If you don't they may think you are not speaking the truth."

No. Marie Michel couldn't do it. She shook like a tree in the mistral.

"I order you," said the judge.

"It's terrible!" she said, sobbing. "I can't . . . Mercy! . . ."

And the court had mercy.

"Very well," said the judge. "Tell the jury what you did after having killed your mistress."

She then explained how, after the murder, she had gone to call Cauvin and had told him she had heard her mistress say she was choking. Subsequently, she told the judge that when Madame

Mottet reproached her, her thumbs were not in the old lady's mouth.

The judge said she had volunteered that because she realized Madame Mottet couldn't speak with thumbs in her mouth.

"You remember there were blood spots?" he asked.

"I didn't notice any."

"There were some. The sheet and Madame Mottet's cap were stained and these things disappeared. Who took them?"

"I didn't."

"The linen was washed and it was to someone's interest to have it washed, and yet you say you know nothing about it. That is peculiar. You also say you scratched Madame Mottet, but the doctors say that the condition of your nails wouldn't have let you make the scratches that were on the dead lady."

"The doctors are wrong."

"You persist in declaring you are alone guilty and the sole motive was the one you have given?"

"Absolutely alone: I had no accomplice."

"You had no lover?"

"Oh! No, Monsieur."

"You did say, at one time, that Cauvin behaved towards you as if he wished to court you?"

"The secretary of the commissaire made me say that. But it isn't true."

"Then it is remorse alone that has brought you here?"

"Yes, sir."

On the following day the weeping girl opened the proceedings dramatically. Cauvin was again in court and she turned to him and with a tearful voice said, "I ask your pardon, Monsieur Cauvin, for having accused you unjustly. I repent of my fault. I am not worthy of your pity after all the trouble I have caused your family. Ah! *Messieurs les juges*, I beg you. Cast a look of pity on this unhappy man and, in the name of Jesus Christ, declare him innocent, for I, alone, am guilty."

And sobs shook her again.

Cauvin went into the witness box and detailed his doings on the day of the crime. His evidence was essential if Marie Michel's confession were to be believed; and the presiding judge had to take the critic's view of Cauvin's story as of the girl's, so that the facts might be arrived at.

Cauvin was not treated as a man who had been wrongly condemned; but as one condemned, so that any and every story seeking to exculpate him had to be most carefully examined.

The judge asked him why he took a revolver and a stick with him when Marie Michel called him. Cauvin replied that he imagined that he might have desperate men to face.

This was the judge's comment: "What! You hadn't the heart to remain there and wait for a sigh that might have escaped her lips. This attitude is inconceivable. It brings out the strangeness of your rôle in this affair . . ."

The fact that Cauvin took a revolver and a stick is all in his favour. Had he been the real murderer he would have known no desperate men had done the deed and would have merely wished to pretend distress. But, if innocent, he might have been afraid. What had happened to Madame Mottet might happen to him: what more likely he should arm himself with a revolver and a stick? That he didn't remain with the corpse was another thing. He was apparently a timorous man and would not even stay with a dead person alone.

He was also upbraided because he took stock worth 50,000 francs out of the house. But he was the heir. The money was his. He may have been dodging the tax gatherer, but it wasn't evidence that he killed Madame Mottet. Now and again the presiding judge in France gives an appearance of unfairness to an accused man; the partiality may not matter in the particular case if the prisoner is guilty, but is hard on the innocent.

The doctors were recalled and one of the jurymen asked, "Does the doctor consider that a young girl of fifteen years of age could have inflicted such damage as was observed on the corpse?"

"Many country girls at fifteen are pretty strong," replied the doctor, adding that if Madame Mottet slept a vigorous pressure could have broken her wind-pipe—one of the facts revealed by the autopsy.

The president asked: "Do you think Marie Michel could have done it?"

"It is quite likely."

The difficulty the jury had was to believe Marie Michel's story. The previous evidence, which was still available, pointed to Cauvin as the interested party and he was, on his own statement, the first person, after Marie Michel, to see Madame Mottet dead. This case was really the trial of Marie Michel; Cauvin's re-trial came later.

One doctor who was called said he did not think Marie Michel could have broken Madame Mottet's wind-pipe.

This seems a singularly foolish statement. Counsel at once asked him: "Have you any precise information respecting the muscular strength of the accused?"

"No."

"Very well, what do you know about it?"

Exactly. And who can tell the strength of one who is in anger and acts furiously? Besides, what is the resisting power of the windpipe of an old lady of eighty?

This same doctor didn't think Marie Michel's hands big enough: Cauvin's were. To which one says: A girl who leaps on a bed meaning to commit

murder has hands much stronger than they look
when they afterwards hold a handkerchief soaked
with tears of repentance.

Not only the physiological but the psychological
view was noted.

One doctor said Marie Michel was in a state of
'latent hysteria'. She might even believe she was
guilty if innocent; and her story ought not to be
accepted.

One feels this queerly. Suppose she were guilty:
then because she is latently hysterical must she be
disbelieved when she confesses? It seems an odd
position.

Counsel said the conclusions of the doctor were
that Marie Michel was not mad, she was not hysterical,
she was a liar.

That she was a liar was true. But when can you
believe a liar? . . . When she accuses other people?
The court had been ready to believe Marie Michel
when she accused Cauvin.

That all is not quite precisely reported is clear
from the evidence of a Madame Senemand, who was
recalled. She was reported at the previous trial as
having said she had seen Cauvin running towards
his villa.

"I did not say he was running," Madame Senemand declared. "I said he was walking quickly,
but the judge said, 'Oh, walking quickly or running,
it is the same thing', and he wrote that Cauvin
ran."

That leaves an unpleasant taste; it suggests that
evidence can be twisted a little, according to the
prejudices of the judges.

Priests and Sisters came forward as witnesses.

Sister Alexandre said she recognized Marie Michel
was capable of a bad action when she threatened one
of her companions in the kitchen with a knife.

"Apart from that, how did she behave?"

"She was gentle, obedient and submissive, but vindictive towards those who crossed her."

Father Marie Breny, who preached the sermon which was supposed to have led to Marie Michel's confession, gave the gist of it. He had spoken of death and judgment, mortification and vanity, particularly vanity. He also dealt with the mortal sin and with ingratitude. And he had told this story, which may be useful to a novelist. Outside the Cathedral at Lyons there was a poor old man, who never went into the church and looked as if he wished to expiate a crime. One day the priest spoke to him and won his confidence. For a time he missed him, but subsequently found him dying in sumptuous surroundings, when the old man told him this story. He was at one time the steward in a Chateau inhabited by a Count and Countess, and their five children, four girls and one son, and was quite happy. When the Terror arrived he, moved by avarice, denounced the Count and his family, saying they had conspired against the Republic. The Count and Countess and four girls were executed—the boy escaped. The old man showed the pictures of his victims, and the priest recognized himself as the escaped son and the dead Count as his father. He gave the old man absolution and was with him when he died.

Marie Michel had heard that story.

Was it sufficient to make her invent a tale of her own that made her sob for days on end? Or merely to confess a wrong she had done, the memory of which might well make her weep if she repented?

There was more medical evidence, tending always to the view that Marie Michel was incapable of committing the crime alone.

Madame Aymes, Cauvin's mother-in-law, swore he came home as usual to dinner about eight o'clock, that he went to bed early and did not get up again till he was called by Marie Michel. She turned towards Marie Michel and said, " Oh ! By her lies she has brought us desolation and death."

And the girl in the dock shook again with sobs. Madame Aymes also mentioned the sad fact that Madame Cauvin, in spite of the black looks of the neighbours, had refused to leave the neighbourhood, so sure was she of her husband's innocence, and had died broken-hearted.

There was more medical evidence. The professor at the Faculty of Medicine at Paris, Dr Gilles de la Tourette, wrote to say he had never heard of such a thing as 'latent hysteria' and didn't know what it meant. His view was that Marie Michel might have broken Madame Mottet's windpipe.

Other doctors thought Marie Michel couldn't have done the deed alone.

Maître Felix Decori addressed the jury on behalf of the Cauvin family. He pointed out to them that if they said Marie Michel was not to be believed then Cauvin went back to hopeless imprisonment; if the girl's confession were to be accepted, he could see the dawn. " What man, " he asked, " can pierce the mind of Marie Michel ? What has thrust her to this confession ? Madness ? The doctors agree she isn't mad. Hysteria ? But we are told she isn't hysterical—merely 'latently hysterical'. Mysticism ? . . . Money ? . . . But what money will compensate this girl for the future she has destined for herself ? "

At the close of counsel's speech there was applause in the court, in which three of the jury joined. Hence a heated scene.

And Marie Michel moaned constantly, " To the scaffold ! To the scaffold ! Condemn me ! Condemn me. . . ."

The Avocat General boldly declared Cauvin the murderer of Madame Mottet, and Marie Michel a comedienne !

P

Irony of ironies, Marie Michel, who screamed to be condemned, had a defender. The law insisted on it. So the girl's counsel did his best to show that Marie Michel couldn't have murdered Madame Mottet alone, which was tantamount to telling the jury not to accept her confession. But he couldn't get over that confession. Was it remorse that prompted it? If not, what was the motive? Money? That wasn't acceptable. Some deep, real sentiment moved her. He found a typically French way out: Marie Michel had been Cauvin's mistress and she wished to sacrifice herself for him!

And the girl interrupted with the cry that she deserved to die. Death was what she deserved, she cried, as her tears flowed.

Marie Michel was found guilty of perjury at the previous trial and sentenced to five years' seclusion.

That was in March; in the following August Louis Cauvin, still a convict, still judicially guilty of the murder of Madame Mottet, fought once more for liberty and honour.

Phase Three

Cauvin was re-tried and Marie Michel was not allowed to be called as a witness at the second trial because she had been found guilty of perjury.

The case was prepared against Cauvin as on the previous occasions. There was little that was new in the evidence. The *acte d'accusation* was black. Take this: " Cauvin had benefited by the murder. If Madame Mottet was not assassinated by him, then she was killed for him or in his interest." This was written *after Marie Michel's confession*, a confession it is difficult to ignore. Apparently the chief point was the medical evidence: Marie Michel could not have broken the windpipe of an old lady of eighty.

The fact that Cauvin was pecuniarily interested in the death of Madame Mottet weighed against him, and everything was shown in its most accusing light.

Dr Flavard, who had given evidence at the first trial, was recalled. He insisted that the strangulation had been effected by a strong hand with pointed nails, such as Cauvin had at that time. When Marie Michel's nails were examined they were short and round. She said she had cut them when she knew that the murderer must have had pointed ones. " But," said the witness, " that isn't true : when I first saw her nails, they were short and round." In his view Marie Michel was incapable of inflicting the damage that was found on Madame Mottet. He maintained the theory that there had been two assassins. Madame Mottet must have fought, and someone must have held her right arm while the other choked her. As a matter of fact, her right arm was found slightly raised in death.

Virginie Chalvet, the servant of the Cauvins in 1892, swore Marie Michel came to the Villa Dahomey to tell Louis Cauvin of her mistress's death. " She was scarcely dressed, " said the witness, " which made me say, ' But you are mad to come like that ; you'll catch your death of cold '. "

When the Cauvin family went to the Villa Mottet, Virginie went with them. She swore there was nothing strange in the death bedroom.

Some contradiction was noted, and she became very animated and said : " They've tried to make me lie and I wouldn't. They kept me sixty days in secret to make me say that Mr Cauvin didn't dine at home and that he didn't pass the night with his wife. I replied : ' Keep me here my whole life, if you want, you won't get me to say what isn't true '."

No wonder Virginie Chalvet's evidence created a '*movement prolongé*'.

One witness said Marie Michel had told him that as Cauvin strangled his victim he said, " Marie, come and hold her hand ", and that she did it.

But what Marie Michel said before no longer carried its weight: besides, that was what she said at the first trial.

A Madame Garnier swore she had been offered forty pounds to swear Marie Michel had committed the murder with someone other than Cauvin.

One is inclined to wonder why this evidence is not sifted better. The witness did not know the man who offered her the money, but she saw him speaking with a Madame Roqueplane, so he ought to have been discoverable. But neither prosecution nor defence seems to have bothered any further in the matter: the prosecution called Madame Garnier. It may have been an idle offer.

Two neighbours swore they did not hear the Cauvins' bell ring and added they would have heard it if it had rung.

On the other hand Madame Braillard said she heard the Cauvins' bell ring about midnight. Mademoiselle Braillard also heard it.

One man's evidence was negative but humanly interesting. He had seen a couple courting the night of the crime. " Perhaps it was Cauvin and Marie Michel, " suggested friends and neighbours. One can almost see the sage heads nodding. But when the witness saw Cauvin and Marie Michel he saw it was neither the one nor the other.

One fact was mentioned by a doctor: he said Marie Michel had confessed to killing her mistress, on account of reproaches. " I killed her," she said, " without hating her at all: I did it as I should have done any ordinary thing."

That was Marie Michel mentality.

The reader has got all the principal facts. There was undoubtedly suspicion of Cauvin because he was the most interested in the death of Madame Mottet. It was difficult for him to clear himself at the first trial when Marie Michel inculpated him. The evidence of his wife and servant and mother-in-law was ignored. But now the case was different in that Marie Michel had been duly recognized as a perjurer at that first trial. Still the old prejudice remained.

It seems on looking over the evidence as if there was more attack on 'motive' and 'interest' so far as Cauvin was concerned, for, apart from Marie Michel's evidence, there was not a shred of convincing testimony to condemn him. Men can't be condemned as murderers because they benefit by someone's death.

The other evidence that made an effect was that of the doctors. Could Marie Michel have murdered Madame Mottet alone? If not, and she had an accomplice, was it Cauvin?

Candidly this medical evidence is not convincing. A young girl, screwed to murder point, has strength no ordinary person can test. To see her afterwards in the dock is to see her in a different physical and psychical condition. Marie Michel was an unusual creature and it surely does not need herculean strength to choke a sleeping old lady of eighty.

Marie Michel was an illegitimate child, inheriting probably tendencies to waywardness. Her upbringing had taken place in a foundling hospital, where discipline was rigid and where the desires and inhibitions of a girl like Marie Michel would not be sympathized with and scarcely understood.

She had to go out and work for other people when she was twelve, at which tender age she fell a prey to some passionate man on the hillside.

Then she became the scullion. Who can tell what her thoughts were whenever she was checked or corrected by her mistress? She had never had, so far as one can gather, a real genuine friend with whom she could romp and share secrets. And she had depths. When her mistress scolded her this little creature of fifteen quietly says to herself, "I'll murder you for that." And does it!

Fifteen can easily be mad. And Marie Michel, lonesome, brooding, reckless, could sit shivering in the cold while the candle gutted, waiting for the moment to find her mistress asleep so that she could kill her. Marie Michel at midnight, letting loose longings and hates in a furious breaking down of repressions, about to murder her mistress who has scolded her, is no timid creature bowing before a judge and jury.

We have found nothing in the case that would persuade us to find Cauvin guilty.

Besides, Marie Michel's confession must be got over. The hysterical girl is dangerous. She can lie with terrible cunning. But Marie Michel was crammed with obvious and genuine remorse. There was no play-acting. She had not the relief of the martyr even, nor the satisfaction of the vain. Her lot was repentance, and the scalding tears were real.

She wasn't mad and she wasn't hysterical; she was like lots of folks—a liar. Only, of course, she had lied hellishly. Her lies had been demonic. But her whole attitude after confession was pain and anguish for what she had done wrong to Cauvin and his family. If he had been her accomplice, could she have behaved like that? Scarcely. If he were guilty and she innocent, could she have behaved like that? It is not likely.

The procureur general Moras pleaded that Marie Michel was innocent and that Cauvin was guilty. This is what he said, turning to Cauvin: "Yes, you went home at eight o'clock; you dined there; you went to bed with your wife: all that is possible;

but at midnight Madame Mottet is ill, the servant fetches you. You go with her. Well it is then, at that moment, between half past twelve and one, you strangled your benefactress."

The procureur general was not inclined to be lenient.

M Decori defended Cauvin. He said the whole case had crumbled since the confession of Marie Michel; that the prosecution had even shifted their ground, for now they accused Cauvin alone of being the guilty party, yet a little while ago they tried to prove that two people were concerned, one of whom held Madame Mottet's arm. He declared that Cauvin had no need to kill Madame Mottet; she had left him everything: he was on excellent terms with her: there was no utility or motive in his becoming an assassin.

The jury took ten minutes to consider their verdict.

Louis Cauvin, after having been condemned for murder, was now held to be innocent and acquitted, amidst the applause of the public.

Marie Michel as a criminal in her teens does not stand alone. Girls at fifteen or sixteen years of age are capable of strange deeds. If they lack balance or commonsense they can do the most foolish—almost terrible things.

IX

CONSTANCE KENT: THE ROAD MYSTERY

FEW crimes have created so great a sensation as the murder committed at Road, near Trowbridge, in June, 1860.

Mr S. S. Kent, a sub-inspector of factories, occupied a house of three stories at Road. Twelve people slept in that house on the night of June 29th, 1860: Mr and Mrs Kent, Mary Anne, 29, Elizabeth, 25, Constance, 16, and William Saville, aged 15, children of Mr Kent's first wife; three other children by the second wife, amongst them Francis Saville, aged 3 years and 10 months, a cook, a nursemaid and a housemaid.

About half past seven in the morning Elizabeth Gough, the nurse, knocked at her mistress's door and asked if either of the children was awake.

Now only one child slept in the room with Mr and Mrs Kent, so Mrs Kent asked what the nurse meant by "either".

"Isn't Master Saville with you?" said the nurse.

"Certainly not."

"He isn't in the nursery," replied Elizabeth Gough.

A little boy nearly four years of age missing. . . .

Mrs Kent got up at once—in fact, the whole household were quickly roused.

Elizabeth Gough said that about five o'clock she saw the cot was empty, but concluded that Mrs Kent must have come into the room and taken the little boy to hers.

The house was searched from floor to ceiling and there was no sign of the missing child.

It was an extraordinary occurrence. The doors were still locked. . . . What could have happened?

Mr Kent set the servants and the gardener to keep up the search and drove to Trowbridge to inform the police.

The news of what had happened spread quickly, and neighbours joined in the search. Two men, one a shoemaker, the other a farmer, examined Mr Kent's grounds, and Benger, the farmer, went almost direct to the privy, near the back of the house.

There was a pool of blood on the ground, and in the privy, wrapped in a blanket, was Francis Saville Kent, the little boy, aged three years and ten months, with his throat cut from ear to ear.

That was the awful crime that stirred the country.

Who could have a motive for killing a bonny little boy scarcely four years of age?

The local police had the matter in hand at first. And not the police only; the public and the press seemed to constitute themselves detectives, magistrates and judges. In the circumstances suspicions flew.

Mr Kent was suspected. So was Elizabeth Gough the nurse. So was Constance Kent, the dead child's half-sister.

It was the accepted notion of the police that the murder had been committed by an inmate of the house. We know who the inmates were. But even then it was not an easy matter to say, " This person had a greater motive than the others for murdering a child."

That the crime had been committed by someone who had slept in the house was concluded from the fact that the place was shut up as usual. The cook saw that the back of the house was secure and the housemaid attended to the doors and windows at the front.

Sarah Cox, the housemaid, had something to report. She said she had fastened everything as usual, but on going down in the morning she found everything as she had left it except the drawing-room. The door of this room and the shutters of one of the windows were open; also, the window was a little way—a few inches—from the top.

Mr Kent went round at night to see all was safely fastened and had found everything in order on the night of the crime.

At the inquest little more than these salient facts was elicited and the coroner, probably to spare the feelings of the family, closed the inquest, at which an open verdict was returned.

But the murder of an innocent child struck the imagination of the people. If there was presumptive evidence that the criminal was somebody who slept in the house, why were not all the inmates called and examined? Why this deference to feelings?

The coroner came in for severe criticism. The storm raised was so great that the Home Secretary was approached; legal proceedings were taken to have the inquest set aside on the writ of *ad melius inquirendum*.

One can gather the state of the public. Everybody was the champion of a little boy of four.

And of course nods and hints and suspicions fell down like manna.

Mr Kent suffered the greatest avalanche. His conduct was rigidly noted and keenly criticized. Almost every minute of his time had to be accounted for. Why had he done this? Why had he done that? What was his explanation of so and so?

The *Morning Post* lashed out. The *Times* reprinted the article as if to endorse it.

"We cannot divest ourselves of the belief", said the *Morning Post*, "that the child suffered death at the hands of someone belonging to the house. We beg to ask what was the antecedent state of the family circle? It has been stated that two of the children once ran away because of some family disagreement. Have there been any recent repetitions of these disagreements? On what terms were the children of the first wife with those of the second? Had there been any previous strife in which the murdered child was involved? Was the father a good father? . . . There are some other questions which ought to be answered. We should like to know why the father went to Trowbridge immediately the child was missed; why he thought that it had been stolen, and how he accounted to himself for the *modus operandi* of the thief; why he did not first search the premises, raise the neighbourhood and call in all conceivable help. . . ."

The *Times* even copied from the *Star* a letter in which the suggestion was made that an appeal should be made to clairvoyants. But clairvoyants, as a rule, appear to restrict themselves to the useless.

However, Inspector Whicher of the Metropolitan Detective Police was sent to investigate, and apparently he sought for someone who might have had a motive for killing a little child.

It is very obvious, looking back, that the motive would be curious, that some psychological kink had pushed the assassin. The mother seemed ruled out. The father was suspected for some strange reason. The *Morning Post's* queries concerning Mr Kent are foolish. At the time Mr Kent drove to the police there was no sign of the child, and that it had been stolen might easily occur to him. The two eldest daughters were not suspected because they occupied the same room. The nurse who slept near the child and Constance Kent, aged sixteen, who slept alone, were suspectable persons. Inspector Whicher fastened on Constance Kent.

It is very likely he started by discovering the atmosphere of the Kent household. He probably learnt of the escapade of Constance and her brother William, who had once, on account of some unpleasantness at home, run away, Constance being dressed as a boy. They were caught at Bath, and the newspaper report of the matter at the time added, " The little girl, we are told, acted like a little hero, acting the part of a boy to the admiration of all who saw her."

Tautologically trying, that sentence has its interest. Constance had resolution. She could act. And when she returned home she thrust the trousers she had been wearing down the privy.

Perhaps Mr Whicher knew these details. At any rate he learnt enough about Constance to make him pursue inquiries.

One remarkable fact had been commented on from the beginning of the case: a night-dress belonging to Constance Kent was missing. It was reported to have been lost in the wash, but the laundress at once notified the fact of the missing article when the list was supplied her. And the police had seen it the morning after the crime when they examined all the linen prepared for the wash. They said this night-dress had on it only the ordinary dirt of the week.

It had disappeared.

One other disappearance had taken place—the weapon with which the deed had been committed. The doctor had suggested a sharp carving-knife, but none of the cutlery in the Kent household showed any traces of blood.

Inspector Whicher pursued his task of convicting Constance Kent with the murder of her little brother. So far as one can gather, the only concrete fact on which the Inspector worked was the loss of the night-shirt. He arrested her and asked for a remand in order that he might gather evidence to suggest a motive for the crime.

What made Inspector Whicher deal so clearly with Constance ? Her bearing perhaps ... The tale of her runaway ... The missing night-shirt ...

Reconstruct the crime. A little child is lifted out of its cot in the dead of night; is carried downstairs, through the drawing-room where the windows were fastened and shuttered into a closet outside and there its throat is cut from ear to ear. The assassin returns, shuts the windows and doors, goes back to bed and nobody hears a sound.

It is an amazing crime, and Inspector Whicher said Constance Kent was the doer of it.

But on the resumed inquiry all the evidence Mr Whicher could produce was that provided by two school companions of Constance who testified that she had spoken of her step-mother in non-affectionate terms.

A missing night-dress and a few words depreciatory of a step-mother are not enough to convict a girl of sixteen of the murder of her little brother.

So Constance Kent was discharged, Mr Kent her father being bound in the sum of £200 to produce her at a future time if called upon.

Contemporary criticism was of this tone :

" ... Whicher, an experienced London detective ... took Constance into custody. ... The grounds on which this accusation was made were so frivolous, and the evidence by which it was attempted to be supported so childish, that the proceeding can only be described as absurd and cruel. The ground of arrest was, that one of the young lady's night-dresses was missing. ... The only other evidence to support the charge was singularly empty and vexatious. Whicher produced two of the poor girl's schoolfellows, who deposed to some silly expressions of jealousy by the young lady, while resident at the boarding-school, respecting the greater attention received by the children of the second family. ...

"Notwithstanding the utter emptiness of the evidence, the magistrates only discharged the accused on her father entering into recognizances of £200, for her appearance, if called upon."

That pretty fairly and adequately represents the attitude of the general public.

People were roused. They meant to have the murderer if possible. After the discharge of Constance Kent the magistrates of the Petty Sessions held a meeting to consider what should be done, and the newspaper of the time says, "We understand that both the police and the magistrates are at a loss what course to pursue in the matter."

Which one might have predicted.

Constance Kent was cheered after the liberation, and the next news of importance was that Elizabeth Gough, the nurse, had been arrested.

All the detecting minds had bent themselves to this affair, and one of the most promising theories was this: Elizabeth Gough had a lover, whom she let into the house at night. The little boy woke up and saw this lover with Elizabeth, who became so frightened he might babble of the matter to her mistress that she agreed with her paramour to kill the little child and so silence him before he could speak. The lover may have done it and gone away. ...

It is quite easy to invent a theory to fit a crime.

There was not a missing night-dress in Elizabeth Gough's case, but there was a piece of flannel which might have served the nurse as a chest protector.

She couldn't be convicted on that, and as there was no other evidence against her of any value whatever she was discharged, being bound to appear again if called upon.

As an example of the zeal and interest of the public the following quotation from the *Trowbridge Advertizer* is interesting.

"That the assassin was not a resident in the house, however, is rendered exceedingly improbable by the fact that further investigation showed beyond doubt that Miss Constance's nightgown must have been stolen, either for the purpose of screening or incriminating that young lady. That it was not accidentally lost is now perfectly clear. Mr Kent himself speaks in a suspicious strain of the two men Benger and Nutt, who found the body. He had, sometime since, a quarrel with them; in the one case on account of the theft of some apples, and in the other for poaching in the river, the fishing belonging to Mr Kent. They are both related to the washer-woman Holley, from whose possession the nightgown is affirmed to have been abstracted; and she again, is nearly related to a servant, named Sparks, who, eighteen months ago, left Mr Kent's service in anger."

One can almost see all the heads in North Wilts nodding as that is noised abroad . . . Benger and Nutt . . . They found the body . . . Hiders are good finders—and so on.

And in spite of amateur detective work; in spite of appeals by the press; in spite of petitions to the Home Secretary; in spite of all the efforts of police, official and unofficial, the Road murder passed into the category of the mysterious.

Until April 25th, 1865. On that day Sir Thomas Henry, the chief magistrate of Bow Street, received information that Miss Constance Kent had arrived in London to surrender herself to justice as the murderer of her little brother.

For five years the Kent family had suffered the slings and arrows of an outrageous fortune. Mr Kent, had been the principal sufferer, but his ill-fortune naturally fell on the others.

Did he suspect his daughter Constance? It is

more than possible. She had the resolution and the temper. Moreover, there was an alleged confession by her twelve months after the crime. The police got wind of it, but there was no more evidence to secure a conviction if Constance pleaded "Not Guilty" than there was when Inspector Whicher failed.

Constance confessed first to the Rev. Mr Wagner of Brighton and added that she wished to confess also to a London magistrate.

She was sent to Trowbridge, where she had previously appeared before the magistrates and was by them committed for trial.

It was at Salisbury on July 20th that the final public act in this tragedy was played.

Mr Justice Willes was the judge and Mr Coleridge, Q.C., defended the prisoner.

"Constance Emilie Kent," said the Clerk of Assize, "you stand charged with having wilfully murdered Francis Saville Kent at Road-hill House on the 30th of June, 1860: how say you, are you guilty or not guilty?"

"Guilty."

Mr Coleridge said, "My lord, as counsel for the defence, acting on the prisoner's behalf, before your lordship passes sentence, I desire to say two things—first, solemnly in the presence of Almighty God, as a person who values her own soul, she wishes me to say that the guilt is hers alone, and that her father and others, who have so long suffered most unjust and cruel suspicion, are wholly and absolutely innocent; and secondly, she was not driven to this act as has been asserted, by unkind treatment at home, as she met with nothing there but tender and forbearing love: and I hope I may add, my lord, not improperly, that it gives me a melancholy pleasure to be the organ of these statements for her, because on my honour, I believe them to be true."

"Constance Emilie Kent," said the Clerk of Assize, "you have confessed yourself guilty of the murder of Francis Saville Kent, have you anything to say why sentence of death should not be passed on you?"

"No."

Mr Justice Willes, having assumed the black cap, said,

"Constance Emilie Kent, you have pleaded guilty to an indictment charging you with the wilful murder of your brother, Francis Saville Kent, on the 30th of June, 1860. It is my duty to receive that plea, which you have deliberately put forward, and it is a satisfaction to me to know that it was not done until after having had the advice of counsel, who would have freed you from this dreadful charge, if you could have been freed thereof. I can entertain no doubt, after having read the evidence in the depositions, and considering this is your third confession of your crime, that your plea is the plea of a really guilty person. The murder was one committed under circumstances of great deliberation and cruelty. You appear to have allowed your feelings of jealousy and anger to have worked in your breast until at last they assumed over you the influence and the power of the Evil One."

The prisoner quietly ejaculated, "Not jealousy."

Mr Justice Willes was so moved that he burst into tears and could not proceed for some time.

The Judge's tears moved Constance Kent, for the court, which had been stretched like a drum skin, was shaken by the sobs of the prisoner.

When Mr Justice Willes resumed, he said,

"Whether Her Majesty, with whom alone the prerogative of mercy rests, may be advised to consider the facts of your youth at the time when the murder was committed, and the fact that you were convicted chiefly upon your own confession, which removes suspicion from others, is a question which it would be presumption for me to answer here. It well behoves you to live what is left of your life as one who is about to die, and to seek a more enduring mercy by sincere and deep contrition, and by a reliance upon the only redemption and satisfaction for all the sins of the world. It only remains for me to discharge the duty which the law imposes upon the Court without alternative and that is to pass upon you the sentence which the law adjudges for wilful murder: That you be taken from the place where you now stand to the place whence you came, from thence to the place of execution, and that you be hanged by the neck until your body be dead, and that when your body be dead it be buried within the precincts of the gaol in which you were last confined; and may God have mercy on your soul."

And then those who had cast stones at Mr Kent or Elizabeth Gough and those who had merely been amongst the amazed public asked the question—how had the murder been committed? Where was the weapon?

Curiosity, which is a psychological craving of a thirsty mind, was satisfied when the following letter appeared in the press:

"Sir,

I am requested by Miss Constance Kent to communicate to you the following details of her crime, which she has confessed to Mr Rodway, her solicitor, and to myself, and which she now desires to be made public.

"Constance Kent first gave an account of the circumstances of her crime to Mr Rodway, and she afterwards acknowledged to me the correctness of that account when I recapitulated it to her. The explanation of her motive she gave to me when, with the permission of the Lord Chancellor, I examined her for the purpose of ascertaining whether there were any grounds for supposing that she was labouring under mental disease. Both Mr Rodway and I are convinced of the truthfulness and good faith of what she said to us.

"Constance Kent says that the manner in which she committed her crime was as follows: A few days before the murder she obtained possession of a razor from a green case in her father's wardrobe, and secreted it. This was the sole instrument which she used. She also secreted a candle with matches, by placing them in the corner of the closet in the garden, where the murder was committed. On the night of the murder she undressed herself and went to bed, because she expected that her sisters would visit her room. She lay awake watching until she thought that the household were all asleep, and soon after midnight she left her bedroom and went downstairs and opened the drawing-room door and window shutters. She then went up into the nursery, withdrew the blanket from between the sheet and the counterpane, and placed it on the side of the cot. She then took the child from his bed and carried him downstairs through the drawing-room. She had on her nightdress, and in the drawing-room she put on her goloshes. Having the child in one arm, she raised the drawing-room window with the other hand, went round the house and into the closet, lighted the candle and placed it on the seat of the closet, the child being wrapped in the blanket and still sleeping, and while the child was in this position she inflicted the wound in the throat. She says that she thought the blood would never come, and that the child was not killed, so she thrust the razor into its left side, and put the body with the blanket round it, into the vault. The light burnt out. The piece of flannel which she had with her was torn from an old flannel garment placed in the waste bag, and which she had taken some time before and sewn it to use in washing herself. She went back into her bedroom, examined her dress, and found only two spots of blood on it. These she washed out in the basin, and threw the water, which was but a little discoloured, into the foot pan in which she had washed her feet overnight. She took another of her nightdresses and got into bed. In the morning her nightdress had become dry where it had been washed. She folded it up and put it into the drawer. Her three nightdresses were examined by Mr Foley (Superintendent of the Wilts constabulary) and she also believes by Mr

Parsons, the medical attendant of the family. She thought the blood stains had been effectively washed out, but on holding the dress up to the light a day or two afterwards, she found the stains were still visible. She secreted the dress, moving it from place to place, and she eventually burnt it in her own bedroom, and put the ashes or tinder into the kitchen grate. It was about five or six days after the child's death that she burnt the nightdress. On the Saturday morning, having cleaned the razor, she took an opportunity of replacing it unobserved in the case in the wardrobe. She abstracted her nightdress from the clothes' basket (as it was about to be sent to the wash) when the housemaid went to fetch a glass of water. As regards the motive of her crime, it seems that, although she entertained at one time a great regard for the present Mrs Kent, yet if any remark was at any time made which in her opinion was disparaging to any member of the first family, she treasured it up and determined to revenge it. She had no ill-will against the little boy except as one of the children of her step-mother. She declared that both her father and step-mother had always been kind to her personally, and the following is the copy of a letter which she addressed to Mr Rodway on this point while in prison before her trial:

"'Devizes, *May* 15.

"'Sir,

"'It has been stated that my feelings of revenge were excited in consequence of cruel treatment. This is entirely false. I have received the greatest kindness from both the persons accused of subjecting me to it. I have never had any ill-will towards either of them on account of their behaviour to me, which has been very kind.

"'I shall feel obliged if you will make use of this statement in order that the public may be undeceived on this point.

I remain, sir, yours truly,
CONSTANCE E. KENT.

To Mr. R. Rodway.'

"She told me that when the nursemaid was accused she had fully made up her mind to confess, if the nurse had been convicted; and that she had also made up her mind to commit suicide, if she was herself convicted. She said that she had felt herself under the influence of the devil before she committed the murder, but that she did not believe, and had not believed, that the devil had more to do with her crime than he had with any other wicked action. She had not said her prayers for a year before the murder, and not afterwards, until she came to reside at Brighton. She said that the circumstances which revived religious feelings in her mind was thinking about the Sacrament when confirmed.

"An opinion has been expressed that the peculiarities evinced by Constance Kent between the ages of twelve and seventeen may be attributed to the then transition period of her life. Moreover, the fact of her cutting off her hair, dressing herself in her brother's clothes, and leaving home with the intention of going abroad, which occurred when she was only thirteen years of age, indicated a peculiarity of disposition and great determination of character, which foreboded that, for good or evil, her future life would be remarkable.

"This peculiar disposition, which led her to such singular violent resolves of action, seemed also to colour and intensify her thoughts and feelings, and magnify into wrongs that were to be revenged any little family incidents or occurrences which provoked her displeasure.

"Although it became my duty to advise her counsel that she evinced no symptoms of insanity at the time of my examination, and that, so far as it was possible to ascertain the state of her mind at so remote a period, there was no evidence of it at the time of the murder, I am yet of opinion that, owing to the peculiarities of her constitution, it is probable that under prolonged solitary confinement she would become insane.

"The validity of this opinion is of importance now that the sentence of death has been commuted to penal servitude for life; for no one could desire that the punishment of the criminal should be so carried out as to cause danger of a further and greater punishment not contemplated by the law.

"I have the honour to remain,
Your very obedient servant,
JOHN CHARLES BUCKNILL, M.D.

Hilmerton Hall, near Rugby. *August 24th.*"

It is an amazing case. Twelve people in a house, and a girl of sixteen can get up in the middle of the night, go into the nursery where a maid and a child are sleeping, take up the child (aged nearly four), carry it downstairs, through the drawing-room, out into a privy at the back of the house, light a candle, take out a razor, cut the child's throat from ear to ear, wait for the end, come back through the drawing-room, examine her night-dress and wash it, go to bed again—and nobody has the slightest suspicion of what has happened.

The novelist would hesitate before such a narrative.

Yet it took place and baffled the police. The doctor may have misled them a little, for he talked of a sharp knife, dagger-shaped, like a carving-knife. And it was a razor. Constance Kent planning this murder and carrying it out so that, save for her own confession, she might have escaped, did no more, as we can see, than pay attention to details. The washing of the night-dress was careful, but the purloining and burning of it was more. Realizing that those tell-tale spots would betray her she had to get hold of that night-dress again. When the linen was ready to be sent away she asked the maid for a glass of water and seized the opportunity to abstract the night-dress. But to burn an article of clothing like that could surely not have been an easy thing for a girl of sixteen with so many other people in the house. Perhaps she did it at night in her own room.

She also managed to put back the razor before its absence was noticed, which also makes one feel how near she was to the edge.

The truth came from the " mob " too. Inspector Whicher was clear-sighted; it was a pity he reaped blame rather than praise. But it was gossip that aided him. What A doesn't see B will in the matter of motives. A may very well have said that Constance

Kent loved her little brother; but B was ready to suggest the jealousy or resentment or that curious psychological kink which egged on a girl to murder. . . .

There is the chief interest in this crime. That a girl of sixteen could kill a bonny little boy, her half-brother, solely because she fancied her stepmother did not give to the children of the first wife the love she gave to her own, is shockingly amazing. We have a long way to go before human nature is purged of folly.

X

CÉLESTINE DOUDET

IS it some old fighting instinct, useful when there was a struggle with tooth and claw for existence, but as superfluous in our morality to-day as the vermiform appendix in our anatomy, that urges human beings to cruelty? The exercise of power gives pleasure, but it is against human reason, when people derive pleasure by inflicting pain. Yet the experience is common.

A testimonial from Queen Victoria, written with the royal hand, was something to be proud of. Célestine Doudet had been a wardrobe maid, and Queen Victoria had been so impressed by her behaviour that she suggested she ought to be something above an attendant on wardrobes—a governess, for example.

Mdlle Doudet became a governess, and with Queen Victoria's valuable recommendation was enabled to secure situations with the Marquis of Hastings, Lady Hay, and other distinguished people.

Then she obtained a post with a Dr Marsden at Malvern. Dr Marsden was a widower with five children and had a nursery governess for the two younger, while Mdlle Doudet took charge of the three elder ones.

Mdlle Doudet pretended to discover that all the Marsden children the youngest aged seven and the eldest aged thirteen—had already given themselves up to secret vices! The father behaved like a fool, as so many fathers and more mothers do in similar circumstance. Instead of talking to his children sympathetically and tenderly, and giving them the benefit of his knowledge and experience, he handed them over to the sole care of this Frenchwoman. It is possible that Célestine Doudet was a Sadist and put ideas in the children's heads.

Madame Doudet died and Mdlle Doudet then informed Dr Marsden that she intended to open a *pensionnat* for young ladies in Paris. Dr Marsden, seeing he was about to lose a governess, who had probably persuaded him that she alone was capable of managing his children (and may have thought that the position of the wife of Dr Marsden was a comfortable one) put Dr Marsden in a dilemma. He decided to let his five children go to France and to pay a hundred francs a month for each of them to Mdlle Doudet.

In the middle of the last century journeys between England and France were not too common for country doctors. However, Dr Marsden, having married again, called to see his children. They were pale and thin, but one says, " Growing girls " . . . In a confectioner's shop he was amazed to see how they wolfed the cakes. It shocked him. It never occurred to him that they were ravenously hungry, which is a little surprising. However, he told Mdlle Doudet to take them to the confectioner's shop every day to eat what they liked till they got sick of cakes ! " To cure them of being gourmands," he said. " Gourmands ! " . . .

But Mademoiselle didn't believe in taking young ladies to confectioners. It was more advantageous to keep the money.

It was in Odiot, where Mdlle Doudet's *pensionnat* was situated, that gossip took wing and flew. First Mademoiselle Doudet's sister, Zéphyrine, left her. The story spread that the sisters had parted because Zéphyrine had no sympathy with a system that seemed to depend on corporal punishment and starvation!

About this time Célestine Doudet refused to allow the Marsden girls to visit people in the neighbourhood, and one of these, a Madame Espert, wrote a very frank letter to Mdlle Doudet.

" . . . Certain reports are circulating of a very distressful character about your treatment of the poor children in your care, and we are very uneasy and disturbed. The confinement of Lucy for more than a month is a matter of such gravity that I must have some explanation of this before I can again treat you as a friend. You don't shut her up alone for the whooping cough. It is a punishment, and it is said that Poppy's cruel accident is the result of too rigorous treatment. People have heard the children being beaten, and their looks show well enough that they live under a regime of terror. That agrees with what your sister says, who only left you because she could not bear to be a witness of your hardness. Also, it is said, your servants have left you. The heart is torn, and one revolts at the idea of an appearance of goodness and extreme sensitiveness with a severity as sustained as it is cruel. I would like to believe, dear Mdlle Doudet, that it is a false system of education. And, believe me, it will be as fatal to you as to the children who are victims of it. If you are a Christian, spread joy and confidence around you, for otherwise you will compromise the health, intelligence and morality of your pupils, and you yourself will cease to be a person worthy of esteem or consideration.

To educate the young is a great and beautiful task, especially when one acts as a sort of mother to orphans. You ought to understand this mission, of which you speak so freely, and I will therefore leave your conscience to answer this question: Did your mother treat you like that? You, who appear to regret her loss, should be moved, for it is in her name that I beg you to re-enter the path of education, more conformable to that you received from your parents.

Formerly the children came from time to time to see us; why don't they come any longer?

CELESTINE DOUDET 241

Believe me, Mademoiselle Doudet, I speak to you as a friend. Soften your educational system, or I shall be compelled to cease to see you, because I don't want to countenance such conduct by keeping up an acquaintance with you. Think over what I have said. But Lucy must be forgiven at once and I must see her near you or I shall not call on you and shall write to the father of the children —I don't stab you in the back. He won't approve such severities, and if he did you ought not to accept such a task. . . ."

A pretty frank letter.

Mdlle Doudet left it without reply for two days, and then asked Madame Espert to call. Madame Espert called and saw Lucy lying in bed in a nice big room, all by herself. Lucy said she was quite happy there.

But other people were not happy about what was supposed to be going on *chez* Mdlle Doudet. A Mrs Maling, aunt of Lord Normanby, a Miss How, a Mrs Hooper, a Madame Poussielgue and Madame Sudre had a meeting to consider what should be done.

It is clear from all this that the reports were very disturbing. At any rate, these ladies (anonymously) informed the police that something was wrong at Mdlle Doudet's establishment.

So M Collomp, the *commissaire de police*, called on Mdlle Doudet and saw nothing to confirm the allegations in the anonymous letter. And the *commissaire de police*, having informed Mdlle Doudet why he had come, Mdlle Doudet on her part, informed him that the anonymous letters came from a group of meddling English ladies, whom she refused to see—and then she went on to tell M Collomp all about these vices of the English girls under her charge. *That* had caused the children to get thin and look pale and be ill. . . .

It seems as if whenever Mdlle Doudet got a

chance, even if it was a visit from the *commissaire de police*, she must seize it to tell the story of the vices of these poor English girls! She told the doctor the same story. It is worth remembering.

M Collomp wrote to Mr Marsden, enclosing a copy of the anonymous letter and suggesting he should come to Paris or send somebody trustworthy to inquire into these charges that were being made.

Mr Rashdall, uncle of the Marsden children, arrived. The first time he called he wasn't allowed in the house. But he called the next day and saw his nieces.

He was terrified—his own words. The children were so thin they were no more than skeletons. Mdlle Doudet explained to him that their father didn't wish them to be too fat! She said they had whooping cough and they were growing girls and—she dragged in the bad habits once more.

His sister, the children's aunt, called and did not get any nearer to facts than her brother. The children were reticent; they refused to say they were unhappy or badly treated, and it was not likely that a visitor would be allowed in at those moments when, if there was bad treatment, it was going on.

Then Mary Ann died.

Dr Marsden came to Paris at once. He took the children from Mdlle Doudet and put them with their aunt, Miss Rashdall. Mdlle Doudet and the Marsden family were on friendly terms and certain letters passed between them. Ten days later Lucy, Emily and Rose went back to England with their father and Alice remained with her aunt.

And Alice was taken a few days later by Miss Rashdall to the police, who showed M Boudrot a lump on Alice's head, cicatrixes of scratches on the hand and the ear.

Madame Esprit then told the police what she had heard from Mdlle Doudet's sister, Zéphyrine.

So what the police heard were accusations on both sides. Mdlle Doudet dragged in the bad habits apparently on any and every occasion, and as she had spoken to the doctors about them, the doctors were ready to agree that the signs of weakness might be attributed to them. The gossips said Mdlle Doudet starved the children, beat them, terrified them and that was the cause of the pale, frightened faces.

Dr Marsden took no action. He had already swallowed the story of the bad habits from Mdlle Doudet and had practically handed his children over to her that they might be cured. With that foolish reticence, which disgraces the average parent, and with a cowardice and shirking of duty which those who can afford do with remarkable unanimity, this supposedly sensible father handed his children to be trained by somebody else in those matters where sensible, sympathetic parents (mothers and fathers) are incontestibly the best advisers. And even now he shrank from a mention of the subject in the court—even when it was suggested that his children had been horribly treated by Célestine Doudet.

His child was dead. Certainly no trial could let her feel the summer again or let her family see her smile. She had had whooping cough and fallen down . . . Well, well, she was dead. He was not to be disturbed.

But those who felt this Célestine Doudet was the villain of the piece, that she had starved and cruelly illtreated these children entrusted to her charge, that she held her head high while her actions should have brought her low, determined that somebody should be disturbed.

The police acted. Mdlle Doudet was arrested.

And in the meanwhile Lucy, who had accompanied her father to England, had died. Whooping cough was probably set down as the cause of death on the certificate, but Dr Black, who attended her, said that the treatment the child had received in Paris had undoubtedly contributed to make the end sure, for otherwise she would easily have overcome the whooping cough.

He obviously had not seen that treatment; but he could judge whether the tales were reasonably true when he attended his patient.

Flore Margarite Célestine Doudet was charged on the 21st of February, 1855, at the Cour d'Assises de la Seine, M Haton presiding, with 'having in 1852 and 1853 wilfully struck and wounded Mary Ann Marsden, which blows and wounds given with no intention of causing death, did however cause it.'

Dr Marsden was the *partie civile* and was represented by M Chaix-d'Est-Ange, who defended Lieutenant de la Roncière.

Mdlle Doudet was defended by M Nogent-Saint-Laurens.

The accused couldn't keep these vices out of her answers, and it is quite possible there was *some* ground for what she said. Only stupid people shut their eyes to facts and come to judgment without studying them.

The Judge: Were all these girls afflicted with this shameful vice?

Doudet: Yes, Monsieur le president.

The Judge: But you have said that only two were?

Doudet: Dr Marsden told me that they all were, and he begged me to take severe measures to correct them.

The Judge: But he only spoke to you of two of his children, and you understand that the cause of the decline of the three others must be found in your bad treatment?

Doudet: All the five had these habits; but they weren't noticeable till they had whooping cough, and that complicated matters and made them get worse.

The Judge: But the whooping cough didn't come till 1853 and in the autumn of 1852 we had had these words, 'They are spectres—shocking to see.' . . .

The Judge: You actually forced these little girls to write to their father a terrifying description of their habits. It is against nature.

Doudet: The father wrote to the children about these habits and they had to reply.

The Judge: But Dr Marsden says it was you who revealed to him the existence of these habits. That was why he wrote to you to be severe in the matter.

All that is interesting. Let us put beside it at this moment an extract from Dr Marsden's evidence. . . . "I believed the accusations of Mdlle Doudet, who told me, with her eyes on the ground, that she loved motherless children; that it was her duty in this world to take care of them; that she had just left a house where there was a girl who had these shameful habits, that she had been obliged to watch her to see she did not become too friendly with the groom; that my children had the same faults, that they were liars, thieves . . ."

And this is the way the letters from the Marsden children began when they wrote to their father:

My dear Father,

    I am sorry to have to tell you that I am still a liar, a thief and given to bad habits, of which I can't cure myself, in spite of the efforts of Mademoiselle Doudet. . . .

Was ever so vile a letter dictated to a child to send to her father? No wonder he wept when he got such letters and implored his children not to write to him like that.

But light is beginning to fall on the case.

Flore Margarite Célestine Doudet was twenty-seven and unmarried. She had praised Dr Marsden when he was a widower. She abused him when he re-married. The bad habits which Doudet attributed to the Marsden children, whose ages were seven, nine, eleven, twelve and thirteen, were probably the manifestation of a morbid sex complex in Mdlle Doudet.

This Doudet creature had been in a situation where the question was thrust violently under her notice, and when she got to Dr Marsden she carried the effects of the disturbance with her. We are still painfully ignorant in the mass of the power and ravages of the sex influence. What it can do to the single woman is unpredictable. Think of Christiana Edmunds sowing death as casually as one throws bread for sparrows. And Marie de Morell, in her world of romance, proudly and disdainfully breaking a young officer's life. . . .

Some day they will be able to say just what was the matter with Célestine Doudet. Our view is that the prosecution was not wrong when it suggested that the accused hoped to be the second Mrs Marsden, and tried to make herself essential by inventing this horrible story. Being foiled by Dr Marsden's marriage, her rage found its outlet on the little girls. It is a suggestion and we write for understanding.

Before arriving at the fatal day we will quote some of the interrogatory between the President and the prisoner relative to acts of cruelty.

The Judge: You are accused of having treated these children horribly. You are accused of having beaten them, of having knocked their heads against the wall, of having bruised their little feet in breaking their chilblains. It is said you tied them to the foot of your bed in winter, that you forced them to remain in a most uncomfortable position, that you scratched their faces, and took the skin off their hands in cutting their nails; that you have hurt them, wounded them, bruised them and that the cicatriced traces of these wounds can be sworn to. Is all that true?

Doudet: There is a good deal of invention and a good deal of exaggeration.

The Judge: But they are all unanimous in accusing you?

Doudet: I believe they have been taught what to say.

The Judge: But your sister, Zéphyrine, was the first to mention these facts.

Doudet: I don't know what she said.

The Judge: The little Rose said you brutally pushed her one day when she was engaged in an act of nature and because, as a consequence of what you did, something was broken, you hit her on the head; and the *commissaire de police* saw the wound?

Doudet: She hurt herself outside, by accident.

The fatal day was the 24th March, 1853. The children had been given a holiday because it was Queen Victoria's birthday. It seems however to have been a strange holiday. Mademoiselle Doudet went out with Emily and Alice. Lucy, so the prisoner said, was left in the front room on the ground floor. Rose was in Emily's and Mary Ann was in the prisoner's room.

The Court suggested Mary Ann was in another place. (The children complained that they had been shut in the closet for hours, and in the cellar, quite naked.) Mademoiselle Doudet contended Mary Ann was in her room, but the prosecution suggested she was downstairs and that when the accused went to fetch her she kicked her with her knee.

R

The Judge: In the dining-room you scolded her ?
Doudet: No.
The Judge: You struck her ?
Doudet: No.
The Judge: You gave her two blows on the chest which felled her.
Doudet: It is false.
The Judge: If the children say it is true, it is a story they have been taught ?
Doudet: Yes.
The Judge: . . . Now Léocadie Bailleul witnessed this scene and has given evidence. You thought the child was dead . . . you were deceived by a few days. You were stunned ! You said to Léocadie (a servant), " Go and fetch a doctor—say she jumped out of the window."
Doudet: I did not say that.
The Judge: She went for a doctor and do you know what she said ?
Doudet: How should I know ?
The Judge: I will tell you. She said, " Come at once. The child has jumped out of the window." Emily ran for help to the chemist, and do you know what she said ? . . . " Come at once ! My sister has broken her arm ! " And afterwards your explanation of the scene was that Mary Ann had fallen in the salon and then had an attack of coughing. . . .
Doudet: I don't remember that.
The Judge: What did you tell Dr Shrimpton ?
Doudet: I don't know. I spoke of convulsions.
The Judge: You told him that the child was lost because of her bad habits.
Doudet: He knew.
The Judge: So that day you wished to make him think the bad habits were really the cause of the accident ? You said to him that you had scolded her in pure affection, that she had gone into a passion, had fallen back and hurt herself ?

Doudet: I don't remember that.

The Judge: Your sister, Zéphyrine wasn't deceived about the cause of death?

Doudet: She wasn't with me.

The Judge: She said that death was caused by the blows you had given the child.

Doudet: She couldn't have said that: her principles wouldn't let her.

The Judge: So that if she did say so, it will have weight. She said, "God keep Mary Ann alive, for if she dies we are lost. . . ."

Dr Marsden went into the box and told the story of how he had confided his children to the care of Mdlle Doudet.

"Mdlle Doudet," he said in the course of his evidence, "has pretended that my daughters were thieves and liars. I had no suspicion of her because there was no reason why I should have. I asked where my other two daughters were and she said she would fetch them. I followed her and saw two children I shouldn't have recognized as mine if I had met them in the street. They hadn't a smile! 'Rose, Rose, my child,' I cried, 'come into my arms!'

"Someone said, 'They are tied to the bed.'

"I looked and saw my daughters were fastened to the foot of the bed. When I saw that I said to Mdlle Doudet, 'If you are not guilty, you aren't capable of being a governess. How dare you tie a living person to a dead body? . . . Who told you to fasten my children?' She told me Dr Tessier. I went to see Dr Tessier, and he informed me he had said nothing of the sort. . . . I took the children away and when they were at home in England they became quite happy. . . . It was three weeks after they had been with me that they began to tell me about the horrible treatment they had received from Mdlle Doudet. Rose was the first to speak.

I learnt they had been struck; that they had been beaten all over; that they were starved, abused, shut up for twenty-four hours in the closet, in the cellar, quite naked, delivered up to fear of the wretched creatures that ran over the floor. . . ."

Lucy, the eldest girl, had never recovered in England. She had slowly wasted and died. Dr Marsden said a distinguished doctor had admitted he couldn't understand what was the cause of her death. She had constantly accused Mdlle Doudet of beating her every day on the chest. She was shut up on the ground floor for weeks at a time; she was deprived of food and knocked down by blows on her chest.

"Was she afraid during her illness?"

"She said that if Mdlle Doudet had told her to plunge a knife into her breast she would have done it. In her last moments she had to hold someone's hand. She said Mdlle Doudet had sworn to come to her dead or alive if she ever told."

"And you probably saw marks of blows?"

"They are on the three surviving children to this day—two years afterwards."

Only three of the five children who had been put in the charge of Mademoiselle Doudet were alive, two were dead. Emily, Rose and Alice were witnesses in the trial.

The children now had to speak for themselves, and by this time they had got over their fear of Mdlle Doudet.

Emily said they were badly treated, that they were beaten and deprived of food. On the 24th she—Emily—with Alice and Léocadie went to the Jardin des Plantes.

"Where were your other sisters?"

"In the house. Lucy was on the ground floor; Mary Ann was in the cellar-kitchen, and Rose was in a room on the first floor."

"Was she free?"

"She was tied to the bed."

"What happened when you came in?"

"Mademoiselle unloosed Rose and went to fetch Mary Ann from the cellar-kitchen. Rose had done her task and had a piece of bread. Mary Ann hadn't done hers. She was scolded, then struck and knocked down. She got up and was then struck once more on the chest and knocked senseless."

Emily was asked why she had written affectionately to Mademoiselle.

"We were not sure we might not go back to her," was the adequate reply.

"For how long were you denied food?" the advocat-général asked.

"From Wednesday morning till Friday evening."

A juryman: "What sort of fault caused you to be treated like that?"

"If we made a mistake in our lessons."

The Judge: "Were you made to get up in the night?"

"If we made the slightest noise in bed, Mademoiselle made us get up, stand in our night-shirts at the foot of the bed, with our arms stretched out."

"When did that happen?"

"After Mdlle Zéphyrine had gone."

"Were things worse after she left?"

"Yes."

"Why didn't you complain when your father came to visit you the first time?"

"We were afraid of Mademoiselle. She told us she would find out if we said anything to father, and she would beat us all the more."

"And she told you you were beaten because your father ordered it?"

"Yes."

"Have you ever been shut up in the closet?"

"Yes, for five hours."

"And once, were you forgotten till eleven o'clock in the evening, while Mdlle Doudet went to a concert?"

"Yes, sir."

The accused interjected, "The door wasn't shut."

And Emily retorted with, "Yes, we could have gone out, but Mademoiselle put something before the door so that she would know if we had been out."

Rose's story was even more pathetic. She was younger and timider and told how she had been frightened by tales of a terrible creature who would come for her. She seemed to be afraid of Croquemitaine even as she stood in the box. And she told of Mdlle Doudet walking on her chilblains!

She repeated Emily's story of Mary Ann being brought up from the cellar-kitchen, being struck and knocked down.

Alice Marsden, aged nine, corroborated.

Léocadie Bailleul, twenty-three, had been a servant with Mdlle Doudet.

"Have you any complaints to make of the accused?" she was asked.

"No, sir. She was always very good to me. But she committed all sorts of atrocities on the children; she beat them, she starved them; she shut them up. I have seen a lot and Mdlle Zéphyrine has told me the rest. She was ill with the cruelty of the place."

"Did the accused know Mdlle Zéphyrine had been confidential with you in this matter?"

"Yes. And she told me not to listen. But I saw with my own eyes what the truth was. Mdlle Zéphyrine often put bread in her pocket to give to the children and handed it to me to give to them."

"You have mentioned bad treatment?"

"I found a handful of Lucy's hair on Alice's bed."

"And on one occasion, when Alice was tied to the bed, she ... made a slight mess on the floor?"

"Mdlle Doudet was angry, lifted up Alice's dress and rubbed her back on the floor till the skin came off."

"The children had chilblains?"

"Yes. And Mdlle Doudet squeezed their toes with her heels. I have seen the children's feet all bloody."

"They have been shut up in the closet?"

"Yes, sir, and I have given them bread in secret."

"What happened on the 24th of May?"

"I ought to say that before then Lucy had been shut up for a month and I hadn't seen her. I had taken her a piece of bread that had been dipped in a pot, which had once had jam, and which Mdlle Doudet had now filled with hot water. When I got to Lucy I didn't recognize her; she was absolutely transformed."

"On the 24th you went to the Jardin des Plantes?"

"Yes."

"What time did you return?"

"Half past five."

"What happened?"

"Mdlle Doudet made Mary Ann, who was in the cellar-kitchen, come upstairs. Mdlle Doudet scolded her on the stairs and then gave her a kick with her knee, which made her books fall. Mary Ann picked them up without uttering any complaint. I was in my kitchen, which faces the dining-room. The door was ajar, so that I heard the blows. When the door was shut I went to hear what happened. Almost at once I heard cries and dashed into the salon, where I saw Mary Ann, whose look was no longer human. Her expressions were horrible—she was dying."

"What did Mdlle Doudet do?"

"She sent me to fetch a doctor. I brought M Gaston Gaudinot, to whom I had said on Mademoiselle's orders, that the young girl had thrown herself out of the window. Mademoiselle sent me to fetch Dr Shrimpton, with whom she spoke English, and I understood nothing."

"While the child was ill, how did the accused look after her?"

"Not much. One day in giving her something to drink she thrust the spout in her mouth. The child took it out and hid it under the counterpane."

Dr Gaudinot told how he had been asked to see a young girl who had fallen through a window. He asked how the accident happened, and Mdlle Doudet said the child had coughed and fallen off the chair. The child did not speak and died without saying a word. He saw the other children and was struck with their appearance. Mdlle Doudet told him of their bad habits. He also ordered better food must be given them. He saw no signs of whooping cough, but she had acute bronchitis. On what they told him he came to the conclusion that the fall had brought on complications which had caused death.

Dr Shrimpton had known the accused for some time. He was called in to see Mary Ann, and he diagnosed tumour and paralysis. He was told she had brought it on by throwing herself down in a passion. And he had been told of these "shocking habits".

The Court wondered how it was that whenever Mdlle Doudet met anybody she talked of the shocking habits of these little girls.

Professor Ambrose Tardieu, who conducted an autopsy on the body of Mary Ann a year after it had been buried, found a lesion on the right posterior of the head, where there had obviously been haemorrhage. In his opinion death was due to haemorrhage, exterior first and then interior.

"Could this interior bleeding have been caused by a fall which took place eight hours before the paralysis?" The professor was asked.

"All that I can say", he replied, "is that it is not absolutely impossible: but it is not easy to admit it."

The doctors, Jobert de Lamballe and Langier, who assisted at the autopsy, agreed with Professor Tardieu.

The concierge, Madame Tassin, said she saw the children when they arrived from England looking bonny and she saw them later when they watched what the children of the concierge ate with hungry eyes. She said that when she went to look at the dead child Mdlle Doudet said, "She smiles, as if she forgave me."

And the concierge had heard of course of these bad habits.

Madame Poussielgue saw how happy and well the Marsden children looked when they first came. When next she saw them she didn't recognize them. Mdlle Doudet said they were "growing". "They were spectres", added the witness. When she went again and saw Mary Ann in bed she was almost heartbroken. It was to this witness that Zéphyrine had said, "If she dies (referring to Mary Ann) we are lost". She had seen the broken chilblains and the marks of kicks on the legs and feet of little Rose.

Mr Rashdall, who had called on Mdlle Doudet, gave evidence, as did also his wife. It was in the course of Mrs Rashdall's evidence that the interpreter enlivened the proceedings with an expression of delicacy that sent the court in a roar.

The President of the Court turned to the interpreter and said, " Ask the witness if, one day, Alice being on the *vase*, she was not hurt by Mdlle Doudet ? "

One can feel the momentary silence. The expression on the interpreter's face is not that of one alert, swift and eager. He looks pathetically at the judge and says in an accent we can all hear, " That's a very delicate question to put to an English woman ".

Madame Maling testified to the healthy English children who arrived in France and the poor spectres she saw later. She told how Zéphyrine had related the stories of blows and the starvations. She said none of the children had whooping cough : they were black and blue with blows.

Louis Tassin had a picturesque phrase. He said Mdlle Doudet could have made the children walk through fire with a single look from her eyes.

Madame Hopper told again the tale of the spectral children. But we got what may be another indication of the morbidly sexual mind of Célestine Doudet. Madame Hopper said Mdlle Doudet said Dr and Mrs Marsden had lived together before marriage.

The accused denied it, but we feel that as one of these two women lied, it is safer to assume it was Mdlle Doudet. Now, why invent such a tale ? . . . Her mind ran on such things probably.

Madame Sudre repeated the starved children story.

More graspable evidence was given by a servant, named Perette, who only stayed a fortnight with Mdlle Doudet. She said the children were punished far too severely, that they were shut up in the closet, even in the night time, and that they only got bread and warm water. Because she (witness) had once secretly given the children some bread Mademoiselle scolded her and she didn't dare to repeat the attempt.

Zéphyrine Doudet was called and there was naturally much curiosity concerning her evidence. But she was not there to stab her sister. She admitted there may have been a little severity, she admitted that: but denied all the other things she was reported to have said. So the witnesses who had repeated her words stood up one by one, reaffirmed what they had already testified, and made Mdlle Zéphyrine feel probably that a still tongue saves a deal of trouble.

Some of the children's letters were read, and they naturally gave no hint of the bad treatment. On the contrary. But that was so natural that the court was probably not misled by them.

A Madame Magny, a dressmaker, said the sight of the children had made her so ill she had refused work.

Dr Marsden's English maids went to Paris to give evidence and they swore they had seen nothing of these " bad habits ".

Since we are always interested in any manifestation of human conduct we should like to insert here a remark made by the Presiding judge when the witnesses for the prosecution had been heard.

" Prisoner ", he said. " We should like to get from you the truth of this matter. You have seen the way the evidence has gone and more than one emotion has been stirred. Now you have been marked as hard, as violent and as dissimulating. All that belongs to character. One is violent and hard by nature; one dissimulates because one is of that kind. At the same time we should like to discover if there is not another motive for your conduct.

A few months ago, a young girl, twenty years of age, was seated in that very spot. She was accused, not of blows and violence, but of the murder of a young girl, an angel, they said. She tried twice to murder that angel, once by asphyxiating, the other time by strangling.

"Now when she was asked to confess the reason for her action she said, 'I wanted to avenge myself on a man; I heard that his young niece had all his affection, so I wished to strike at him through his niece, whom I didn't know.' We caught the drift of a word in this trial—the word *jealousy*. You said to a doctor whom you saw for the first time: 'Dr Marsden is very popular with ladies. He is a man of pleasure and for his own satisfaction has neglected his children and just got re-married.' The doctor was struck with the note of jealousy that ran through these words. If we compare them with what you have said of Mrs Marsden—that she was a light woman, that she was hiding her past under the veil of an honourable union—we are inclined to suggest you have been moved by a double sentiment, one of jealousy against Dr Marsden, and one of hate against Mrs Marsden, and to satisfy that double emotion you have flinched from striking the head of the family?"

"No, Monsieur."

The 'No, Monsieur' doesn't interest us. At that moment she was bound to say it. But the judge's theory has probably the heart of the matter in it. Mdlle Doudet's nature had been repressed sufficiently to have started a revolution. The sadness is she treated five little English girls as a shameful world.

There were naturally a number of witnesses to come forward and say what a splendid person Mdlle Célestine Doudet was, and that they had never seen her doing any of these violent and hard things.

Madame Schwab had come all the way from England to testify to the esteem in which she held Mademoiselle Doudet, who had been a governess to her children. Her children had not been beaten. Mdlle Doudet would almost imitate Queen Victoria if one of the children transgressed. . . . "We are not amused . . . *Sortez!*"

In the court that kind of evidence would probably have equal weight with evidence on the other side. Madame Schwab coming all the way from England was something. But if we get at the motive that egged Célestine Doudet to her cruelties, we can see that when she is living with the Schwabs she has no need to imagine herself other than a wardrobe Queen Victoria, and play the majestic dame. But when she is with Dr Marsden, a widower . . . and other dreams enter the situation . . . the matter is complicated because Célestine Doudet now is in her own house, almost mistress, Queen. . . . And then Dr Marsden marries . . . and his children are with her. . . . "His brats!" one can imagine her saying.

It is all a matter of finding the true key to unlock the cupboards of her conduct.

One item of evidence bearing on that ulcerated spot—the bad habits.

Madame Walter had made some drawers of a particular kind for three of the Marsden children. The following short dialogue carries its own dramatic value.

"Open the packet, witness."

Witness opens the packet.

"Have those things been worn?"

"Never!" (Sensation.)

"Prisoner! Why weren't these things worn?"

"Because M Marsden wrote that he didn't wish me to use them."

Dr Marsden rising. "I never said anything of the sort."

Counsel will make mention of these *caleçons de chastite*. If the accused must talk of this matter to almost everyone she met, and if she had set herself the task of eradicating the bad habits from the children, why didn't she see they wore these caleçons? One must conclude that either she didn't want to cure them or there was nothing to cure.

Before the speeches of counsel, Mrs Marsden's evidence, taken on oath in England, was read by the Judge. She said that Rose bore on her body marks of blows and violence; that Rose had confessed to her that she and her sisters were continually being beaten by Mdlle Doudet. The other sisters, on being questioned, made similar answers. Lucy, the most affectionate of them all, was always haunted by fear. In her last delirium the figure of Mdlle Doudet pursued her ceaselessly.

In its simple directness that burns like acid.

M Chaix-d'Est-Ange then addressed the Court as the representative of Dr Marsden. Speeches of counsel, as a rule, are a superfluity of words in a work of this kind; but every now and then there is some flower to be culled with advantage. We shall be able to pick one or two flowers from M Chaix-d'Est-Ange's finely argued and finely presented speech.

"Let us recall the situation of the Marsden family in 1852, when Célestine Doudet goes there. The family was happy, proud to be in the world. Célestine Doudet enters, and with her a procession of fears, pains, injustice, defilings, and following the defilement—death. She comes there, as here, surrounded with the best testimonials; they have been given her by the highest families, by her gracious Majesty the Queen. She speaks with a voice full of unction, a honeyed voice, so that one can't resist her. She fascinates everybody—except the grandmother! 'Take care, my son', said this venerable lady, 'That woman wants to be mistress here'."

One is glad to record these penetrating flashes into human nature.

M Chaix-d'Est-Ange mentioned the caleçons to demonstrate the hypocrisy of the accused. He boldly declared the prisoner had invented the theory of the bad habits and turning to her said, "You have killed the body; I accuse you of having also killed the soul!"

Another hint at human nature's terrible varieties.

"There are depths of iniquity that the thought can't penetrate. I won't search for examples in the odious theories that certain diseased minds have seen fit to develop in these days: I will go to a philosopher—to Montaigne." Here M Chaix-d'Est-Ange read from the chapter on 'Cruelty'. He continued: "This thirst for blood, this need of torture, all this is practised not on strong, vigorous beings, but on weak ones, on children. It seems in truth that the redder the blood, the more life and innocence there is, the greater is the attraction to crime. Shall we find in that an explanation of this case? . . . Every month judicial records give us examples of this sort."

M Chaix-d'Est-Ange then told a story of a case that happened early in his career. A Marchioness went to a hospital at Rouen and took children away. "What a charitable woman!" people said. Nothing of the sort. The woman took the children to torture them! "*Elle leur fait manger leurs excrements.*" He had defended her, because he couldn't believe her guilty. But she was guilty.

M Nogent-Saint-Laurens scoffed at the gossip, said the children weren't to be believed, that the evidence of the maid, Léocadie, was worthless, and that his client ought to be set free.

The Avocat général spoke and M Nogent-Saint-Laurens replied, and the verdict of the jury was, " Not guilty."

It was a verdict received with amazement.

But Célestine Doudet had not heard the last of the matter. She was charged with having beaten Emily, Rose and Alice Marsden; also with having acted similarly to Lucy Marsden.

The case was tried in Paris on March 9th, 1855.

A good deal of the evidence was a repetition of what was heard at the previous trial, but now the incidents of cruelty were more numerous, were more detailed.

Dr Marsden said it was Rose who had first informed him of Mademoiselle Doudet's cruelties. Lucy told him the accused had dragged her by the hair, calling her a devil with red hair. He said they had all had to drink soapy water and they had scarcely a hair on their heads.

Emily gave the menu. Breakfast: bread, water and a little butter. Evening: milk, bread and butter. They had never enough to eat. She said Lucy had been dragged by the hair and beaten. One day Mademoiselle Doudet broke a ruler over her and made her go up and down stairs fifty times. One day she threatened to pull Alice's tongue out—and did, in fact, try at it.

The sickening story of cruelties was repeated, and the children swore that the letters they wrote were written at the dictation of Mademoiselle Doudet.

When Zéphyrine Doudet went into the box she admitted she had received letters from Lucy and Emily and returned them because she believed them to be dictated,

Célestine Doudet was found guilty and condemned to two years' imprisonment and fined 200 francs.

But Justice was not satisfied. Just as there is an appeal for mitigation of sentence so there is an appeal for its aggravation.

And though the suave tongue of the eloquent Berryer was added to the persuasiveness of M Nogent-Saint-Laurens, Célestine Doudet was finally condemned not to two years but to five years' imprisonment and to pay the costs of both trials.

XI

MADAME JONIAUX

THE socially ambitious woman, big in body, big in little ideas, married to a book-worm, does not suggest the happy conjunction.

Madame Faber was perhaps a good wife after her fashion (and it may have suited her husband, in which case it is nobody else's business), but that she was not wholly and entirely in sympathy with the things her husband loved, we conclude from the things she did.

M Faber was the secretary of something or other: really, he was something to do with books. He wrote *A History of the French Theatre in Belgium*, and paid for its publication. He probably wrote other books as well. He spent a fair amount of money on his library too, considering his financial position. He received 2,000 francs (£80) a year for his secretaryship, and his parents allowed him 3,000 francs; so that altogether M and Madame Faber had an income of £200 a year. Not very much if you have a fancy for first editions; but "before the war" in frugal Belgium, an income of five thousand francs represented the bourgeois. Madame Faber was the daughter of General Jules Ablay and presumably liked to mix with the friends and acquaintances of Generals. But her people had no money, and her marriage to M Faber was a good one in the circumstances.

And M Faber, reading and writing books, probably did not bother over much about his wife's expenditure on dress and other matters. Soon he ceased to bother about books, for 'finis' was written on the last page of his life.

Madame Faber, who had a daughter, then married M Joniaux, an engineer, and the Joniaux household enjoyed an income of about 14,000 francs (£560).

But Madame Joniaux had social ambitions which cost money, of course. It may have been she had run into debt with her first husband. Her story was that when M Faber died she had 200,000 francs' worth of debt. She said the library had swallowed the money. But the late M Faber's books were only valued at 3,500 francs. So she was probably mistaken.

Madame Faber—subsequently Madame Joniaux —was constantly borrowing money. She borrowed 80,000 francs; her mother-in-law lent her 20,000; someone else lent her another 20,000. And she said her mother-in-law wasn't nice because she wouldn't pay her debts !

A phrase of the mother-in-law's might be quoted. " She is a gulf and " . . . a pause " she won't hesitate at crime ! " It cuts like a razor.

What was it that pushed this stout, middle-class woman to search continually for money ? She borrowed right and left. When she had to explain these things she talked of 'sacred debts'. But she was sensible enough to say that all debts were sacred —even those of tradespeople !

She denied she had expensive tastes, but a letter of the late M Faber's was found in which he had told his mother they were living in a miserable condition and yet she was dealing in almost wholesale fashion with dressmakers and milliners.

Almost as soon as Madame Faber became Madame Joniaux she was borrowing again. And her second husband seemed to have as little control over her expenditure as her first. She was the type of woman who was not easily interfered with, determined, resolute, unswerving. And she would be a society woman.

Every day almost this amazing creature must have wondered from whom she could get money ... She borrowed 2,000 francs from a M Stevens. ... Another 1,000 from General Baron Van de Smissen. ... She pawned a watch and a pin at the *mont-de-piété* at Brussels.

She was accused of cheating at a friend's house!

She faced the accusations with astonishing force. At her trial, when the cheating incident was mentioned, she showed she felt the lash of that charge.

"It is an odious calumny," she said. "It has been fixed up solely out of revenge. I am the victim of a woman's spite—Madame Neyt, who has waited till I am in trouble to attack me. I protest against her infamy. Of all the charges which are laid against me this hurts me most."

That, in itself, is an interesting remark. Did she feel it most because all her being had been absorbed in the wish for money and cheating betrayed it? ... It is interesting.

The president said: "You were found holding cards under the tablecloth!"

At Spa there was trouble. She was accused of having tried to bribe one of the officials to give her blue cards instead of red ones.

That she did not do very well at Spa is a fair conclusion from the fact that she borrowed 100 francs from a shop girl, tried to borrow £20 and 40 from people in the hotel and visited the *mont-de-piété*.

Ever this search for money.

She went to Monte Carlo. When this incident was mentioned to her she replied, "I was never such a fool as to think I could make a fortune by gambling."

People who are always hunting for money, who

gamble at Spa and Monte Carlo do hope to make money. Madame Joniaux was always after an elusive fortune and that class of person snatches eagerly at small sums.

A Madame Van Setter, who went with Madame Joniaux to Monte Carlo and lent her 400 francs, has a tale to tell of cheating at cards.

"In 1891," said Madame Van Setter, "Madame Joniaux came to dine with us and in the evening we played cards. She suddenly said she wasn't well, asked for a candle and left the room. When she did that a second time we thought it singular. . . . We counted the cards. . . . There were some missing. We were amazed. When she came back we saw her replace the cards. The mirror betrayed her. I did not dare to say anything. I was so upset. Madame Joniaux noticed my manner and went away earlier than usual. I didn't see her for a long time. . . ."

Then came the incident of the death of her nephew. He was found drowned.

Georges Ablay received an anonymous letter:

"Chance and Providence have made me master of a terrible secret. I am not a dishonest but an unfortunate man. I know all the circumstances of the death of that poor child. Who profits by it? . . . It is in your interest to avoid a terrible scandal. I hold in my hand the irrefutable proof of the crime. You will weep tears of blood. I shall write it big. The papers will talk of it—take care!"

And then the usual demand—25,000 francs, to be given to a commissionaire.

The experts swore the letters (a similar one was delivered to M Joniaux, which was a clever idea) were the work of Madame Joniaux.

Of a woman's scheming this is illuminating: she borrowed 300 francs from the landlady of her sister, Emily, in Brussels; she begged with tears in her eyes for a loan of 30,000 from Mdlle Van der Vorst—without getting it; she asked for 2,000 francs from a M Antoine Gillis, who let her have 500. She pawned a watch for 35 francs. She wrote to those who had lent her money that she couldn't repay them at that moment. She begged for a loan from the lady superior of a convent—without success.

What a life!

If the history of crime teaches us nothing of human nature it is no more profitable than a handful of sand in the desert.

Was it this daily urge that pushed Madame Joniaux, the daughter of a poor General, to the terrible idea? Money . . . If she had been born of humble stock she might have been a good and capable wife. She was the daughter of a General and poor. . . . She would move with the well-to-do and she hadn't the means. She struggled daily to climb the ladder. And it needed money . . . Always money. . . .

Madame Joniaux insured the life of her sister, Léonie Ablay, for 70,000 francs. Six weeks after the insurance had been effected and the premiums paid by Madame Joniaux, Léonie Ablay died.

That was in 1892. In 1893 M Jacques Vandenkerckhove, an uncle of Madame Joniaux, lived at Ghent with his mistress. Madame Joniaux—so it was asserted—had hoped to be included amongst his heirs. He was sixty-four years of age, lusty and healthy. More than that, he had decided, as many old roués have done, to marry his mistress. In all probability it was not morality that moved him so much as a desire to do fairly by the woman and their child. For M Vandenkerckhove had a son, and his marriage with the mother would legitimise this son.

This news would not be pleasing to Madame Joniaux, who was suffering from money hunger. She did not know the contents of her uncle's will, but she realized it wouldn't interest her at all once he was married and had a son.

So she gave a party. M Vandenkerckhove was invited. He died the next day.

That was in 1893. In that same year Madame Joniaux was writing here and there for money and begging her creditors for time and money. She got a loan from her brother-in-law of 4,000 francs. She bought some silver ware on credit for 900 francs and at once pawned it. Again she went to the jewellers; this time she got 10,000 francs' worth of silver. And again she pawned.

Early in 1894 she persuaded her brother, Alfred Ablay, to stay with her. He arrived at his terrible sister's on the 4th of February, 1894. Before a week had elapsed he was insured for 100,000 francs. In a month he was dead!

Léonie Ablay had been insured with *la Société Générale Néerlandaise* and *La Baloise*. Alfred Ablay's insurance had been accepted by the *Gresham Assurance Coy*.

The Gresham Assurance Company refused to pay the 100,000 francs due on the death of Alfred Ablay, and the police arrested Madame Joniaux, who was charged with the murder of her sister, her uncle and her brother.

This woman of forty-nine stood in the box and faced her judges with an ease, confidence and readiness of speech that can rarely have been surpassed, though all criminals have ease before their judges.

The case was tried at Antwerp in 1895 and was the most sensational judicial event in Belgium since the Peltzer trial in 1882.

It will be noticed that it was the death of Alfred Ablay which aroused the suspicions of the police. M Vandenkerckhove had died in 1893 and Léonie Ablay in 1892.

Autopsies were practised on the three bodies,

but it was obviously not an easy matter to testify to poison after so long a period had elapsed.

This is what the *Acte d'Accusation* said about the death of Léonie Ablay—*acte d'accusation* being the case for the prosecution as set out before the actual trial.

"The autopsy and chemical analysis of the viscera do not, of themselves, provide us with the proof that the cause of death was poison; but that proof is found in the results of the autopsy with other elements in the case.

"The autopsy though mute on the positive cause of death shows it was not due to typhoid fever as was thought by some doctors, nor to cerebral haemorrhage. . . ."

The accused was in this situation: her daughter was about to marry and would soon be a major. If Léonie Ablay had died twenty days earlier or three months later than she did, the prisoner could not have touched the money paid by the company.

The prosecution suggested that Madame Joniaux had used morphia, and consequently there were no traces left in the bodies after the long lapse of time.

A jury naturally prefers to have everything not only clear but convincing. Legal proof is no more than common sense for a jury. If a doctor says, "This person died of morphia; the prisoner bought morphia and had an opportunity of giving it to the deceased and had a strong motive for wishing his death", the jury feel morally satisfied when they give their verdict of guilty. But if the doctor says, "We have found no poison in the deceased though we do say he died of something which wasn't typhoid", then the members of the jury have to take into consideration a number of things.

In the case of Madame Joniaux there were two charges where poison could not be definitely stated as the cause of death by the doctors; but the autopsy in the case of Alfred Ablay showed morphia in all parts of his body. Doctors could say that Alfred Ablay had died of morphia poisoning. Though naturally there were other doctors to differ. There generally are.

It was the business of the prosecution to bring home to Madame Joniaux the deaths of her sister, uncle and brother. In the course of the trial it was essential to understand what her motive had been, and these pages from her borrowing life were an illuminating part in the trial.

But Madame Joniaux stands out as a prisoner, who preserved her coolness and audacity to the last. Crimeless people have a feeling that when the guilty are discovered they betray themselves by their emotion in some way or other. Certain hard types can lie with the sun in their eyes.

Criminal trials in France and Belgium impose on the prisoner a terrible ordeal. The judge examines them day after day if need be. Madame Joniaux submitted to an examination that lasted for five days, and after that was called on to reply to or contradict or supplement witnesses. And she stood in the dock, like an injured lady from a comfortable, detached house somewhere in the suburbs, replying to charges with ease, readiness and point, now and again breaking into denunciations of those who dared to suggest she was capable of doing the things of which she was accused. This well-dressed, stout *bourgoise* amazed the court in her dialogue with the President.

"You are accused," said the President, "of having poisoned your sister, Léonie, your uncle, Vandenkerckhove and your brother, Alfred Ablay. You deny it?"

"Absolutely."

"Their deaths occurred when you were most pressed."

"Not at all. . . ."

"Didn't Dr Ruelle think your sister might have died of meningitis?"

"I am not responsible for his diagnosis. . . ."

"For fifteen years you have been living on and by expedients."

"For fifteen years I have struggled like a wretch against a situation which I didn't make."

She affirmed that her first husband liked going out in the world, clearly desiring to show that he spent money.

The President: "Did M Faber pay any attention to the housekeeping?"

"As much as a man can."

"More than M Joniaux?"

"M Joniaux knew the difficulties and responsibilities I had to face."

"I suppose M Joniaux didn't know the name of your dressmaker?"

"No."

"In your family you were treated like an oracle?"

"They put everything on my back."

"Your brother, Alfred Ablay, was particularly docile, wasn't he? And wasn't M Faber somewhat weak?"

"Yes."

And later:

"You had considerable influence over your daughter. . . ."

Madame Joniaux's character as seen by others comes out in these remarks. This resolute woman had clearly run her house as she wished. She moulded her daughter (dictated her letters on occasions), and begged from or was furious with her husband's family as the circumstances prompted. But nobody ever dominated her.

Asked if she had pawned things she quickly retorted: "Yes. That isn't a crime."

Taken through the incident of the death of her nephew when the prosecution alleged she had written the anonymous letters she never hesitated.

"The experts who have examined the letter addressed to Madame Meskens have declared it to be your writing."

"They are wrong."

"A similar letter was addressed to your brother, Charles."

"I know."

"George Ablay came to see you a fortnight afterwards and you then showed him a similar anonymous letter which you said you had found in the letter-box."

"Perfectly true."

"Weren't you the author of that letter? How do you explain the coincidence?"

"Chance. I couldn't do such an odious thing. Lionel was buried that day and I cried the whole day."

"And you had an important bill to pay at that time?"

"That's possible, but it isn't a reason why I should be the victim of an infamous charge."

The death of Lionel Ablay was in itself a tragedy. He was the son of Alfred Ablay and he was found in a pond, in a sack with a rope round his neck. Suicide had been suggested. Perhaps the family were glad to let it pass as that, for Alfred Ablay hinted (perhaps without foundation) that Lionel Ablay had seduced a farmer's daughter and his death was the result! The suggestion was: Madame Joniaux, by writing anonymous letters, wished to exploit that situation to her profit.

The President had been going into the debts owed by the accused in 1892.

The President: "Did you warn the future parents-in-law of your daughter that she had no fortune?"

"I told them she had only a pension of 75 francs a month."

"And the expenses of the wedding?"

"I wasn't responsible. It was the duty of Madame Faber, her grandmother, to help."

"Must we go so far as to admit that the granddaughter of General Ablay, the daughter of the director Joniaux, might be married without a reception?"

"Mon Dieu! Monsieur le President, I don't push pride as far as that. Besides, anything can happen —*I am here, to-day!*"

Few women in the dock can have been so ready and so little discomfited before a judge. And she too had her very human moments. She was taken through the details of the assurance and death of her sister. She spoke clearly and lucidly. She said her mother on her death-bed, had confided in her sister, Emilie, the secret of a sacred debt of 30,000 francs. The prisoner and Léonie had considered how this debt could be paid. Hence the insurance.

The President: "You were to get 30,000 francs, which came just in time for the wedding and your daughter's trousseau."

"Possibly. It remains to be proved that I poisoned my sister."

"It will be proved."

"How can you poison without poison?"

"This sacred debt—there seem to be a good many of them in your family. It is an honourable family yet, according to you, it has been frequently compromised."

"You will agree that, at least, I have done all I could and that I haven't spared myself to keep that honour intact."

And then came the emotion.

"Your sister Léonie was very fond of you?"

"Yes, she was only happy with me."

And then Madame Joniaux sobbed. She had poisoned that sister—that was the charge—and after discussing lucidly and calmly other matters, the note of affection is struck and out pour the tears. It is interesting.

The President: "Did you buy morphia on the 3rd of January?"

"I did not take morphia at that time."

"Why did you hide from the judge the fact that you had bought morphia?"

"Because I hadn't bought any."

"On the 8th of January you bought some more?"

"No. I didn't even know that the prescription had been ordered."

"How much money did you get when your sister Léonie died?"

"Nothing."

"But you had 70,000 francs."

"No. I paid my mother's sacred debt and my daughter had the rest."

"You nursed Léonie?"

"Yes."

"Do you know the effects of morphia?"

"I have never made a study of poisons."

"Have you taken morphia yourself?"

"Yes. But not since 1883." (This dialogue took place in 1895.)

"If at this time someone had suggested to Dr Ruelle that you were poisoning your sister, do you think he would have believed them?"

"I don't think he would have believed it."

"The public prosecutor didn't wish to believe it."

"He didn't wish to believe it! Well, of course not!"

"The insurance companies were not quite satisfied with your sister's death."

"That's their custom. There is one thing they haven't discovered, and that is to give with the policy of insurance a guarantee for a long life."

"*La Baloise* considered the question of having an autopsy on your sister Léonie."

"I am sorry they didn't do it."

"They didn't do it because it was represented to them that it concerned a respectable family and the scandal would be enormous."

"They were wrong."

"You have, however, described as 'unqualifiable' their inquiries into Léonie's death."

"Because they never told me anything about it."

"*La Baloise* offered to pay half the policy?"

"I said, 'Prove you owe nothing or pay all'."

A letter had been found presumably written by 'Emilie Ablay' in which reference was made to the 'Sacred debt'. The prosecution alleged that this letter had been forged.

"The experts," said the President, "say this letter wasn't written at the date it bears. Wasn't it written to help your case?"

"Experts! . . . Some will swear white; others will swear to black."

The Judge came to the death of M Vandenkerckhove.

"Did you know he had made a will in favour of his son, and that he intended to marry and so legitimize his son?"

"No."

"If M Vandenkerckhove died without leaving a will, who inherited?"

"My mother-in-law and his brother."

"Didn't you believe he had made a will in your husband's favour?"

"Never. Besides, I thought his fortune was more supposed than real."

"But you had written to the notary, M Bellinghen, that you were heirs of your uncle and that when he died you would be able to pay all your debts."

"When I wrote that I had learned what was in my uncle's will—I saw it the day after he died."

"Had your uncle frequently refused to dine with you?"

"No. He fixed his own day. We were on very good terms with him."

"On the 7th and the 9th of March you bought atropine?"

"I used it as a lotion for my eyes."

"Who prescribed it for you?"

"Dr Coppée prescribed it for Georges Ablay many years ago."

"Hadn't M Vandenkerckhove some apprehensions about visiting you?"

"If he had, why did he come?"

"He sat on your right at table: you were generous with the wine with him. Did he take coffee?"

"Yes."

"Did he ask for more?"

"I think he did."

"When he was leaving he felt ill and you sent for Dr Molitor?"

"Yes. The doctor asked me what my uncle had done and suggested apoplexy. He ordered leeches behind his ears."

"Who watched the sick man?"

"My husband, my brother-in-law and myself."

"Did he vomit?"

"He vomited blood and died the following day at noon."

The judge asked a question concerning the will, and Madame Joniaux replied: "You are asking me a question of law; how do you expect me to answer you?"

And a little while afterwards she said: "Those who listen to this case would think I was charged, not with poisoning, but with being a fraudulent bankrupt!"

The Judge linked each death with which Madame Joniaux was charged with a monetary crisis, and consequently she was run through a series of pecuniary transactions and difficulties and then to the death.

The President: "How did you expect to pay your debts in 1894?"

"None pressed."

"Didn't your son-in-law help you?"

"I don't want to speak of my son-in-law. A mother-in-law who speaks of her son-in-law is always wrong."

"Still?"

"I regret to have spoken to my son-in-law in these terms. He made a scene with my daughter when she was about to be confined and I boxed his ears. But I was so far in the right that his father made him apologize to me."

Boxing her son-in-law's ears! ... An indication of this woman's character.

"Wasn't it at this time that you asked him for 15,000 francs?"

"No. I wouldn't ask him for anything."

The President ran through a list of names to suggest to Madame Joniaux that there was nobody at that time from whom she could borrow money. She protested she was not pressed.

"Did you insure your brother's life?"

"He insured himself."

"Was it made in your interest?"

The accused gave an evasive answer. But she made a strange declaration later: "I have prayed to Providence to shed light on the whole matter," she said. "And He will, of that I feel sure."

The Judge replied coldly, "Providence hasn't got your papers."

Questions were put to her suggesting that sums of money which had been given to her for transmission to her brother had not been forwarded in their entirety.

"So the conclusion is," she replied, "that I lived on Alfred and not he on me!"

Madame Joniaux's story was that her brother had forged and she had to raise money to help him.

"Each time you are embarrassed you say there was a debt of honour."

"I am not at all embarrassed."

"You have an answer to everything."

"I am before my judges: I defend myself as I can."

There were moments when this amazing woman broke down and wept. But she had her moments too of indignation, when she dominated the whole court; these occurred when her husband's name was mentioned. She said that no members of her family knew of these 'sacred debts' and what they entailed. When the question cropped up of a debt of 4,000 francs, which Madame Joniaux had incurred " to save her brother's honour ", the Judge asked:

"Did M Joniaux know of this debt?"

"No."

"But he knew generally what your financial situation was?"

"That only proves how I can keep a secret even from my husband when it is a question of the honour of a member of my family."

She was disconcerted a moment or two later.

Being asked the name of the money-lender who had let her have the money she replied:

"Loriot."

"That isn't true. Loriot had been dead a year before then. I have a copy of his death certificate here."

For an instant Madame Joniaux looked awkward, but the next moment she said simply:

"I suppose I have mixed the dates."

The insurance of Alfred Ablay was gone into.

T

His premium was 3,286 francs and all he earned was 3,000 francs. Madame Joniaux was to help with his first premium.

"And so long," said the Judge, "as the policy was not made over to his creditors you had an interest in his death?"

"That doesn't prove that I poisoned him."

For three solid days this woman had faced the judge, and a writer present at the trial said: "In this difficult part of her interrogatory the accused showed astonishing lucidity and facility in reply. She corrected a question of detail so that the President said: 'You have a marvellous memory.' No tears, no emotion: it was the clear discussion by a woman who had faced financial difficulties and mastered them with a sure hand. If, by any chance, she makes a slip in a date she explains it away and excuses herself that she is carrying hundreds of dates and figures in her head."

It was suggested to her that her brother, Alfred, had understood her situation. He saw she was embarrassed for money and realized that his policy for 100,000 francs might be of some use to her. He wrote to that effect to his mistress in Paris.

Madame Joniaux retorted: "I am not responsible for what he wrote to Marie Roguet."

Marie Roguet had not trusted her lover's sister. She had said to him when he left her in Paris: "God knows if I shall see you again."

The purchase of poison had to be shown.

"On the 8th of March you bought morphia?"

"I bought a lot."

"Why? Are you a morphomaniac?"

"I was."

"Since when?"

"Since June, 1893."

"But you never had any other prescription than that given you by Dr Molitor?"

"That may be so. On certain days I took six centigrammes of morphia. At the seaside I didn't take any. If I wanted to commit a crime should I have bought morphia from the druggists to whom I benevolently gave my name and my address?"

"And when you were buying morphia you were also telling your tradespeople you would pay them."

"I reckoned on the money which usually came to me at that time."

"Not on the insurance?"

"It wasn't completed."

"What were the symptoms in his illness?"

"My God! The other day you gave me a lesson in toxicology when you spoke of the death of Léonie. But the reality wasn't at all like what you said."

"Why did you take your brother to Dr Max?"

"I don't know."

"Didn't you aid the doctor in making his diagnosis?"

"Oh!" (Imagine the accent and gesture.)

"What did Alfred complain of?"

"Dizziness, itching, palpitation."

"Were those Léonie's symptoms?"

"No."

"And Alfred died the next day?"

"Yes."

"Now after your brother had seen Dr Max he went to visit your sister and you went to a chemist's and bought some morphia?"

"Yes."

"You had taken care to buy your morphia at different chemist's."

"You were with your brother in your house the night before he died?"

"I went to see how he was. He said he was going to sleep like a piece of lead."

"And he never woke again?"

"He never woke again," repeated Madame Joniaux calmly.

But the Gresham company, as we know, refused to pay. Someone said this was the third mysterious death in three years in that same house. M Joniaux, himself, seemed struck with the melancholy business. "It is a fatality," he said when his brother-in-law died. "I live amongst hearses!"

And so the police were informed and Madame Joniaux arrested and tried.

The witnesses followed.

Chemists proved the buying of morphia: doctors declared that Alfred Ablay had died of morphia poisoning. Experts were produced by the defence, who said that not enough morphia had been found in the body of the deceased Alfrey Ablay to allow them to say he had died of morphia poisoning. There was the usual difference of opinion amongst the doctors and experts. The jury were even treated to glasses in which they saw morphia precipitates. The avocat-général Servais was heroic enough to take some morphia to see what it felt like. He was able to say it had no taste.

The doctor Van Vyve, who was the principal medical witness for the prosecution, said Léonie Ablay had not died of typhoid or of cerebral haemorrhage. He could not swear to the cause of death, which took place two years ago. He also swore that Vandenkerckhove had not died of cerebral haemorrhage. He had found no poison, but the death occurred thirteen months ago.

He swore that Alfred Ablay had died of morphia intoxication; they had found traces of the poison in the viscera. Two professors from the University, of Louvain and a M Druyts, a chemist of Antwerp, agreed with Dr Van Vyve.

M Depaix disagreed; he said not enough morphia had been found to account for death.

Witness followed witness. Some swore to the borrowings, some to the cheatings, to purchases of morphia, to details of insurance. They filled in the picture of this eager, anxious desperate woman looking with argent eyes at the dawn of a golden sun, with "Money! Money!" as her morning prayer.

And it didn't matter who the witness was, Madame Joniaux was ready with her accountancy mind to contradict with stolid and warm assurance.

An undertaker loosed a horrible remark. He said he had remarked to Madame Joniaux after the death of M Vandenkerckhove, "You will have luck during the Exhibition, for none of your relatives will come near you. They will be afraid!"

The closing speeches had that odour of oil that addresses to juries in criminal cases frequently have, particularly in countries where rhetoric is obligatory.

M Servais, the avocat-général, went laboriously but lucidly through the life history of the accused since her marriage to M Faber. Figures abounded. One saw the picture of a woman swimming desperately in a sea of debts, and snatching at any straw for safety. He fixed on the time when her daughter was about to be married as that when Madame Joniaux decided on the desperate course.

"Everything crumbles around you, and Jeanne is engaged to Mertens. You tell the family that you will find money. And up to the marriage you have to give an illusion of luxury and have money for the marriage itself. Madame Joniaux, mère, has nothing to give you. Vandenkerckhove refuses to help you. Where can you get the money? And you have got to keep up your style of living for some months yet. And your resources have dried up. All doors are closed to you. Do you think that this woman, who has minted money out of the honour of her family, who has tried blackmail, who has cheated at cards, is going to be beaten ? . . .

"And the accused has with her Léonie Ablay, a weak mind in a strong body . . . The idea of the crime was born. . . .

"In January, 1892, Jeanne was betrothed and you (the accused) said to a witness : ' Jeanne Faber will be rich by the end of the year.' At the end of the year Léonie Ablay was dead."

Counsel described the death of M Vandenkerckhove and came to that of Alfred Ablay. Money was necessary. The prisoner had said, to justify her need of money, that her brother had forged and must be saved. It wasn't true. He led to this : "Morphia has been found in the body of Alfred Ablay; you (the prisoner) had morphia in your hand : you had bought it the night before. There is your signature to the crime."

Mr Hendrickx for the defence cried, "Fatality", when he had to deal with the deaths. "It was that fatality in which one believes for oneself, but which one won't admit for others. Fatality holds us, surrounds us." And he added this, which is a curiosity, "On the bare walls of her cell, where for ten months she has prayed, waiting for the verdict, she has put the portraits of her victims ! Strange criminal, who not only slept with a light heart in the bed of M Vandenkerckhove the morning after his death, but who for a year has willingly passed before the eyes of those she has killed. That is beyond human force; that fact will tell you that this woman is innocent."

The views of the morally healthy on the possibilities of the criminal are full of innocence and ignorance.

Mr Graux dealt with the arguments of the prosecution as well as they could be dealt with. He suggested that not enough morphia had been found

in Alfred Ablay's body for anyone to say he had
died of morphia poisoning.

President Holvoet asked the accused if she had
anything to say. 'Nothing!'

And the jury found Madame Joniaux guilty of
having poisoned her sister Léonie Ablay, of having
poisoned her uncle, Vandenkerckhove; of having
poisoned her brother Alfred Ablay.

She was condemned to death. But Leopold II,
with a mercy that may not have been suspected in
him, refused to sign a death warrant, and so Madame
Joniaux was imprisoned for life.